SEEING IS BELIEVING

SEEING IS BELIEVING

America's Sideshows

A.W. STENCELL

ECW PRESS

Published by ECW Press, 2120 Queen Street East, Suite 200,
Toronto, Ontario, Canada M4E 1E2
416.694.3348 / info@ecwpress.com

CANADIAN CATALOGUING IN PUBLICATION DATA

Stencell, A.W.
Seeing is believing: America's sideshows / A.W. Stencell.

ISBN 1-55022-529-4

1. Sideshows — United States — History. I. Title.

GV1835.S74 2002 791.3 5 0973 C2002-902163-4

Cover and text design by: Tania Craan
Layout and Typesetting: Gail Nina
Printed by: Shanghai Chenxi Printing 2 3 4 5

Author photo © 2002 Peter Sibbald

This book is set in Joanna and Futura

The publication of *Seeing Is Believing* has been generously supported by the Government of Canada through the Book Publishing Industry Development Program.

Canadä

PRINTED AND BOUND IN CHINA

ECW PRESS
ecwpress.com

CONTENTS

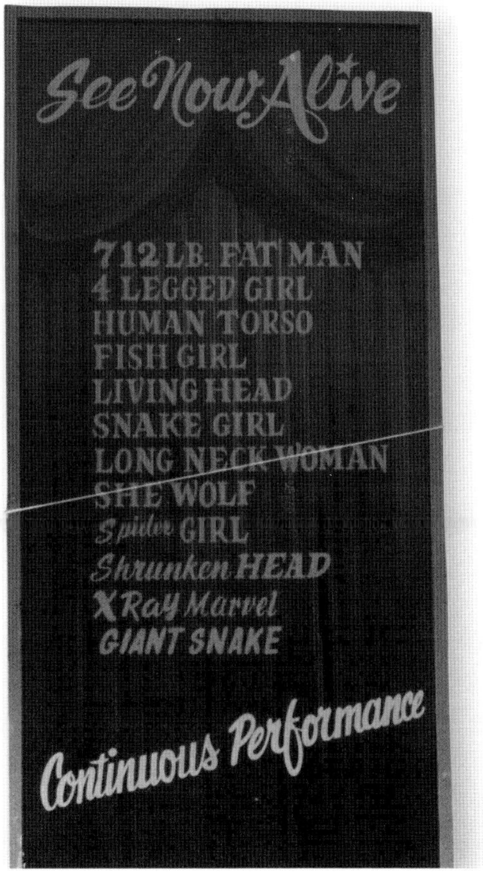

See Now Alive
712 LB. FAT MAN
4 LEGGED GIRL
HUMAN TORSO
FISH GIRL
LIVING HEAD
SNAKE GIRL
LONG NECK WOMAN
SHE WOLF
Spider GIRL
Shrunken HEAD
X Ray Marvel
GIANT SNAKE
Continuous Performance

Dedicated to the memory
of three good friends I met on the sawdust trail:

Larry Sellon

Dave Mulaney

Fred Phillips

Acknowledgments

First, gratitude and thanks to my wife Shirley for all her help, especially her computer skills in rescuing portions of text I had sent to computer Siberia by accident. Chronicling the history of back-end shows on midways over the last century couldn't be contained in just one volume. I apologize to those whom I interviewed and who loaned me material that will not be in this book; your stories will appear in the next book.

Thank you to publisher Jack David for his patience and Tracey Millen for her persistence. Thanks to Tania Craan for the book cover design, and to both her and Gail Nina for the fine book layout. Editor Stuart Ross waded through G-strings to produce my first book, *Girl Show*. He has dodged racecar-driving monkeys and avoided breaking jars of pickled babies to clearly bring you *Seeing Is Believing*.

Without the stories from various show folks there would be no life to the facts borrowed from various trade journals. I want to thank Michael Saiber, Tim Deremer, Jack and Ruth Sands, Harry Fee, Malcolm Garey, Jimmy Dixon, Lee Kolozsey, Jack Constantine, Bill Cadieux, Frank Hansen, Bill Hall, Dickie Marchant, Faye Renton Frisbee, Betty Renton, Alvin Cube, Dallas King, Johnny Meah, Philip Morris, John Moss, Jeff Murray, Michaelle "Lucky" Orr, Lefty Johnson, Joe Pelequin, Dick and June Johnson, Chris Christ, Ward Hall, Bobby Reynolds, Bobby Noell Jr., Billy Burr, Dean Potter, Bill Karlton, Diana Phillips, Don Prevost, Verna Mae Smith, Shirley Bates, Ray Chambers, Don Hurst, Barbara Pedrero, Henry Thompson, Charlie Roark, Bill English, and the late Walter Wanus for their wonderful recollections from their years on show lots.

During this project my friend back-end showman Harvey Lee Boswell passed away. We had been friends since my first season working on a carnival in 1963. Certainly when he was made they threw away the mould. Other friends shared their collections of circus and carnival material. Gail and Bob Blackmar also put me up in their home and fed me the best homemade pie next to my mother-in-law's! Bill Peacock loaned me boxes of material from his dad's collection. Laura Sedlmayr went out of her way to loan me items from Royal American Shows.

I want to thank Barbara Fahs Charles for letting me use images from her C.W. Parker archives and for generously making time for me, with Bob Staples, during a very busy period in their museum design business. Historian Dick Flint has again come through with some rare images from his collection, as did John Polascek, Dave Price, Kent Danner, Bob Paul, Bill Jamieson, Paul C. Gutheil, Scott McLelland, J. "Furry Couch" Shipley, and Ken Harck. Special thanks to Bill Cooker for all the photos and material I used from his collection and to Fred D. Phening Jr., editor of the *Bandwagon*.

Gretchen Worden of the Mütter Museum in Philadelphia and John Dodge of the Dodge Company were very helpful in explanations of early preservation techniques. Current "gaff" makers Mark Frierson, Dick Horne, Doug Higley, and John Hartley told me about their endeavors to carry on a delicate art. Shad Kvetko was extremely helpful in relating information on his relative Homer Tate. Mike Sappol shared information on Arnold Schenkenburger he found while researching material for his fine book, *A Traffic In Dead Bodies*. Brett Mizelle generously let me use material from his paper on early animal exhibitions in America. Photographer William Eakin let me use his fine motordrome photos, and Henry Meyers sent me a photo of his Dillinger banner. Thanks to Peter Sibbald for taking and providing me with the author photo on the flap.

British fairground writer-historian Paul Braithwaite has provided me with material on wax works and peep shows. Research director Vanessa Toulmin has been generous in providing both images and information from the National Fairground Archive at the University of Sheffield.

In America entertainment historians would be lost without the Circus World Museum in Baraboo, Wisconsin. The fine library staff, headed by Fred Dahlinger Jr. and assistants Lori Czajka and Meg Allen, provided images and information quickly and professionally. Dick Bennett has been a great help at the Carnival Museum operated by the International Independent Showmen's Association at Gibsonton, Florida. Writer and circus historian Steve Gossard used his days off from work to lead me through the vast circus collection at the University of Illinois at Normal.

Cameron Campbell at the Canadian War Museum provided information on Hitler cars. John A. McKinven sent me his booklet "Roltair–Genius of Illusions," which contains a review of historical levitation patents. A big thank you goes to Dan Bell at the Capac Historical Society in Michigan for supplying me with images and material from the Kempf Collection. Lorain Lounsberry and Lynette Walton of the Glenbow Museum in Calgary, Alberta, have been extremely helpful.

The next generation of sideshow men and women are hard at work, but not always in traditional carnival or circus venues. In the last decade Harley Newman, Tod Robbins, Doc Swann, Johnny Fox, and Jim Rose have catapulted the sideshow arts into mainstream popular culture. Keith Stewart and the Biddlestiff Family Circus, Tim Cridland (a.k.a. Zamora the Torture King), strongman and banner painter John Hartley, George the Giant MacArthur, Enigma and Katzen, Slymenstra Hymen's Girly Freak Show, Matt Bouvier, and Felecity Perez are all out there on the road making a living at swallowing steel, eating bugs, sticking pins into their flesh, and blowing fire.

Jan Gregor was the first manager of the Jim Rose Circus Sideshow and has been a friend, author, collector, and a solid contributor to this book. His knowledge of the new avant-garde, worm-eating, vile-drinking, penis-lifting sideshow troupes has been invaluable. When putting the manuscript together became tough he came through with e-mails and phone calls of encouragement. There is no better "blow-off" to these acknowledgments than to say, "Thanks, Jan."

A.W. Stencell
Toronto, September 2002

KING REID'S HOLLYWOOD
MONKEY RACES
DARE DEVIL DAN
WORLD'S CHAMPION
RACING

INTRODUCTION

Hurry Along — You Used to be Just in Time

STREET FAIR,
DALLAS, TEXAS,
One Week, Commencing MONDAY, MAY 28,
Under the Auspices of DALLAS LODGE, B. P. O. ELKS, No. 71.
THE BEST FREE ATTRACTIONS
That money can buy will be furnished to draw the CROWDS to DALLAS. FAKIRS, SIDE SHOWS, MIDWAYS, FERRIS WHEELS, ETC. For concessions, terms and privileges, address J. L. VERONEE, Theatrical Agency, Lyric Theatre, Chicago, Ill.; or P. G. CLAIBORNE, Gen. Mgr., Dallas, Texas.
WANTED.—Troupe Japs, Midway Dancers, Casting Act, Etc. Write or wire.

The carnival midway has come a long way since its early years. The first touring midway companies that emerged after the 1893 Chicago World's Fair had no rides, only shows. These shows were independently owned and often operated by showmen who had been visiting fairs on their own with various attractions since the 1870s and '80s. Some of them had banded together to share baggage car space and comradeship on the way to the same venues. Their complaints of unfair business treatment at some fairs made a collective organization a welcome proposition. By the early 1900s, there were several dozen large midway companies and twice as many small-time carnival operators playing fairs and street celebrations.

Showmen with individual attractions such as an illusion show, snake eater, or stuffed alligator could now book on with one midway company for a whole season. The

Opposite: A nice crowd graces the back end of Reid Lefebvre's King Reid Shows midway in the 1950s.

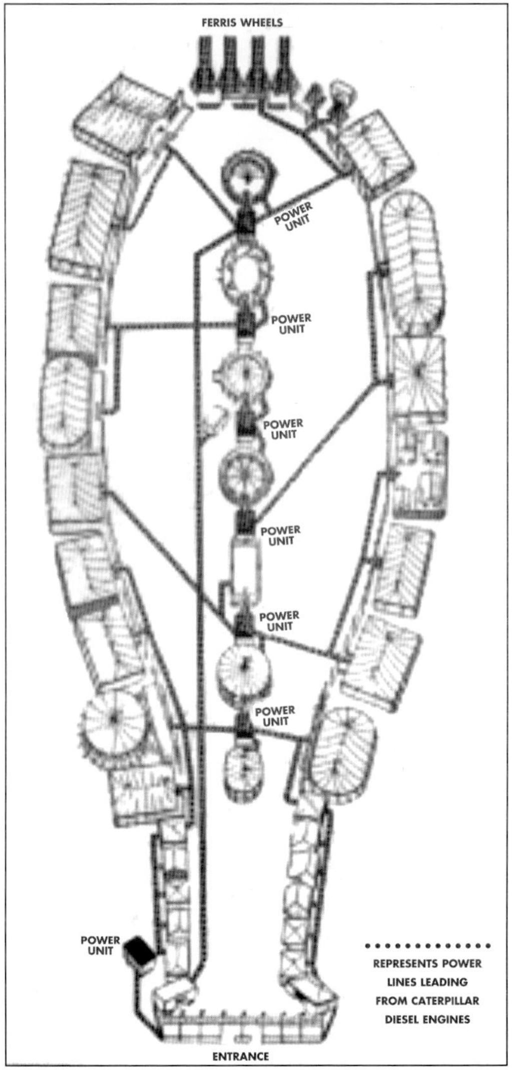

A sketch illustrating the electrical layout on a big carnival also shows the typical elongated horseshoe shape of a carnival.

A smiling crowd exits Lee Klozsey's Man Eating Chicken show in the 1970s. Inside, the crowd saw a seven-foot man eat fire and consume chicken from a fast food take-out bucket.

midway owner played a prebooked route and took care of licenses, electricity, and water, and in some cases transportation, in exchange for a percentage of the attraction's gross. Other showmen preferred to hopscotch their show, ride, or game from one carnival company or fair to another. A fraternity of showmen grew, and carnies, regardless of what show they operated or where they went, stuck together.

Back-end showmen brought their skills — learned from working in vaudeville theaters, dime museums, circuses, medicine shows, minstrel shows, and magic shows, panoramas and lantern slide presentations — into the new midway business. The first touring carnival companies were a rich stew of vaudeville acts, Wild West shows, dog and pony circuses, freak shows, Swiss bell ringers, glassblowers, minstrel acts, illusions, mind-reading acts, snake eaters, and hundreds of dead, stuffed, pickled, embalmed, or mummified monstrosities, both human and animal. The art of the pitchman and the flash of the showman combined on the carnival midway. Seldom did a patron visit a show without being charged for a special after-show or leave without being pitched something.

Until World War I, the merry-go-round and Ferris wheel were the main rides on midways. After the war, new rides were designed and the ride-manufacturing business was in full swing. New rides debuted every few seasons. The baby boom in the late 1940s gave rise to rides designed for children, and every midway now featured a kiddieland area. Until the 1960s, back-end shows were still a big part of a carnival's overall gross. That all changed once high-capacity rides arrived. Today, rides dominate the business not only on touring midways but also in amusement parks.

The biggest growth in carnivals may be in the food business. Midways once had a grab joint or cookhouse and maybe a few ice cream, popcorn, candyfloss, and candy apple stands. Now food joints outnumber game booths at fairs — you can buy fried dough in a myriad of shapes, sausages of every description, and full chicken and souvlaki

ROYAL AMERICAN SHOWS
SHOWS & EQUIPMENT FOOTAGE - 1966

GIRL SHOW	93F x 160D	(8 feet blow on left side of front.) (Top over stakes 85 x 160.)
HARLEM	99F x 155D	(8 feet blow on left side of front.) (Top over stakes 85 x 155.)
MOTORDROME	66F x 65D	
SIDE SHOW	Full banner line 152 ft. Full top 164 ft over stakes. Middles can be taken out in 20 and 30 foot sections as needed. Small banner line 110 ft. 70 feet deep over stakes. Banner spreaders are 12 ft.	
SLIDE	60F x 21D	
HOFBRAU HAUS	65F x 43D	(Trailer extends 7 feet back in center of ride.)
FUN HOUSE	61F x 10D	
GHOST SHIP	54F x 10D	
MONKEY SHOW	111F x 68D	(11 foot spread on banners.)
SNAKE SHOW	40F x 10D	
GLASS HOUSE	66F x 20D	
SNOW MAN	65F x 12D	(Can cut to 55F)
UPSIDE DOWN MAN	50F x 35D	
CREATURE	40F x 14D	
SAFARI SHOW	57F x 20D	
WAX SHOW	35F x 20D	
MAD WORLD FUN HOUSE	60F x 40D	
ARCADE	43F x 107D	
FRONT GATE	65F x 12D	
POWER PLANTS	7 towers - 14 ft each.	2 towers - 15 ft. each.
FLIGHT TO MARS	84F x 45D	
GRAND PRIX	120F x 58D	
ROCK-O-PLANE	48F x 25D	(With wagon 55D)
SKY DIVER	36F x 66D	
CATERPILLAR	60F x 60D	
FLYING COASTER	55F x 55D	
TWISTER	50F x 50D	
ZOO CHOO-CHOO	55F x 25D	
GUN EXHIBIT	55F x 8D	

ROYAL AMERICAN SHOWS
RIDE & KID RIDE FOOTAGE - 1966

M-G-R	50F x 50D	
GIANT WHEEL	50F x 80D	
SPACE WHEELS	50F x 96D	
TILT-A-WHIRL	50F x 50D	
OCTOPUS	55F x 55D	
ROLL-O-PLANE	44F x 55D	(With wagon)
COASTER	200F x 50D	
WILD MOUSE	64F x 134D	(This allows tractors to work completely around ride.) (Requires 15 feet extra on left side of ride in back section to erect.)
DODGEM	90F x 46D	
LOOPER	42F x 42D	
TRABANT	55F x 50D	
ROUND-UP	32F x 32D	(Allow 8 feet extra for steps in back on tight lot.)
SCRAMBLER	62F x 62D	
FLY-O-PLANE	74F x 74D	
PRETZEL	58F x 54D	(Gypsy Joy Ride)
OLD MILL	78F x 60D	
EXPRESS	66F x 54D	(28 feet from front to center.)
CALYPSO	66F x 66D	(Set center wagon back 28 feet, 6 inches.)
SWISS LIFT	Short cable 373 feet over wagons plus tractors. Long cable 516 feet over wagons plus tractors.	
METEOR	52F x 55D	
BAT CAVE	80F x 36D	
TIP TOP	54F x 50D	
PARATROOPER	54F x 50D	
SKY FIGHTER	30F x 30D	(In #46)
TANKS	28F x 28D	(In #46)
JOLLY CAT	28F x 28D	(In #32)
CHOO-CHOO	24F x 24D	(In #32)
BOATS	24F x 24D	(In #48)
KID WHEEL	18F x 18D	(In #48)
HELICOPTER	36F x 36D	
PONIES	36F x 36D	
MOTORCYCLES	24F x 24D	
TOY AUTOS	24F x 24D	
ORGAN	20F x 8D	
GERMAN M-G-R	36F x 36D	

Lot layout card used by the staff on Royal American Shows in 1966 showing the dimensions of some of the rides and shows. Note the dimensions for the girl and Harlem shows, both big sit-down revues.

Right: The 1917 wooden frame and canvas minstrel show front on the Clifton Kelly Show at Hattiesburg, Miss., was typical of many show fronts of the era, especially on gilly shows or with showmen traveling their outfits via baggage car.

Carl Sedlmayr's Royal American Shows, founded in 1921, became the largest railroad carnival in America. Here, four Ferris wheels anchor the back end of 12 shows in Shreveport, La., in 1959. Harlem in Havana (lower right), Club Lido revue (half way up on left), and the 10-in-1 (next to girl show) are in the big tents. The motordrome's round canvas roof can be seen across the midway from the 10-in-1.

ELKS'
JUBILEE
Carnival
Bennett Park
BASE BALL GROUNDS
Cor. Mich. and Trumbull Aves.
BEGINS TOMORROW,
JULY 14-26
7 O'CLOCK P. M.
Indisputably the Best Thing in Town

Caskill-Mundy's
MAGNIFICENT ORGANIZATION OF SENSATIONAL AND SPECTACULAR CARNIVAL ATTRACTIONS.

READ THE GREAT LIST OF FEATURES

KILPATRICK
In His Famous Ride for Life.

PHILION
In His Great Spiral Tower Act.

The Burmese Midgets
Smallest People in the World.

Splash and Spray
The Champion High Divers of the World. PAUL SPLASH dives from a 80-ft. ladder into a 4-ft. tank of water.

SLIDE FOR LIFE
MLLE. GILMORE IN A THRILLING ACT.

BALLOON ASCENSION
With Monkey Parachute Drop from the Clouds.

THE ORIENTAL PARADE IN THE ESPLANADE

The Cycle Dazzle.
Johnstown Flood.
Statue Turning to Life.
Under the Red Dome.
The Dancing Girls.
The Magic Swing.
Mt. Pelee Horror.
The Glass Workers.

The Performing Wild Animals (Greatest in the world).
The Dog and Pony Show.
Trained Goats and Monkeys.
Wild Rose, the ½-Monkey Girl.
The Gypsy Camp.

THE STADIUM SHOW,
With Its Six Great Acts

THE GERMAN VILLAGE
CONTINUOUS VAUDEVILLE
TODD'S METROPOLITAN BAND,
In Daily, Afternoon and Evening Concerts.

SPECIAL ACTS ADDITIONAL FROM DAY TO DAY.

dinners. Food joints have evolved from humble wooden stands to state-of-the-art, sanitized $100,000 mobile kitchen trailers.

Over the years, every aspect of the carnival business has expanded except the shows. Into the 1960s, patrons to even the smallest pumpkin festival could see a variety of back-end shows as showmen hopscotched around, looking for fresh spots. Now, the few shows that remain are found only at very large fairs. One carnival owner told me that when his carnival was set up on a mall parking lot, people came and put their kids on a few rides and left within a half hour. There was nothing to hold them, no shows to entertain them. The carnival industry has forgotten that it is not only a business of riding, playing, and eating — gawking and gazing are part of the overall picture.

It takes a special breed of person to be a showman. It takes a longer apprenticeship than learning to cook sausages, dip candy apples, or put up a ride. Imagination and intestinal fortitude are essential, but there are countless skills and hundreds of pieces of midway knowledge to learn to run a successful midway attraction. Showmen didn't learn their trade at schools; there were no textbooks. They simply started in the business and learned from experience,

New high-capacity rides the industry called "spectaculars" started to dominate the business in the 1970s. Typical of these big rides was the "Sky Wheel" seen here on the 1972 RAS midway. It became the carnival's new bidding tool in securing the best fair dates. The space required for these rides left less footage for shows, especially those with large fronts like revues and 10-in-1s.

Today dark rides are one of the growth areas in the carnival and amusement park industry. Outside animation and vivid artwork that often borders on extreme eroticism best attracts today's young midway crowds. Dark rides have even become multi-leveled like this Wicked Witch dark ride on RAS in 1971.

Jack Constantine put one of his small ladies inside this 20-by-20-foot metal framed enclosure, with vinyl walls and roof, on the James E. Strates Shows midway at the 1999 Hamburg, N.Y., fair.

often painful experience, as in the case of a fledgling fire-eater, but always educational. It's still the only way to learn the business.

Sex and horror along with the unusual have always been the staples of midway shows. Monkeys driving tiny autos around a small steel speedway might seem offbeat. But, they appeared tame next to jars of pickled, deformed babies or walk-through shows of over-embalmed gangsters, papier-mâché or wax figures arranged in scenes portraying Underground China, Opium Dens, A Gangster's Last Trip, or the ultimate horror: Medieval Tortures! Showmen framed shows around freaks, both human and animal, or around any curiosity or subject they felt could make them money. And whether they were fake or real — the shows were always entertaining. At a nickel a glance or ten cents a laugh, how could you complain if the horse advertised with his head where his

In the 1970s, carnivals replaced ticket sellers on each attraction with central ticket boxes. The pricing of midway attractions by coupons hurt independent show operators. The remaining show operators say that the best solution for them is to accept the coupons as well as take cash and sell their own tickets.

tail should be turned out to be just a horse turned backwards in his stall? Can you blame the showman for the mark's surprise at seeing a pickled fetus in a jar after he had purchased a ticket based on seeing a banner depicting a two-headed baby on a rocking horse billed as "Real" or "Born to Live"?

At the higher scale, you could pay a dollar for a half-hour minstrel show equal to anything in a high-class supper club. Midway girl revues and variety shows were often better than the tabloid productions playing theaters. Revues, illusion shows, and acts in the sideshows were often the same acts you paid more money to see at the local vaudeville theater in the wintertime. On a per dime or quarter basis, your money and time were well spent on North American midways.

There are still shows on carnivals, but these days they're very rare. Almost all of those who my generation calls the old-timers, showmen who started in the business around World War II, have died or retired. Back-end showmen — those who worked on the back end of the carnival lot — have always considered themselves the real show folks. They considered front-end people flatties and hustlers.

Visit a midway today, and on the back end you'll find the funhouses and dark rides. These, along with spectacular midway rides, are the growth areas in the amusement industry. As rides and funhouses grow, they need more midway footage, and this space has come at the expense of the small independent attraction owner. The last grind showmen have gone from exhibiting their shows in small trailers to still smaller portable structures enclosed by vinyl so their show can fit in the pie-shaped areas left open where the fences surrounding the large rides meet.

There are a few midget horses and huge cows, a couple of extremely large pigs, an alligator or two, a log house, a few wild men gone on one drug trip too many, a couple of aliens, a few freak babies, and several girls-becoming-gorillas left on the midways. But you won't see more than two or three of these, even at the big fairs.

The carnival industry has a future, but showmen are a dying breed. This book is about these showmen and the shows they have enticed their marks into over the years. There have been a half dozen books on freaks and sideshows but none come close to explaining the sideshow or back-end business on carnivals. Sideshowman Ward Hall sums it up best: "Nobody's an

Filmmakers and writers still arrive each winter in Gibsonton, Fla., hoping to see carnival freaks. The days have long passed since the 1940 volunteer fire department, consisting of the town's founder and eight-foot-four-inch giant Al Tomani, three dwarfs, and driver Ralph Doremus, responded to the town's fire siren. But you can still eat at the Giant's Camp restaurant.

authority on sideshows unless they have sat up all night with a sick fat lady, or helped the midget lady bury her midget husband, or changed a flat tire for the frog woman in the pouring rain in the middle of the night alongside the highway." Novels and movies have portrayed only the grim side of the carnival business, exploiting the freaks and the sideshow end of the business. Documentary filmmakers continue to show up in Gibsonton, Fla., the town with the largest showmen's colony, expecting to see midgets and three-legged men ambling along Route 41.

But, the worst insult for show folks is that nobody looks upon the circus and carnival as businesses — people have a hard time legitimizing the nomadic occupation of exhibiting mummified remains or racecar-driving monkeys. The carnival business appears to be a haphazard affair until you find out that every small detail involved in extracting money from the showgoer has been carefully studied and put into practice.

NOAH'S ARK

LOOKEE HERE!

English Showmanship Comes to America

The 17th-century kings and queens of Europe shared an interest with all classes of people in dwarfs, giants, hermaphrodites, scaly men, and other freaks of nature. Visits to see the lions at the Tower of London in 1692 included a viewing of the two-legged dog. The influence on America of showmen from this era started with the first settlers from the English Isles. Blow-offs, dings, lecturers, the selling of pitch cards or booklets, and other subtle means of caging a few extra coins from the curious were all practiced by English showmen, and were quickly imitated by their counterparts here. Along with the shows, illusions, and attractions brought from overseas came the patter, lectures, deceits, and general principles of operation.

Opposite: The elaborate wood carved front of the Ferari Brothers' Noah's Ark show on a lot in England. Note the trumpet organ and the big bass drum that are used to draw the crowd. The two front wagons also double as accommodations. This style of show front was copied by American showmen once the midway business got rolling in the early 1900s.

England's famed St. Bartholomew Fair started in 1102 in London and ran until

Chapter 1

The Bostock-Wombwell menagerie on the road outside Ballater, Scotland, in 1896. Animal shows, wax figure shows, and small circuses had been moving in this manner since the early 1800s.

England's Chittock animal show, 1885. It would be several decades before American back-end showmen would produce similar elaborate show fronts to attract the public.

1855. At the 1631 St. Bartholomew Fair, a showman exhibited something in a box called the Turkey Horse, which stood just over two feet high. Other rarities on shows included a mother and daughter with three breasts; a baby with four arms and four legs; a man with one body but two distinct heads; a child with three legs and 16 toes. Displays involving elements of sex, horror, and strangeness consistently opened the public's purses. The rules for midway poker were quickly established — dead or alive, anything with two heads trumped anything with only one.

By 1784, author Thomas Frost tells us, "men with wooden mummies in show boxes were found straggling about the fair" among shows featuring human freaks, enormous pigs, double-bodied cows, and menageries.

By 1830 St. Bartholomew Fair was awash with such attractions, including two magic acts, Ballard's Beasts, a learned pony, a pig-faced woman, a living skeleton, a fat boy and fat girl, a fire eater, a diorama of Navarino, a Scotch giant, and a couple of exhibits showing the late George IV lying in state, at a penny a show.

The art of showing something for profit starts with "the story." It's the tale that convinces a would-be voyeur to pay his money and peer into a peek box, go into a room, or enter the tent where the showman's attraction is tucked away from non-paying eyes. While street performers could give a show and pass the hat, the showman was careful to keep his attraction out of sight, and only after you paid were you allowed to see it. And so his spiel was his most important tool in getting you inside. Asked to define a showman, Claude Bostock, the nephew of animal showman Frank Bostock, replied, "A man who can incite the curiosity of the public, then make them pay to satisfy it."

Making a racket with a trumpet, drum, or gong were the best ways of pulling a crowd in front of a booth. By the 1700s, British fairs tried to license the use of trumpets and drums by showmen. The management of the Chicago World's Fair in 1893, where the word *ballyhoo* was coined, banned talkers and outside demonstrations because of their noise. Talkers soon switched to pantomime hoping scantily

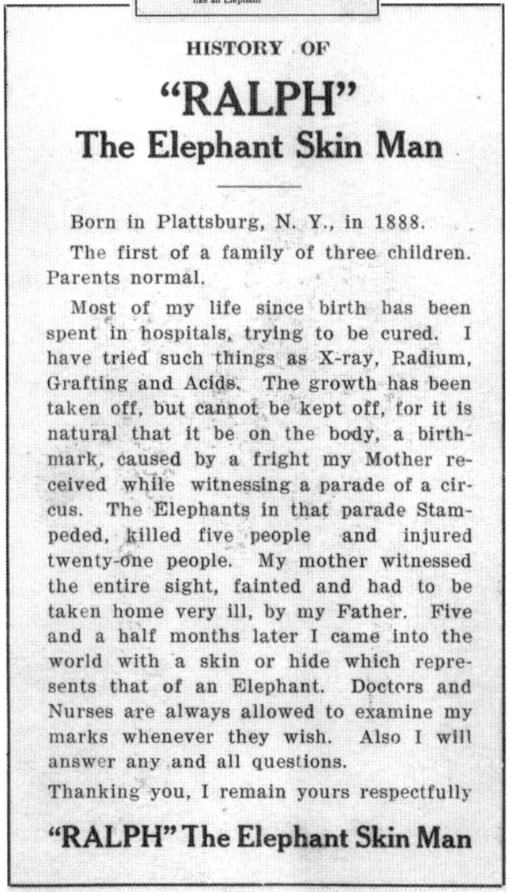
HISTORY OF

"RALPH"

The Elephant Skin Man

Born in Plattsburg, N. Y., in 1888.

The first of a family of three children. Parents normal.

Most of my life since birth has been spent in hospitals, trying to be cured. I have tried such things as X-ray, Radium, Grafting and Acids. The growth has been taken off, but cannot be kept off, for it is natural that it be on the body, a birthmark, caused by a fright my Mother received while witnessing a parade of a circus. The Elephants in that parade Stampeded, killed five people and injured twenty-one people. My mother witnessed the entire sight, fainted and had to be taken home very ill, by my Father. Five and a half months later I came into the world with a skin or hide which represents that of an Elephant. Doctors and Nurses are always allowed to examine my marks whenever they wish. Also I will answer any and all questions.

Thanking you, I remain yours respectfully

"RALPH" The Elephant Skin Man

Above: An early fairground booth at St. Bartholomew Fair demonstrates how showmen of the 20th century adopted their ideas for banners and the bally. The high bally platform seen here enabled a free flow of spectators in and out of the show booth and also put the free show above the heads of the crowd so everyone could see it.

Left: Some of the surviving remnants of early exhibitions of freaks and strange wonders are the small handbills used to advertise their presence and the small bios and pitch cards sold at the venue. Here Ralph the Elephant Skin Man has combined his photo card with a short bio on the back.

Talkers were the heart of the sideshow, pit show, and grind show business. "Eeka's inside. If she gets out, we all get out"; so goes the talker's spiel for that wild snake eating creature, Eeka. Faye Renton Frisbee said her dad chose the name Eeka for their geek show because it was easy to say, especially when you had to say it hundreds of times a day. Another catchy name for the snake eater used on many geek shows was "Zoma."

A pantomime artist draws people to the show, after fair officials forbade the use of talkers in an attempt to curb the loud racket on the bally.

clad dancing girls giving the crowd a "come in" wave from a doorway would fill their shows. In America, the portable stage set up outside the exhibit tent and in front of the banners became known as the "bally stage," and the free show given on it, the "bally."

Door talking became a profession. Operators were willing to pay good money to those who could tell the tale and pack their exhibit spaces. Bona fide freaks needed very little selling, but gaffs or hoaxes needed a smooth orator who could draw people inside with a good knowledge of suggestive and evasive words.

The "talker" — earlier known as the boomer, blower, orator, and spieler — became the most important person around midway shows. Most were paid 10 percent of the door, and the good ones were never out of work. One showman's letter to *Billboard* in 1911 provides a good description of their wiles: "I heard one of the best talkers I ever listened to make an opening in which he used the most beautiful English. His talk was interesting, imaginative, and in no way pertained to the show or any part of it. He filled the tent on the first opening. The people saw the show, which lasted exactly three minutes. It was the worst that could be seen anywhere. On the way out, a lady accosted the talker: 'Mr. Man, where is the show you were telling us about? I am afraid our party went into the wrong tent!'"

The outside display of painted images on a square of canvas suggesting the wonders inside the show booth was a necessity. Most of the showmen's early clientele couldn't read; only the educated could be enticed in with lettered signage. As a result, pictorial banners were the midway showman's main form of advertising — he pointed to these images to reinforce his spiel.

But American show business was held

A sketch of a ram with six legs exhibited at St. Bartholomew Fair in 1790.

One of the oldest and most pleasing animal acts presented by showmen at fairs from the 15th century on was the "pick-out pig." The educated hog could add, tell time, and even spell his name. The sketch depicts Toby, an 1833 performer at St. Bartholomew Fair, that did all the above and more while blindfolded with 20 handkerchiefs.

in check by the Puritanical crowd that had fled Britain hoping for a liberated world, only to become persecutors themselves. David Brett Mizelle pointed out at the 2000 Circus Historical Society convention in L.A. that after the 1796 Sabbath Day Act (U.S.A.), showmen framed their acts to appeal to women and children, tempering their presentations to bring in a wider audience. In 1804, pig-faced women were the entertainment rage, but when they turned out to be bears with shaven faces the public rebeled against such vulgar shows. Audiences wanted novel but moral

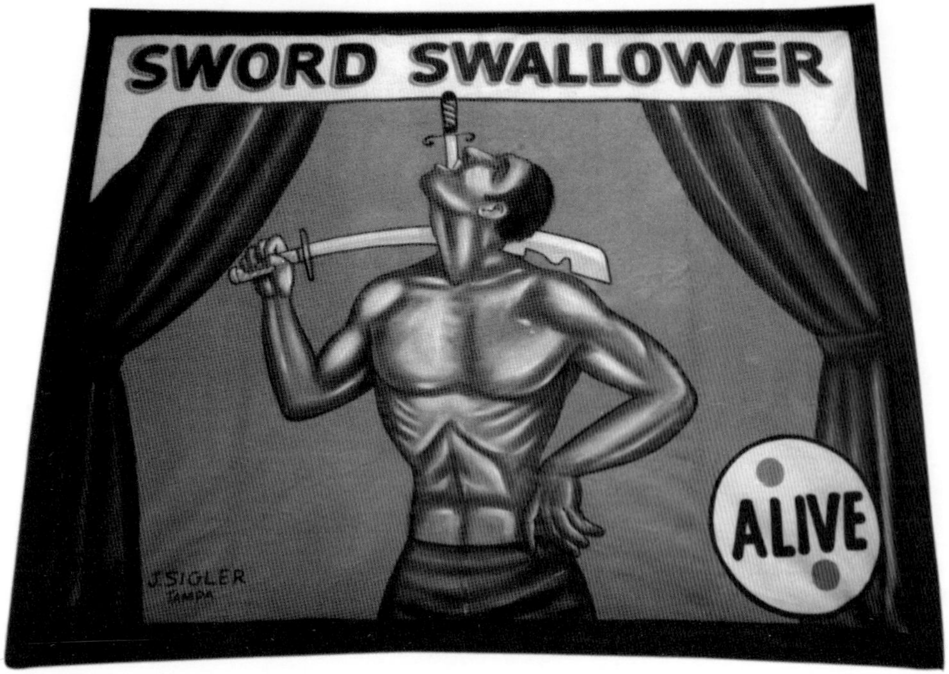

Showmen in 19th century America were quick to distance themselves from fake or phony presentations by marking on their handbills that their attraction was "real" and "alive." This carried over to 20th-century circus and carnival banner painters who put such wording inside a circle (known as a bullet) in one corner of the painting.

entertainment. There has always been a debate in the public's mind about what it is willing to look at and what is worth viewing.

In the summer of 1860, Van Amburgh's menagerie was touring New Hampshire and Vermont. To avoid offending the moral standards of the area, the show went by the title Van Amburgh's Great Moral Exhibition of Pious and Well Disposed Animals. The *New York Clipper* at that time was speaking out on behalf of show people, claiming: "There never was a more reviled, slandered, or generally abused professional class than show people; nor did a more outraged, cheated, plundered, persecuted, and at the same time enduring set of victims ever invoke public justice or appeal to popular sympathy. Showmen have been robbed from the stable boy to the ugly official. The stable boy shorts the horses on oats and the city official wants bribes or passes to let the show into town. They seem like legitimate prey from all they have dealings with." Showmen viewed the public as marks, but because of the showmen's transient nature and low reputation, the public felt show folks were easy prey as well.

Animal exhibitions started in America around 1720 and continued until the Continental Congress in 1774 banned cockfighting, horse racing, and animal exhibits. After 1785, showmen once again presented animal exhibits.

One of the oldest animal acts, the pick-out pig act, can be traced back to the 15th century. One of the routines involved the pig picking out letters laid on the ground and spelling PORK, the trainer cueing the animal by changing his breathing or making slight sounds by rubbing his finger-nails together. The pick-out act is still performed today, with animals that have the appearance of dumb creatures, like pigs, birds, and mules, providing the best impact.

American showman Wiliam Frederick Pinchbeck began exhibiting his "learned pig" in 1770. Pinchbeck developed practices that would be followed by many traveling exhibitors. His handbills always stated his attraction would only stay for a short time, so those interested should attend right away. He established reserve-seat tickets for those scared they would not get a seat when the venue had limited seating. To set his show apart from the many fake exhibitions, he emphasized that his exhibit was "Alive" and "Real," terminology 20th-century banner painters picked up on.

Like their ancestors in Europe, the first itinerant American showmen walked from town to town. Richardson Wright's book, *Hawkers and Walkers in Early America*, lists showmen among the crowd of peddlers, preachers, lawyers, doctors, and others who tramped for a living. Tavern and inn proprietors were glad to give showmen exhibition space, knowing they could sell food and drinks to the crowds the showmen attracted. By the late 1700s, puppeteers, wax figure showmen, ventriloquists, owners of peep shows and automatons, and showmen with trained bears, performing dogs, and educated pigs were showing up in town squares and at tavern doorsteps.

By the beginning of the 19th century, freaks appeared on exhibition in larger settlements. Such curiosities as armless or legless men and women; giants, midgets, dwarfs, and albino women; and man-made wonders such as mummies and mermaids could be viewed for a price. The famous Siamese twins, Chang and Eng, landed in America in 1829 and were on exhibition for 23 years. Show business in the middle of the 19th century was dominated by P.T. Barnum and other exhibitors who cashed in on the public craze for curiosities.

Steamboats and stage coaches made traveling life easier for the showman and

S. Calkins' Busy World Show was exhibited in a wagon, making it easy to transport from one fair to another. The two panels, which can be lifted to enclose the miniature village, are beautifully painted.

The Beautiful Spotted Negro Boy exhibited at St. Bartholomew Fair in the 1830s.

British entertainment historian Paul Braithwaite's sketch of a peep showman. The windows accommodate three viewers and the showman changes the scenes by levers on the side. When he is done, he folds up the stand and carries it on his back to another venue.

enabled him to broaden his itinerary and carry a more elaborate show. Some of the early showmen traveling in this manner were the magic-lantern and dissolving-view exhibitors whose shows didn't require a lot of heavy gear and who could make a living by performing for a few dozen people in a small space. Another show that early showmen favored was the "Panstereorama" model. These miniature recreations of towns, countries, buildings, and so on were made of paper, wood, paste board, and cork. On tour were detailed models of Jerusalem, St. Peter's Church in Rome, Mt. Vernon, Windsor Castle, Washington's Tomb, and the Lord's Last Supper. Early in his career as a showman, P.T. Barnum traveled the country exhibiting a Panstereorama model of Solomon's Temple. Barnum wasn't the only showman to start this way. For example, Yankee Robinson, a prominent 19th-century showman and lifetime circus owner, started his career exhibiting a model known as the Raising of Lazarus. The show was moved around the country in a small wagon drawn by a horse.

Wright mentions the 1748 *New York Post Boy* recording the visit of an itinerant showman with what he called a Philosophical Optical Machine. The peep show was one of the first exhibits on North American fairgrounds. New York journalist A. Pember's 1874 book, *The Mysteries and Nisaries of the Great Metropolis*, tells about his meeting with two peep showmen from "Canady" working on Baxter Street. The showmen had a good stock of pictures and could change the views to suit the proclivities of the natives of the land they were traveling through. The viewer looked through eight openings and saw the three great presidents of the United States — Washington, Lincoln, and Grant — in a group, as well as views of the Battle of Gettysburg, the Capital of Washington, Sheridan's Ride, the Falls of Niagara, the Hudson River by moonlight, Central Park, and New York Bay. The charge ranged from one to five cents depending on the viewing time. At fairs such showmen did terrific business, often taking in 15 to 20 dollars daily from fair patrons, many of whom visited the show three or four times a day.

The glorious extension of the peep show was the panorama. In the 1840s, P.T. Barnum brought Huldon's diorama called The Obsequies of Napoleon from Paris, and from London, England, he brought a copy of the panorama titled The Ascent of Mt.

Blanc that had been on exhibition at the Egyptian Hall for several years. By the 1850s, there were many touring panoramas with such titles as The Life of Christ, Dr. Kane's Arctic Expedition, and Tours of Europe, as well as panoramas of Paris, London, and other great cities. Pilgrim's Progress and Milton's Paradise Lost dealt with morals, while other panoramas such as The Revolutionary War reenacted military battles.

Amos Hubbel, a formidable panorama showman for many years who traveled by horse and wagon, exhibited The Burning of Moscow. He booked the show, set it up, sold tickets at the door, and did the lecturing. He wrote in the *Clipper*: "In the late 1850s I went to England on behalf of Barnum and brought back Thiodon's Theater of Art for exhibition here. It was a diorama of pictorial, mechanical, animated, and moving figure representations of noted battles that had been fought on land, naval engagements on the high seas, and other noted scenes of the world. There were many moving figures of men, horses, soldiers, and ships. These figures were very neatly cut out of sheet brass and painted natural and lifelike on one side. Each was set with a clog wheel that ran over a strip of felt, which set the figures into their natural movements when hooked on a revolving belt running in front of the painted scenery. You could show a town, city, or street scene and have a whole army marching through! The natural movements of the limbs of the soldiers, people, horses, and the guns and cannons on the ships and forts were so fixed that the operators behind the scenery could puff smoke through them and the boom noise would be imitated on a bass drum."

A sketch of the "Sea Nymph" exhibited inside a booth during the 1830s at St. Bartholomew Fair.

One of the exhibitions at the Crystal Palace Fair in London, England (1851), was that of Herr Ploucquet from Stuttgart, Germany. Ploucquet conceived the idea of setting up stuffed small animals such as foxes, ground hogs, cats, and mice into comic scenes. They were an instant hit on the fairgrounds and in museums. Here kittens serenade a pig.

THE SOUTH CA
WEARS A
THE YOUNG LADY
SPECTIVELY
AGE.
FAIL
WOMAN LIVING
PAC FIC

A RICH MIDWAY STEW

Early Fairground Shows and Showmen

Chapter 2

In the early days of fairs in North America, people were happy to stare at anything, and to the showmen's good fortune, they did. For the most diverse entertainments, New York City was the place to be. The Tammany Museum started in 1790 and was acquired by Barnum in 1842. Within a decade, he had lots of competition. Just below Barnum's museum at 300 Broadway was the Anatomical Museum, where crowds could view wax reproductions of various parts of the body. Further along Broadway, at the Stuyvesant Institute, was the Museum of Egyptian Antiquities. At Hope Chapel, on Broadway, you could see a Panorama of Niagara for a dollar, the most expensive ticket on a street where most amusements cost a quarter.

For a quarter, you could also see magician Signor Antonio Blitz and his wonderful performing canaries at 659 Broadway. Blitz

Opposite: Showmen displaying some of the banners to their shows on the way to the Stanley, New Brunswick, fair in the early 1900s. In our age of disenchantment, why must we doubt the genuineness of The South Carolina Camel Girl?

had been performing in America for two decades. His show consisted of magic, ventriloquism, and over 500 canaries. And at 7 p.m. nightly, also for a quarter, crowds were admitted to Banvard's Georama of Egypt-Petra and Land of Eden. Just before buying a ticket to see Wood's Minstrels at 444 Broadway, you could step into an establishment that had on view a painting of the Battle of New Orleans. Across the street, there were demonstrations of "Spiritual Manifications," [*sic*] and a rhinoceros was on display at Driesbach's Menagerie. Bowery and Chatham Square had similar shows. The Temple of Graces at 6th Ave. opposite the Crystal Palace opened early afternoons to give hourly shows of model artists (tableaux vivants). These were just some of the happenings recorded by the *Clipper* for one week in 1853.

At World's Hall, on Broadway, Prof. J. Woodman Hart displayed a celebrated model of San Francisco and Prof. Hart's Panorama of the Holy Land. Hart advertised $300,000 in gifts for those paying a dollar admission to his shows. Everyone was given a ticket that guaranteed the bearer one item from a list of expensive and inexpensive gifts and told they would be notified when the gifts were awarded. In Hart's pitch, he promised everything from building lots and gold watches to 80,000 engraved maps of New York City. You can be assured everyone got the map. This venture fostered the origin of lotteries as well as the candy pitches found in burlesque, canvas repertory theaters, circuses, and on carnival shows.

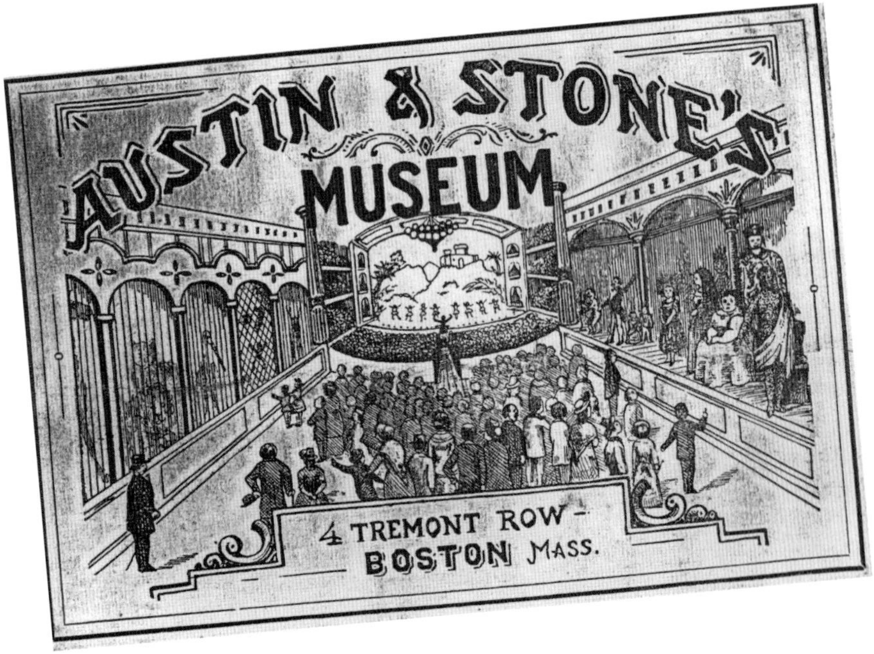

There were more suckers in the sticks! Magician Gus Hartz played two- and three-day stands. On the last night in town, he put on a gift show that he had ballyhooed at earlier shows. Patrons got a numbered slip of paper with each admission. The slips were placed in a box and drawn by an audience member on closing night and the gifts distributed. Except for a few good prizes to smother the heat, the gifts were slum.

Most *Clipper* references to freaks on tour in the 1860s have them showing in dime museums, theaters, and lyceums. Tom Thumb toured such venues, playing one- and two-day stands booked in month stretches by his agent, Alfred Cately. The midget would return home for a short rest

A rare look inside a combination show with a stage for plays and variety acts. Note the aerial ladder act plus the movie projector with gas cylinders.

This early fairground show is as plain as you can get. Consisting of a single crudely drawn and lettered banner, a small 20 x 20 tent with low side wall, and a small fold-up ticket box, the whole show could be gillied in several trunks and travel via railroad baggage car.

between stints on the road and head out again. To hold the crowd and entertain them enough to sell the pitch cards and booklets, Cately added some musical acts.

"Remember the Aztec Children here some years ago?" the *Clipper* reported in November 1860, "Barnum has them back after a couple of years in Europe. Now they are much older and nasty children. One look at them turns the stomach. While gazing upon the Aztec children, reflect that the self same ugly devils you are now looking upon have been looked upon in like manner by Queen Victoria, Emperor Napoleon, etc. What you now are, they have been!"

Around the same time, the *Clipper* noted the Peak family of Swiss bell ringers would open their 16th annual tour in April playing one-night stands along the New York and Erie Railroad. W.H. Peak claimed they were the original troupe of bell ringers and traveled with 170 bells, including the only set of silver bells ever made. Peak's family had been members of the church choir in Bedford, Mass., before joining temperance preacher John B. Gough on tour in 1829. Gough and the Peaks parted ways after a few seasons, and the family soon had two troupes, one managed by the father and one by the son.

Clipper reports starting in the 1860s indicated showmen were taking various attractions onto agricultural fairgrounds. An August edition reported: "We are glad to hear that the properties of the smaller or curiosity shows expect to reap a good harvest in the fall, on the occasion of their visiting the agricultural fairs." Later the same month, the *Clipper* listed Loveli and his Australasian Bear, and Carter the Indian Giant as two shows exhibiting at the Cynthiana, Ky., fair. At the fair in Easton,

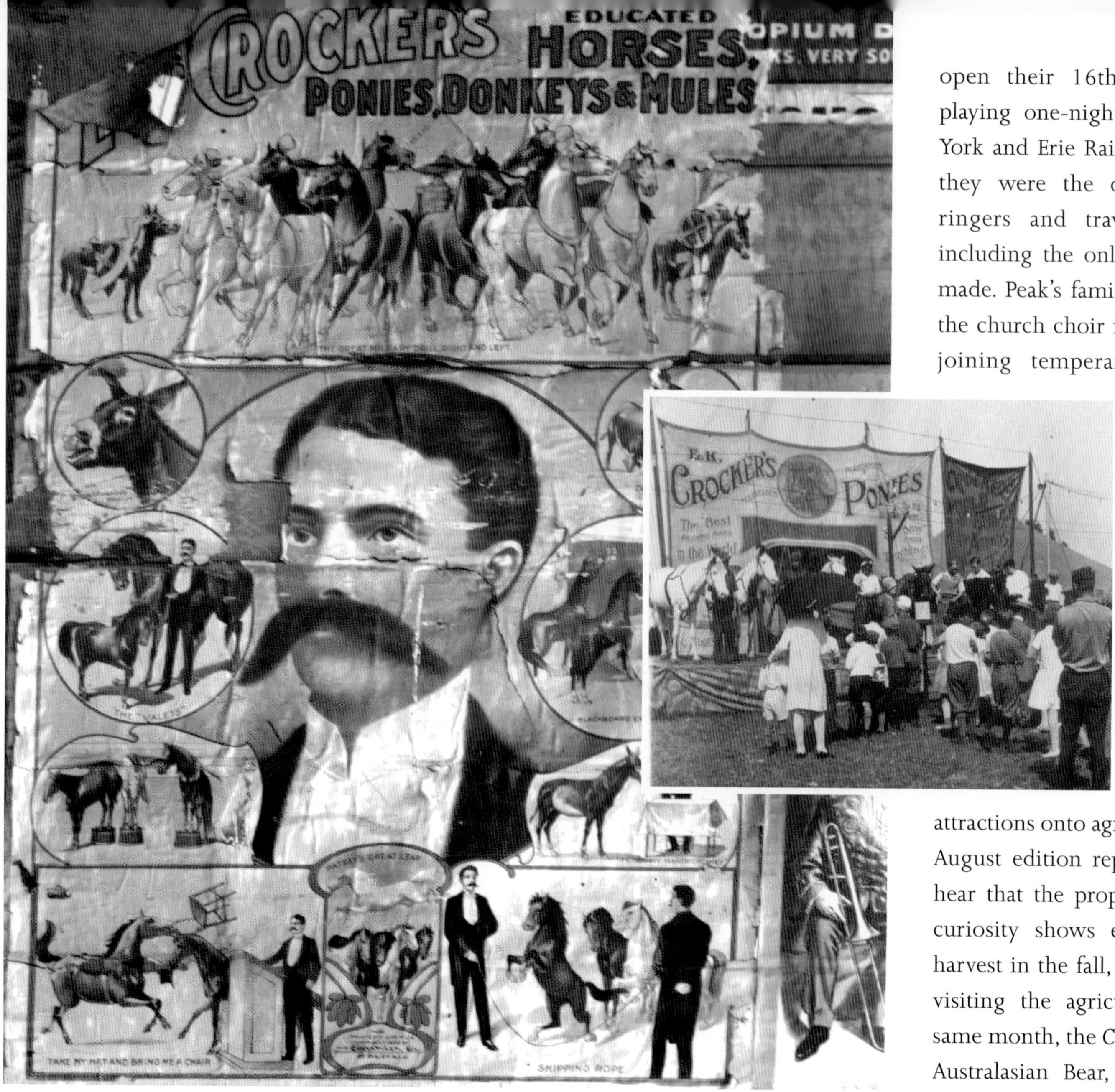

E.K. Crocker's educated horses, mules, donkeys and ponies show (inset) set up on the 1926 midway of Harry Lottridge's Royal Canadian Shows in Guelph, Ontario, and a poster advertising the show in vaudeville.

La., patrons viewed S.W. Bancker, billed as "the American Hercules," a skeleton man, and Whitby's Circus Co.

"Numerous shows in Indianapolis Fair. Some with more monstrosities than people could ever imagine exist," the *Clipper* noted in November 1860. "Men without arms or legs, who could play the flute. Three Bearded Children, skeleton man. Hogs with nine legs, and calves with six!" A small item in the trade paper a month later mentions the opening of the Cotton Plantation Fair in Macon, Ga., on December 10. This three-week fair started after the southern crops were harvested. It attracted big crowds and was the major event for showmen working south for the winter. On the grounds were shows comprised of Chinese jugglers; L. Hubbell, the American Samson strong-man show; Jane Campbell, the Connecticut Fat Girl; and Colonel Vedder and Major Bunnell's Museum of Living Wonders. This museum, the largest show on the grounds, featured Vantile Mack, Infant Giant; the Walters Dwarf Family; a mammoth anaconda; Japanese mice; and "wax figgers."

References in diaries, the *Clipper*, and in freak pitch-book bios indicate there was plenty of activity in sideshows playing fairs by the mid-1860s. Perhaps the best of this information comes from the pitch book for John Powers, the Kentucky Fat Boy. His sister Mary Jane Powers was ten years older and even heavier than he was, and first exhibited at Barnum's New York museum in 1867. The next year she joined her brother on a sideshow that left the circus to play fairs in the fall. The Powers left a show they were on several seasons later and bought a tent, snakes, and birds in Cincinnati and played fairs. At one point they added a professional talker, a midget lady, and two bears to their sideshow, playing fairs, storefronts, race meets, picnics, and firemen's musters, setting up in town squares and on lots adjacent to circuses. Each week was a mad scramble to pay fairground privileges and boarding bills for themselves, their help, and their horses. They would make money one week, only to lose it at the next venue. Snakes were constantly dying and their horses were often sick. By the fall of 1875, fed up with the struggle of running their own show, the Powers went to work for Colonel Woods at his Philadelphia Museum.

The early 1860s marked the end of many showmen's southern runs for a few seasons. The January 6, 1861, *Clipper* reported: "A deplorable state of affairs exists on either side of Dixie and the poor player sees his bread and butter gradually diminishing, without the power to save even a few crumbs of comfort from the vanishing substance. Some stars who have always played to full houses in the south, have this season performed to business as low as 18 dollars! Nigger Minstrels don't even find favor." Many showmen sought work for their troupes in Cuba. One-night-stand gift shows, dramatic troupes, minstrels, and

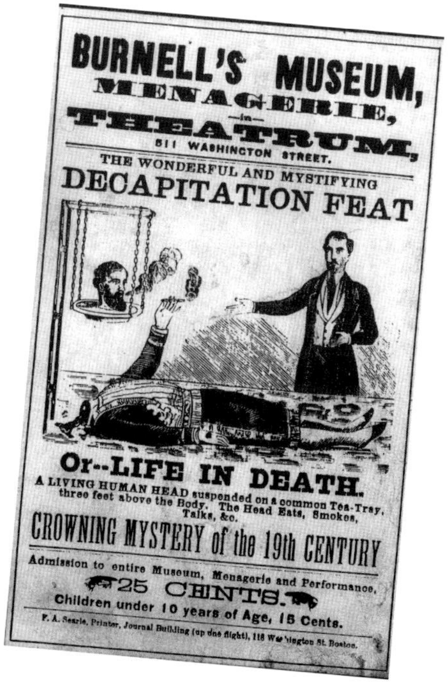

A fat ladies' convention at a dime museum in 1898.

even freaks kept their routes north of Dixie for the next few seasons. The 1861 circus season saw a lot of menageries and circuses going on lengthy tours in Canada. The resurgence of the touring panorama business, which had been losing public interest at this time, was one of the few amusements that directly benefited from the Civil War.

The 1880s, however, ushered in a new growth period for shows. Circuses and other amusement entrepreneurs worked the kinks out of moving a show via the railroad. Small amusement areas and beach resorts ran ads in the *Clipper* seeking showmen with flying horses, striking machines, shooting galleries, weighing machines, cider presses, and fruit and popcorn stands. George Bartholomew's Equine Paradox Show, consisting of 20 educated horses, was offering his attraction to fairs and claiming "the only touring animal entertainment endorsed by Humane Societies." New York City was still the place to go if you wanted to buy amusement supplies, from animals to sea serpents. Donald Burns on Roosevelt Street offered showmen snakes of all sizes that were guaranteed good feeders. He also had on hand monkeys, macaws, some cockatoos, a large tapir, and a tiger. The New York-based Martinka Co. was now the largest maker and seller of illusions and magic supplies to showmen.

Dime museums were also clipping along and organized into various chains so that freaks and working acts could easily get 15 to 20 weeks of continuous work. Between 1880 and 1900 there were hundreds of such museums — at least one in every city with a population over 10,000 — usually located in two- or three-story buildings. Customers bought a ticket and proceeded to the top floor to see the permanent collection of artifacts, then back down to the second floor to the curio hall where the current freaks and working acts performed. Ground level contained a theater where admittance to a 50-minute variety show was free but seats cost a nickel.

Attractions presented were the very best in the freak and variety act line. They were booked in by agents who took a modest 5 percent cut. All acts worked museums at one time or another and they had to be up to standards to get booked. Museums opened around 10 a.m. and ran continuous hourly shows until closing at 10 p.m.

The latest museum craze in 1887 were the Fat Lady Conventions. Managers booked in a half-dozen fat ladies and featured them in various contests — the 50-yard dash in the street outside the museum always drew large crowds. That same season, J.E. Sackett presented his Japanese Village in dime museums, advertising it as "a correct reproduction of a street in Japan with opera booths on either side hung with a perfect forest of lanterns." Each booth had an artist doing clay modeling, bamboo work, and so on. Another strange act making the dime circuit was Miss Agness St. John, billed as "A LIVING DEATH" and described as "eating, sleeping, and passing her existence floating in a miniature lake from 80 to 120 hours." Over 31,000 people paid to see her at G.E. Lothrop's World Museum in Boston.

The big highlight of Austin and Stone's museum in Boston in the winter of 1888 were 12 tattooed men and women billed as the Twelve Martyrs of the Needle. In the winter of 1892, Angola the Gorilla was a big draw on the museum circuit. His billing claimed he was the hero of a hard-fought battle in which he killed Warren Wilson's thoroughbred bulldog in 1 minute 50 seconds, thus winning a purse of $2,000. His owner, Frank Fletcher, said he stood four-foot-six and weighed 146 pounds. Angola joined a long list of chimps billed as gorillas.

Medicine shows were another popular touring entertainment, and a great source of talent for fairground showmen who obtained experienced and savvy talkers, pitchmen, and performers. Haley and Bigelow's Kickapoo Indian Medicine Show consisted of four Indians, a manager who was also the lecturer, a magician, and two musicians. Some seasons there were 30 or more units of the Kickapoo show out across the country. Next to the newly forming vaudeville theater circuits, the Kickapoo enterprises were the biggest employers of variety acts in the 1890s.

Beginning in the 1870s and continuing up to the turn of the century were touring shows the *Clipper* referred to as "Traveling Combinations" or "Pavilion shows." Presented under canvas, usually for a week, these shows offered performances that were a cross between a dime museum and a small circus. Many featured the hottest act or entertainment item, such as stereopticon views or phonograph demonstrations, and presented different shows each night of the week. The tents weren't as large as those on circuses, but smaller 50-by-90-foot tents with seating for several hundred. These shows often presented small dramatic or comedic theatrical pieces as well as sideshow acts, vaude and circus acts, illusions, and curio pieces. The candy pitch, food and drink sales, jewelry sales, fortune telling, glassblowing, and other concessions comprised a big part of their income.

November 7, 1885, marked a watershed in amusement coverage by the *Clipper*. A column titled "Circus and Sideshow" appeared for the first time, and a column titled "Miscellaneous" gave more extensive coverage of medicine and pavilion shows, as well as the first mention of the attraction known as "the fair ground show." The September 19 *Clipper* had carried route listings for 296 touring amusement enterprises, which included 201 dramatic, 28 musical, 25 variety, 14 minstrel, 12 circus, and 16 miscellaneous troupes. There were many more show operators who chose not to send in their routes, wishing to keep their whereabouts from competitors.

By the end of the 1800s showmen were mounting their pit show attractions and exhibiting them on city streets and show grounds. This uptown wagon (special pit show wagon built by circuses) is on Gollmar Brothers Circus in the early 1900s.

Several other factors reflected the growth in showmen exhibiting their attractions on the fairgrounds. Ads for support industries such as banner painters, tent makers, and gaff freak makers began to appear more often. By 1887, J.C. Goss' Detroit Tent and Awning Co. advertised: "Sideshow tents a specialty." There were ads for showmen seeking door talkers, snare drummers, and various acts, while talkers and acts were advertising their availability. The larger fairs, too, were advertising for sideshows, museums, and illusion acts.

Most early sideshows on circuses were independently run. These first operators had a baggage wagon for the tent, poles, stakes, stages, lanterns, and knock-down ticket boxes. Another carriage transported their acts and help. Overland show wagons were small and built light, with high wheels so they could ford streams. Paintings that could be rolled up provided colorful fronts for sideshowmen with limited space. An 1870s view of Barnum's one-pole, round-tent sideshow on his circus shows a half dozen banners of various sizes, each brought by individual acts.

More reports came into the *Clipper* about fairground showmen and their shows. G.W. Donaldson's fairground show opened its 1886 15-week season on August 20. He needed a strong woman, a lady to sing and play banjo, a Punch and Judy man who could lecture and do magic, plus a talker for the show. B.L. Bowman, meanwhile, wanted sideshow people with paintings for his New York Museum and a novelty show to play fairs, while Frank Uffner, manager of the Brooklyn Museum, took a show out during fair season. In 1892, he was manager of one of the best freaks, Tocci the two-headed boy, who he claimed he had been showing for 58 consecutive weeks without missing a single half-hour.

In the 1880s snare drummers and small hand organs (a barrel organ operated by crank) were used on these shows to attract people. Almost all the ads selling complete sideshow outfits list a hand organ among their goods for sale. Showman Ruben Hoffman of Niles, Mich., offered for sale a show consisting of a five-legged cow with two bags, double twin calves, and a double-headed calf, along with other curios, a tent, and a good crank organ. Freak cows seemed to be popular. Showman E.A. Franklin said his six-legged cow show came with a 40-by-60-foot tent and three outside paintings.

In March 1892 the Metallurgy Electro Co. of Syracuse, N.Y., was selling the property of a fairground show to settle a mortgage. The show consisted of performing bear cubs, two sacred Japanese dram fowls, a pair of Norway chickens ("Silk hair instead of feathers"), three alligators, three deer, "one buck with long antlers," several cases of stuffed animals, two music boxes playing several tunes, a dozen automatic figures, an Egyptian mummy, a Devil Child, wax double babies, a mermaid illusion, a 70-foot round tent, and more.

Artists and writers give us visions of the early circuses and medicine shows moving by horse and wagon. Independent sideshows and fairground shows traveled this way too. W.A. Roddy, from Danville, Ind., moved his fairground show in 1892 by six horses and mules pulling three wagons. His acts featured "the heaviest person alive," a Circassian snake charmer, a guitar player and singer, plus a door talker and lecturer.

The modernization of the showgrounds was slow but steady into the 1890s. Wagons built especially as show-exhibit wagons started appearing for sale in the *Clipper*. Circuses used exhibition wagons, which they referred to as "uptown wagons," mainly to get a location uptown on the circus parade route and capture some of the business from people who didn't go out to the circus grounds. The wagon was also set up on the grounds to catch the matinee and night crowds. Snakes, midgets, and freak animals were all good attractions for uptown wagons — one circus even exhibited an Oriental hoochie-coochie dancer in one.

There were maybe 50 or more independent fairground shows touring a few years prior to the 1893 Chicago fair. Those appearing in 1892 *Clipper* route columns included W.D. Ament (Mexican Billy); Wichita Jack's Wild West; C.E. Jordon with his devil child, sea turtle, and alligator show; J.A. Jones' Museum Show; Prof. E.S. O'Dell's Living Vampire, mind reader, mechanical talking figure, half lady, and midget; and F.R. Blitz touring the famous attraction Millie-Christine.

In the outdoor show business, showmen knew they'd reached the pinnacle of success when show owners and fairs

directly advertised in the trade papers for them or their attractions. In the early 1900s there were frequent ads from show owners wanting Frank R. Blitz, Mexican Billy, and H.L. Montford. Blitz and his wife, Louise, whom show people affectionately called Aunt Lou, were fairground show pioneers. Blitz, the son of famous musician Signor Blitz, had been on the fairground with museum-type shows since 1870. He and his wife knew every museum manager, every sideshow exhibitor, and every place in America where freaks and curiosities could be exhibited profitably.

Blitz became the road manager in 1878 for Millie-Christine, one of the greatest living curiosities then on exhibit in the U.S. Billed as the Famous Carolina Twins, the Two-Headed Nightingale, and

Frank Blitz's Millie-Christine fairground show as it appeared in 1899. Possibly Aunt Lou in the ticket box and Blitz behind her.

Millie-Christine, the famous Carolina twins.

the Double-Tongued Nightingale, Millie-Christine McCoy were black Siamese twins born near Whiteville, N.C., in 1851 to slave parents on a plantation owned by Alexander McCoy. The twins, who weighed 17 pounds at birth, had separate upper and lower bodies joining into one waist and pelvis. Although two separate people, they preferred to be addressed as one. McCoy was quickly fed up with the gawkers and sold them to a Mr. Baxter for exhibition. Baxter paid $10,000 with a note backed by local businessman Joseph P. Smith.

In 1853, Millie-Christine were the sensation of North Carolina's first state fair. Baxter was conned out of the twins in New Orleans when he tried to exchange them for land in Texas. He couldn't pay the note, nor did he have the twins. Back in North Carolina, Smith paid off McCoy and hired a detective to find the twins. The detective located a New York City cab driver who had driven them to the docks for a ship to Liverpool. Smith and the twins' mother sailed to England, where they found them on exhibition. Mrs. Smith was made the twins' guardian, and she home-educated them. Millie-Christine became skilled dancers and excellent singers, harmonizing in two different voices. In 1860 Smith died, leaving his son Pearson in charge of promoting Millie-Christine. They toured Europe for seven seasons. On their return to the U.S. in 1878 they hired Blitz as their manager.

Over the next 27 years, Blitz exhibited Millie-Christine as part of Blitz's Mammoth Museum, which he claimed was the largest fairground museum show on tour. In 1899, Blitz had Millie-Christine on Gaskill's Canton Carnival Co., one of the first organized carnival companies. But he preferred to book independently on fairs, because he felt the Millie-Christine show didn't belong on the midway — with so many fake attractions on the fairgrounds, he feared fairgoers would assume the same about his exhibit. He promised fair boards 10 percent of his gross, and backed up his statements by citing the 22,000 patrons who paid a quarter each to see the twins at the Winnipeg fair.

By 1909, Millie-Christine had retired from the road and bought a farm in North Carolina. They died, a day apart, in 1912.

Blitz, meanwhile, sought out bookings for a midget he named "the Russian Prince." A newspaper ad showed the prince being held up in the palm of a hand, and Blitz claimed his midget could gross more money in an hour than any of the other midgets out there could gross in a week. The Russian Prince, he said, could sing, dance, buy government bonds, build houses, and make money — and he had just entertained President Taft at the White House. At the 1909 Winnipeg fair, Blitz's Russian Prince grossed $2,631 on the midway of the big Kline Shows. Frank died at age 57 at the end of the 1910 season.

J. Augustus Jones started his outdoor show career as a fairground showman but quickly rose to the ranks of a circus owner. Jake Friedman stands on the pit show ticket box of Jones's 1917 two-car Cooper Bros. Circus.

J. Augustus Jones, better known for his two- and three-car circuses, more or less wrote the book on this type of circus operation. But, he started as a fairground showman. We first see mention of him in a July 1892 *Clipper* ad seeking freaks, curiosities of all kinds, a strong man, a fat lady, a glass-blower, a woman with snakes, and a man to do Punch and Judy shows and make openings. Working out of Warren, Pa., Jones opened his fairground show in Plainsville, Ohio, and went as far south as the Danville, Va., fair that season. In 1894, Jones was operating a show consisting of three small cages of animals, a den of snakes, and Jocko the performing monkey. In 1895 he was selling a 2.5-foot mermaid (with painting) and going into the circus business.

By 1910, Jones owned a large flat-car circus. In the teens, when the struggling carnival business was trying to clean up grift (con games) on shows, *Billboard* printed letters from people describing show grift they had witnessed. After several letters of complaints about his show appeared in *Billboard*, Jones wrote back saying it would

H.L. Montford made a good living with both his fairground and dime museum shows. He was also a dealer in "Devil Fish." These stuffed octopi appeared on many fairground shows floating in water, and were good attractions for small platform shows like the one here playing on the 1914 Parker and Kennedy Shows lot.

be very impractical for his circus to have grift on their two-car show as they were traveling in general passenger service and often laid over for the night in the towns on their route. A few weeks later, a small item in *Billboard* noted that Jones had reinforced his stateroom in the sleeping car on his show with two-inch bullet-proof steel.

Jones was not the only circus man to start a rich career on the fairgrounds. The December 1891 *Clipper* reported that Frank A. Robbins was in his 15th week touring fairs with a show. As the circus business progressed rapidly and showmen acquired more horses, elephants, exotic menagerie animals, and railroad cars, the show expenses soared as well. Many circuses stopped leasing out concert, sideshow, and candy-stand privileges and simply hired managers in an attempt to grab a bigger share of the money generated by these extras. This may be why more sideshowmen went onto the fairground circuit. Other circus showmen turned to the carnival business, because circuses paid higher licences for a one-day exhibition than carnivals paid for their whole week's stay.

H.L. Montford could be described as the Devil Fish King. He started his fairground show career in Detroit in the 1880s before moving his operations to Toronto. During fair seasons, he toured Ontario, Quebec, New York, and Pennsylvania with a museum-type show that featured both live acts and stuffed curiosities, mainly devil fish or "octopi," which he also sold to other showmen.

In winters Montford operated dime museums, alternating between Toronto, Ottawa, and Montreal. In a July 1886 *Clipper* ad he advertised for a fat lady, a tattooed lady to handle snakes, a Circassian lady to sing and play banjo, a lecturer to do Punch and Judy, and "talking heads." He also wanted two loud snare drummers who had lively sideshow specialties. Door talkers had to make strong and loud openings, he warned: "Only hustlers need apply." That season his was one of the few shows set up at the Toronto fair. His September 3, 1892, *Clipper* ad offered showmen two devil fish Montford described as genuine octopus accompanied by 12-by-12-foot paintings. They were exhibited in tanks of water and could be bought from him en route. Montford put lots of showmen in business — the devil fish was among the shows on the first carnival companies.

One difference between the circus sideshow and the fairground sideshow in this era was that while few fairground shows featured real freaks, half the acts presented in any major circus sideshows were freaks. Circus sideshow men had limited time to fill a tent — and freaks were a big draw. The talker had to turn a high percentage of the people on the grounds into the sideshow with just one or two openings. By contrast, on the fairgrounds, the sideshow was exposed to crowds from the time the fair opened until it closed, and operated at a far less frantic pace. Fair crowds came to be entertained, and the working and variety acts seemed to satisfy them. But as more and more shows appeared on the fairgrounds, the need for a strong freak to put people into the sideshow certainly increased. Peter Conklin, working fairs with a sideshow in 1892, added Congo, an armless performer, to his roster.

The hottest freak attraction on the 1892 dime-museum circuit was Laloo, a gentleman who had a second body emerging from his stomach. His fame had even crossed over to the gaff makers, who were turning out papier-mâché likenesses of him. Among the working acts in museums, the top attraction was the Tank Act or Man Fish, in which a performer simply swam in a glass tank and did unusual things underwater for long periods of time without surfacing for air. At the top of his field was Enoch, who could stay underwater for up to three and a half minutes while playing the trombone.

One of the real characters of outdoor show business in this era was W.D. Ament, who billed himself as Mexican Billy. In August 1891 he opened his 16-week fairground tour in Homer, Ill., with his California Museum in a 40-by-75-foot tent. The *Clipper* called his Wild West fairground show the neatest, largest, and strongest of its kind. It was the only show selected by the Springfield, Ill., fair out of 50 applications. The show consisted of magicians, cowgirl singers and dancers, a tribe of Indians, and cowboy musical artists, with

In the early 1890s, Laloo from India, with his twin sister growing out of his stomach, was a big draw at dime stores and circus sideshows. He was one of the early human freaks that the fake freak builders created images of from papier-mâché and wax.

By the end of WWI the style and operation of the carnival 10-in-1 was fixed and has remained that way. This one is operating with pits and an open front as Walter Sibley pioneered them. With the exception of the fat couple, the rest are working acts including glass blowers, a paper tear act, a fire eater, a magician, and a tattooed man.

Billy himself doing sharp-shooting.

In March 1892, Mexican Billy played museums west of the Mississippi and advertised for recruits for his fairground show: "Recognized show people who are sober and reliable." In October 1893, after his fair season closed at Belle Plain, Iowa, he placed an ad in the *Clipper* offering his skills as the world's champion fancy rifle shot, musical artist, and vent, and promoting his wife, Princess Nanna, as a gifted mind-reader. They were soon working on the Midway Plaisance in the Chicago World's Fair before moving on to the California Mid-Winter Fair. Two years later he was touring W.D. Ament's Big Ten Cent Shows. In 1900 he had out a good-size circus called Capt. W.D. Ament's Vaudeville Circus, presented under an 80-by-140 main tent, with a 16-by-20 stage for the show plus a 30-by-60-foot black sideshow tent.

Ament also put the first ghost shows on the American midway. In spring of 1901 he wrote *Billboard* to say he had been in Jackson, Tenn., when a cyclone went through town. Houses were flattened, but his new U.S.A. Tent and Awning Co. 50-by-120-foot tent stayed up. In his 20 years of trouping, he hadn't seen any tent withstand a wind like that! In July he took out a "Plantation" show with a 50-foot front that featured a 50-by-80-foot tent along with the ghost show. He had ten employees on the ghost show and 30 on the minstrel show. He also had an arcade on the midway. In 1903, his March *Billboard* ad offered his ghost show and another show to carnival managers, warning, "Don't ask for more than 95% as I need 5% to pay the actors!" In 1909, he built a theater for black people in Jackson.

This is your typical dog and pony circus at a street fair. People have the mistaken impression of "dog and pony shows" being of poor entertainment value. Most had high-quality acts and some were medium-sized railroad circuses with good reputations. The title was used to avoid licences.

This is a very early "well show." The patron went up a set of high stairs and stared down into the bottom of the pit shaft where a naked female image made the climb worthwhile. This show worked with a mirror similar to the mermaid illusion and was one of the first shows banned on fairgrounds.

As one of the showmen who periodically wrote the *Clipper* and *Billboard* to relate excessive fees charged him by fairs or carnival managers, Ament joined California Frank, Joe Ferari, J.H. Johnson, and others to found the Showman's Association in 1909. They hoped to weed out all the fakers and immoral exhibitors from the profession and reinforce the reputations of independent showmen with worthwhile shows. As Ament told *Billboard*, "Showmen do not want to be classed as a pack of thieves and grafters to be robbed and imposed upon by unfair managers who demand every dollar of profit from our business."

After his ghost show and arcade days, Ament ended up on the west coast. In 1922 he was on Foley and Burk Shows with a large combination illusion and freak show that included the Spidora, Zenobia, and

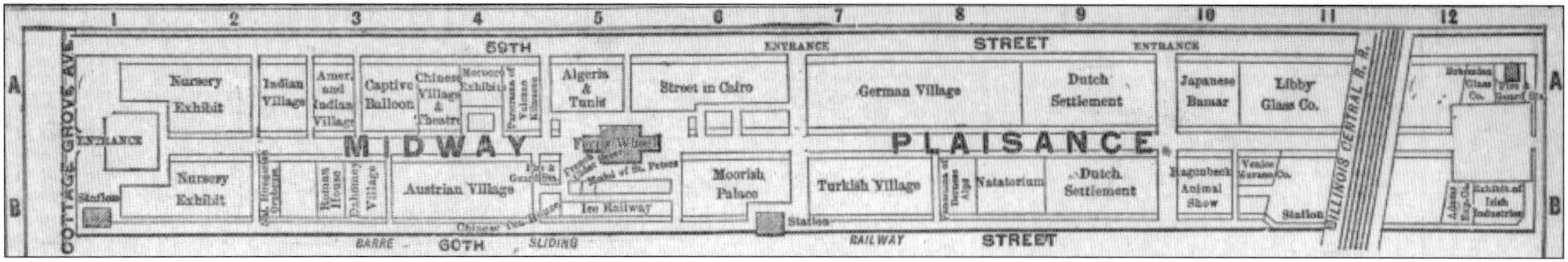

The midway plaisance area of the 1893 Chicago World's Fair.

Long, single banner fronts with a doorway cut in the middle like this girl show set-up dominated show front architecture on carnivals until WWI.

Sawing a Lady in Half illusions, along with Marietta the Armless Wonder, the mind-reader Madame Fremini, and a two-headed baby. The following year, he put his show up for sale, ending his long career in the outdoor show world.

At the 1893 Chicago World's Fair, the cry was "Have you seen the midway!" People everywhere talked about going to Chicago and seeing the midway shows. The midway was a novelty — the public had never seen so many quality attractions gathered in one area for the sole purpose of entertaining them. The unique ways of presenting the various shows were so different and intriguing to the public that even old shows seemed new. The cooch dancers in every circus sideshow annex and carnival girl show were now called the famous and original World's Fair Dancers. The public lapped up the stories of Little Egypt. They didn't know truth from fiction and they didn't care; what they wanted were the latest in entertainments.

As the 19th century wound down, many social factors were in place for a whole new era in the growth of show business. The biggest obstacle to the expansion of fairground entertainment had been the lack of electricity, but the 20th century and the "electric era" would revolutionize both the fairgrounds and the amusement park. Another boost to the fair business was the arrival of the automobile — families could easily drive in from surrounding towns and farms, with far less time and effort than it had been via horse and buggy. Families could visit the fair several times during fair week, while from the showmen's point of view, greater numbers of cattle and horses could be trucked in, enlarging these displays and drawing more rural folk.

The industrial age and the growth in manufacturing and commercial ventures made employment available to those who wanted it. Now ordinary people had spare money for entertainment and looked upon leisure time as an important aspect of a full life. By the early 1900s, employers were letting workers off a half day on Saturdays and some employees were even taking small vacations. American cities grew rapidly from 1870 through to the 1920s, and local showmen provided them with arcades, dance halls, cinemas, amusement parks, and vaudeville theaters. People enjoyed the company of strangers, and by the 1890s there were few restrictions at public events based on gender, religion, or occupation. The only enduring barrier to where an American could pursue his or her pleasures was race.

Until flat car and wagon carnivals flourished in the years after WWI, the average carnival showman moved his show or ride in baggage cars. If show people bought enough coach tickets the railroads threw in the baggage cars for free. Here we see the Flack's Great Northern Shows moving gilly style in the early 1900s.

On the fairgrounds, things were changing too. Better technology and lighter but stronger materials led to the arrival of the first merry-go-round and then the Ferris wheel on touring midways. An 1896 *Billboard* report of the Springfield fair said the fakers had gathered in an open area by the horse and cattle barns and offered such shows as a Petrified Woman; a circus with

Cars helped to swell attendance at fairs. Based on the number of cars at this fair, there seems to be a good crowd. The popular whip ride in the foreground had just made its first appearance on midways.

Oriental dancing girls; "he, she, or it" views for scientific purposes at ten cents extra; a lady said to have a horse's mane and a lion's claw; a Mexican wild man; a wild double-woman; and "20th Century Dancing Girls." The barkers were openly advertising "Men Only Shows" and part of their spiel was a promise the show was "Nothing tame like ladies and children could see in downtown opera houses."

Billboard took a swipe at the fair officials, suggesting such entertainments wouldn't do so well on the fairgrounds if fairs put less emphasis on horse racing and betting and more on dog shows and trained animals. The Wisconsin fair the same year declared for the first time it would have no fakers and no sideshows, "nigger babies," cane racks, educated pigs, museums of anatomy, living pictures, or snake ladies.

But, the showmen would never be off the midway for long. By the early 1900s, a fair wasn't a fair without a midway; fairs needed them to attract the people and their money. Neither midway nor fair could do without each other, and a love-hate relationship between carnivals and fair boards began. And it continues to this day.

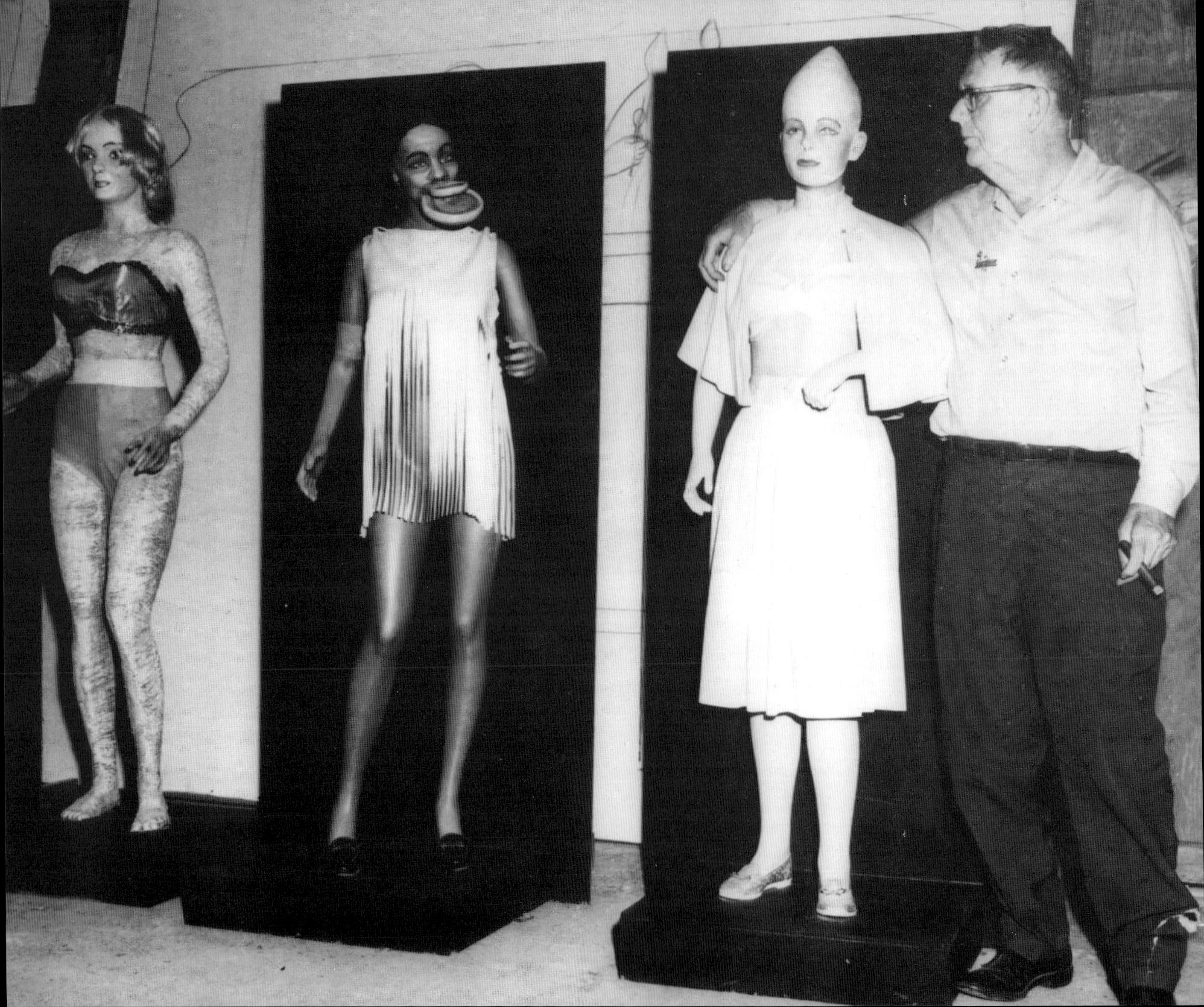

WHERE DO YOU BUY A POLY-MOO-ZUKE?

Suppliers of the Unusual

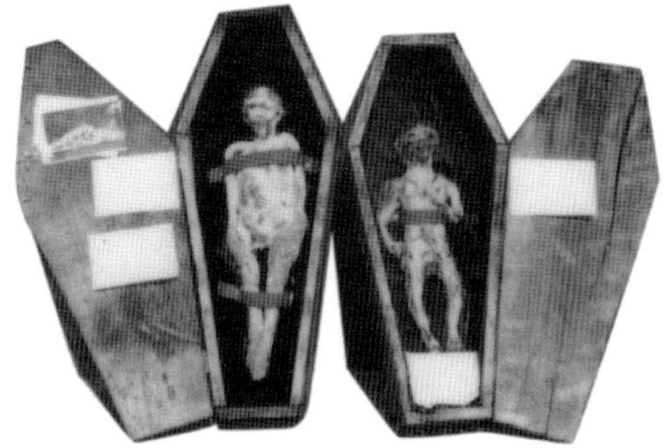

Inside the old semi-trailer, the air was stale and hot. Its doors hadn't been opened in years. Showman Dick Johnson moved poles, trunks, bundles of old canvas, folded-up ticket boxes, and crates holding illusions. He unloaded half the trailer before finding the Little Men From Mars. Their black coffins poked out from under more bundled canvas.

He had offered to sell them to me in the mid-1970s. I remember the winter day I got his letter and the four Polaroid shots of these guys. I was in the kitchen and I showed them to my wife. How about these for a show on the circus midway, dear? The look of horror, then disgust, on my wife's face told me we wouldn't be adopting them.

With the interest in sideshow relics heating up in the 1990s, I hunted up Dick in Florida to see if he still lived with the Little Men From Mars. I wanted another look. Dick removed the lids from their boxes. The two

Opposite: Banner painter Snap Wyatt also made show displays using various papier-mâché freaks like the ones he poses with here in his Tampa, Fla., studio.

Chapter 3

little men lay against a background of red satin. One had a broken leg. They looked like they were made of old cork, maybe even a strange concoction of wood filler and papier-mâché stained with chewing tobacco. Their limbs protruded from their bodies like twisted tree roots. One thing they didn't look was real. On today's midway, you couldn't fool even the most ardent tabloid junky with these guys and a story that they once lived on Mars. But five decades ago, people stared into a canvas pit at them and wondered what they ate, whether they played ball on Mars, how they got here, and how they "did it." The lecturer may have told them all that and more, before selling them the pitch book or postcard.

Homer Martin Tate's people arrived in Utah with the early pioneers. They were of Irish descent and eventually became followers of the Mormon faith. In 1898, they moved to central Arizona. Homer had been a miner, farmer, sheriff, still breaker, and head of a boy's reformatory. Out of the blue in the 1940s, he began making strange creatures and selling them to showmen. Homer seemed to be the only Tate that took a wrong turn.

One of his first ads in *Billboard* in 1942 was headed "THE SHRUNKEN JAPANESE SOLDIER. SEE THE TINY SHRUNKEN BODY." It went on: "Once being a mighty fighting soldier, now a shrunken midget. Genuine reproduction of the Japanese body in shrunken condition. Every detail true to life. Crowds flock to see this one. It has black hair, eyelashes, brows, mouth, ears. Cannibals actually shrink heads and bodies. We tell you all with lecture. Fill your show every night. Weight about seven pounds. Length over all about three feet. Shipped in nice casket post paid — only $15. Biggest window attractions in America. Stops all. Carnivals, museums, circuses, store shows, window attractions. Order today."

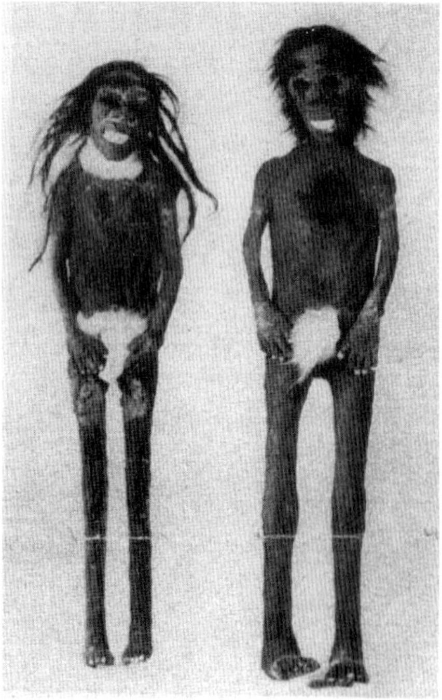

Tate moved to Phoenix around 1945 and had several museums. In 1946 he was advertising "Native shrunken heads, Devil's Child, Fish Girl, Wolf Boy and Ape Boy." He was the main gaff maker to showmen after World War II.

In 1948 Tate was specializing in "Shrunken Heads as the natives of the jungle prepare them! White native and others, also female heads with long hair." He also made life-size mummies. By 1950

Tate figures on display in Jack Constantine's museum show in Hamburg, N.Y., in 1999.

Tate was advertising for other dealers to handle his shrunken heads. The next year, he offered "the Wild Boy from the Jungle of Borneo" and "Dried Pigmy Bodies." In 1952 he claimed business was so good that he was even shipping shrunken heads to South America.

Tate was now offering a "Two-headed Bisexual Baby and also a Morphidite." His family viewed him as the black sheep of the fold and in the early 1960s he went to jail for reasons unknown. When he got out of prison, he reformed and worked in a church. He died in 1975. Like many folk artists or creators of what the art world now calls "outsider art," Tate's fame arrived only after he was gone. His creatures are now highly sought after by collectors of the bizarre.

Shad Kvetko, a step-great-great-grandson, told me Homer gathered animal parts in the desert to make the hands of devil's childs, and used claws from dead animals for other figures. Shad had seen several of Tate's bigger pieces and said it looked like he had used broomsticks for the arms and legs, then covered them with a skin of toilet paper and horse glue. His shrunken heads also had an opening in the neck the size of a broomstick and Shad suspected Homer formed the head around a broomstick. Tate colored his figures with

A Mark Frierson painted banner, depicting little people from Borneo, that could be used to ballyhoo most of Tate's shrunken jungle figures.

A Tate "devil man" figure on display at James Taylor and Dick Horne's Baltimore Dime Museum. This establishment is in its second year of operation. The collection is a potpourri of showman artifacts and man-made freaks, plus other curiosities such as human hair art.

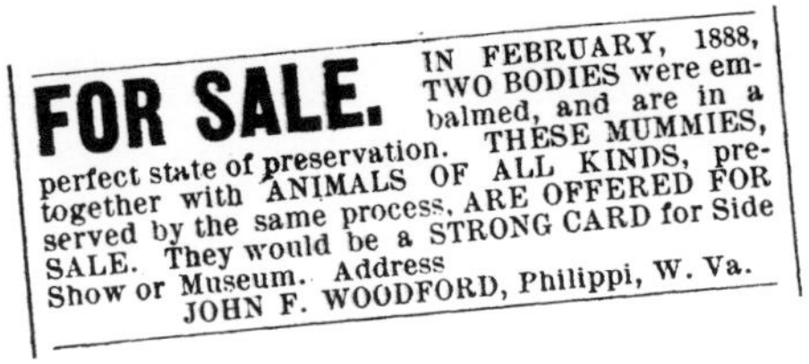
FOR SALE. IN FEBRUARY, 1888, TWO BODIES were embalmed, and are in a perfect state of preservation. THESE MUMMIES, together with ANIMALS OF ALL KINDS, preserved by the same process, ARE OFFERED FOR SALE. They would be a STRONG CARD for Side Show or Museum. Address
JOHN F. WOODFORD, Philippi, W. Va.

shoe polish, which gave them that mummified, earthy look. Mark Frierson, a sideshow gaff maker of the 21st century, autopsied some Tate figures and found that they also contained a lot of newspaper.

A Fiji Mermaid currently on display in Scott McClelland's Carnival Diablo grind show on Conklin Shows midway in Canada. Scott's grandfather, Nick Lewchuk, who was a magician, showman, and carnival owner in Saskatchewan since the mid-1920s, owned it.

As long as there have been showmen, there have also been people making fake attractions for them. Richardson Wright's *Hawkers and Walkers in Early America* describes a mermaid on exhibition in New England in the early 1800s — its lower part was made of a stuffed cod fish and neatly connected to the breasts and head of a baboon. Barnum's Fiji Mermaid was obtained on a lease percentage basis from Moses Kimball of the Boston Museum. Kimball claimed the embalmed mermaid had been obtained by a Boston sea captain near Calcutta in 1817. It was described as the body and tail of a large fish and the shoulders, arms, and upper torso with drooping breasts of a female orangutan, with the head of a baboon. It went on display at Barnum's Museum in 1842 but was pulled off tour a few months later when a fuss was made over its authenticity.

The makeup of the Fiji Mermaid suggested just some of the skills a taxidermist needed to disguise the original components. An average person with little knowledge of zoology or anatomy in the 19th century could be easily fooled, and some taxidermists and gaff makers were so good, even medical people were taken in by their creations.

A curious public will look at anything, and memory of past humbugs or fakes is a moot restraint once the mind's curiosity is stoked by the showman's spiel or the lurid banners displayed in front of his show. By the early 1890s, several New York City naturalists were advertising embalmed human freaks as well as petrified and mummified curiosities. As the sideshow business on the fairgrounds grew and city dime museums flourished, the trade in dead, stuffed, and mummified curios increased.

Certainly many preservation techniques and display methods were well-known to taxidermists, naturalists, and makers of gaffed attractions for showmen. No doubt some had their own "secret" formulas. Early man-made freaks were made from wax, papier-mâché, various compounds, and combinations of embalmed or natural animal and human parts.

From the 1840s, most living freaks earned good money in museums and theaters. They could remain in one location for weeks or months. But circus and fairground work would not be their first choice; for the small-time sideshowman, freaks were simply too expensive and hard to look after on the road. Living freaks often had short life spans because of the medical conditions that created their uniqueness. Working acts blew the show without notice, and freaks often got sick or died. As a result, gaffed freaks and illusions became the showman's insurance policy. Certainly limited space on early wagon circuses and limited boarding rooms made gaffed freaks popular to the early circus sideshowman. Two or three man-made freaks, like mermaids, two-headed calves, and devil fish, could be packed away in a few boxes and each could be featured on a banner and in the talker's spiel to make the show seem bigger.

Automatons and mechanical figures were some of the earliest wonders presented by showmen. In the late 1860s, P.T. Barnum found Wesley L. Jukes working as a glassblower at Wood's Museum in New York City and hired him at $250 a week to be in charge of building mechanical figures and effects for the museum. In 1871, Jukes produced the Dying Zouave, described in William L. Slout's *Olympians of the Sawdust Circle* as a "life-sized figure draped in French Zouave military uniform, breathing and struggling from the effects of the final bullet, the wound emitting a stream of warm, red blood." Jukes also built a Magic Drummer that answered questions in arithmetic, geography, and history, and Sleeping Beauty, breathing precisely as if alive, plus automatic trumpeters, lady bell ringers, and mechanical birds. Barnum also exhibited Jukes' mechanical Lord's Last Supper from 1876 to 1880.

Julius S. Hansen, a New York City taxidermist and nature specialist, was one of the earliest suppliers of the strange and wonderful gaffed freaks for showmen's use. His September 10, 1887, *Clipper* ad informed sideshow managers he was ready to ship a 13-foot sea serpent in a 10-foot box for $45; a 4-foot mermaid for $28; a 4-foot-6 alligator boy for $25, and 4-foot-6 Egyptian mummies for $22 each. A year

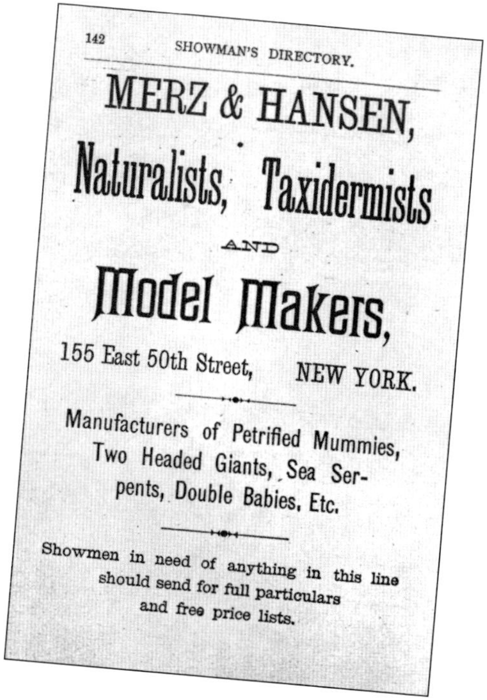

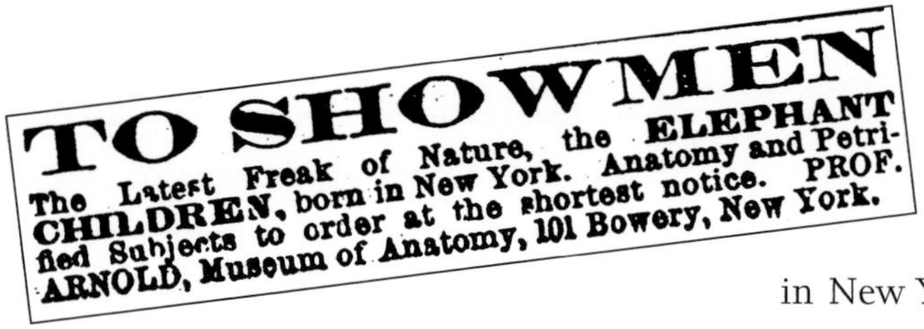

later he was offering the Demon Child, 3 feet high and priced at $35. He was also selling mummies, petrified bodies, and embalmed human freaks.

In 1891, Hansen took on a chap named Merz as his partner. They now listed themselves as taxidermists, naturalists, and model makers. The next season their ads read: "Showmen, want a Mummy?" They were offering an Egyptian mummy, an alligator boy, a crystalized baby, and an Indian head. By 1899 they were creating petrified mummies, two-headed giants, sea serpents, and double babies.

Used devil childs and other stuffed creatures turned up regularly for sale in small *Clipper* ads. The "Gorilla Man" was listed for sale in the fall of 1891 by H.A. Davenport, who stated: "He is one of the finest mummies on the road. I have just closed four successful years with him. He is in first-class shape and easily carried. If you want to work streets, rooms, fairs, and picnics, this is the attraction for you."

Merz and Hansen had competition in the freak-making field. Arnold Schenkenburger and Ernest Bruggemann, working out of E. 51st Street in New York City, were advertising themselves as anatomists and naturalists, offering sideshow presenters sea monsters, mummies, and an illustrated catalog of such works. Bruggemann was the naturalist, while Schenkenburger was the modeler and had a reputation for excellent creations.

Schenkenburger's history as a freak-maker reached back to before the 1890s. The November 6, 1887, edition of the New York City paper *The World* carried an article titled "The Sea-Serpent Factory." The writer, riding on the Third Ave. elevated train, observed what he thought was a body dangling out of an upper-storey Bowery window. He got off at the next stop and backtracked to the building. At the entrance he was given a series of excuses why he couldn't go up there. After an hour or so of haggling, he was let up to the top-floor attic, where an old man and a boy were working in a room surrounded by "freak objects."

The reporter identified that old man as Arnold Schenkenburger, an Alsatian who claimed to be a naturalist and anatomist. Looking around the room, the writer observed all kinds of freaks in various stages of construction. Among the pieces were mummies, unicorns, griffins, dragons, mermaids, and sea serpents. Schenkenburger also made human bats, gnomes, devil fish, crocodile boys, octopi, man-faced dogs, turtle boys, and anything to order.

Asked how he made a mermaid, the curious craftsman replied, "A strange fish was caught and sent to Fulton market. I bought it, cured it, and put human shoulders, head, and arms on it. The shoulders,

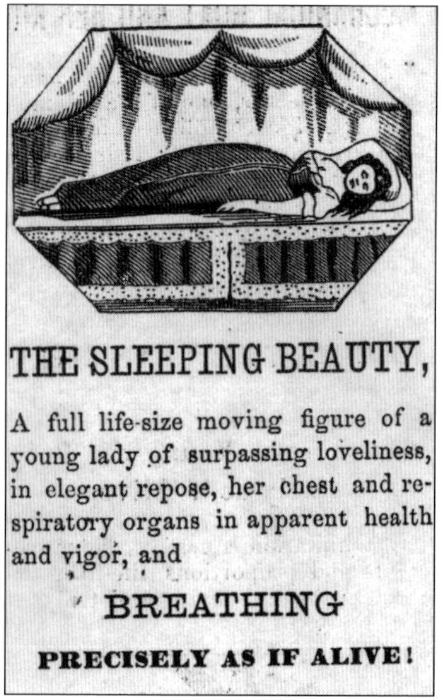

head, and arms as you see are anatomically correct and made of composition. The teeth and hair are natural. The skin is human skin, prepared and shriveled by a process known only to me. The nails of the claws I make myself from horn. So long as you don't cut or chip my mummies, you can't tell them from the ones in Central Park." The mermaids were his best sellers.

The reporter asked about the man-ox and was told, "the ground work of the man-ox is a composition; the skin covering the bones is natural but preserved, the teeth are natural and so is the hair. The sinews are made of glue and chamois, the fingers and toenails that look so real are made from polished horn, and the ribs are sheep ribs. We call it a man-ox because it resembles a man in all but the body." For a higher price, Schenkenburger made figures with detailed insides including lungs, heart, liver, and all internal organs, so the freaks could withstand semi-scientific inspection.

William Nelson was a showman. Somewhere along the way in his adventures he also turned to making and selling freak attractions. One of his earliest attempts was advertised for sale in an August 1890 *Clipper*, just in time for the fair season. His "Wonderful SERPENT CHICKEN" (a chicken with a snake's head) and "CAT WITH TWO HEADS" were mounted exhibits that sold for $20, including an 8-by-10-foot banner. His first gaffs must have been convincing, as he sent each one out by express agent so the buyer could examine it before purchase.

In 1895 Nelson believed he had found a new sensation. He described it as the "Japanese Devil Fish Child imported from Japan. It is strange, wonderful, hideous to behold; an attraction standing solitary and alone, as hard to duplicate as the Pyramids of Egypt; a whole show in itself." The price for this wonder was 20 bucks.

Next year he was offering showmen Nelson's X Ray Illusion for looking through a person's body. His ad claimed: "Taking nine and ten hundred weekly. Everybody wants to look through pretty girls. It's getting all the money at the fairs; it's bankrupting all other attractions. It holds the push and nothing can break it. The old attractions ain't in it. They have had their day. Fakirs, showmen; it is not yet too late. Get one at once. The fairs last but a few weeks. It may put thousands in your pocket. Price: $25."

In 1903 Nelson was in charge of the show wagon on the Pawnee Bill Wild West, which featured Eugene Berry, the big-footed boy. In *Billboard* ads, Nelson offered sideshow and platform men the "Two-Headed Hockadola," which he claimed was

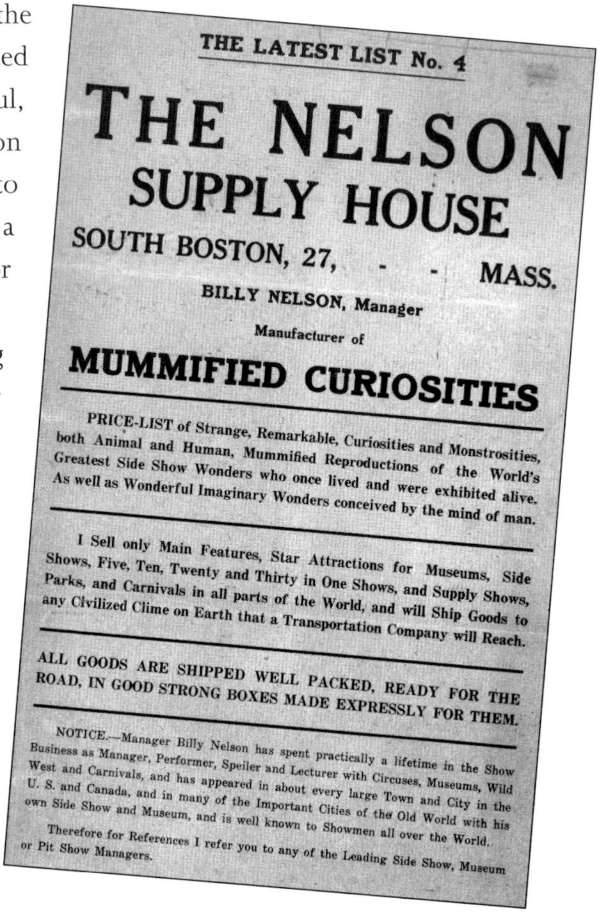
THE LATEST LIST No. 4

THE NELSON SUPPLY HOUSE

SOUTH BOSTON, 27, - - MASS.

BILLY NELSON, Manager

Manufacturer of

MUMMIFIED CURIOSITIES

PRICE-LIST of Strange, Remarkable, Curiosities and Monstrosities, both Animal and Human, Mummified Reproductions of the World's Greatest Side Show Wonders who once lived and were exhibited alive. As well as Wonderful Imaginary Wonders conceived by the mind of man.

I Sell only Main Features, Star Attractions for Museums, Side Shows, Five, Ten, Twenty and Thirty in One Shows, and Supply Shows, Parks, and Carnivals in all parts of the World, and will Ship Goods to any Civilized Clime on Earth that a Transportation Company will Reach.

ALL GOODS ARE SHIPPED WELL PACKED, READY FOR THE ROAD, IN GOOD STRONG BOXES MADE EXPRESSLY FOR THEM.

NOTICE.—Manager Billy Nelson has spent practically a lifetime in the Show Business as Manager, Performer, Speiler and Lecturer with Circuses, Museums, Wild West and Carnivals, and has appeared in about every large Town and City in the U. S. and Canada, and in many of the Important Cities of the Old World with his own Side Show and Museum, and is well known to Showmen all over the World.

Therefore for References I refer you to any of the Leading Side Show, Museum or Pit Show Managers.

Midway show featuring Nelson's Mother and child mummy. Note the black carnival band providing the music to attract a crowd for the talker.

The Poly-Moo-Zuke

"a thousand miles ahead of dancing girls, wild men, or snake eaters. A dead man can get money with it."

By 1909, Nelson was manufacturing "mummified curiosities." He pitched his products as "Strange, Remarkable Curiosities and Monstrosities both Animal and Human and Mummified Reproductions of the World's Greatest Sideshow Wonders who once lived and were exhibited alive."

His specialty was "Wonderful Imaginary Wonders conceived by the mind of man." Elsie, the Wooly-Faced Girl, who Nelson described as "Alive, alive, has more legs than any human on earth," was his leading seller for platform showmen.

Among these creations were King Mac-a-Dula, the Two-Headed Patagonian Giant; King Jack-a-Loo-Pa, the Three-Faced Man, described as having one head, three faces, three hands, three arms, three fingers, three legs, three feet, and three toes; the six-legged Poly-Moo-Zuke, the Centipedian wonder ("Something horrible and different from anything ever shown"); "Antonio," the Italian Twins with two heads, four arms, four shoulders, one stomach, and two legs; the Gigantic Moa or

Mummified figures last used by Ward Hall and Chris Christ in their combination sideshow and museum show (1990s).

Devil Bird ("A new up-to-date attraction. A supposedly extinct monster that science believes to be a Gigantic elephant-footed Moa or Wingless Serpent Bird"); "Labow," the Egyptian Double Boy with Sister Growing from Breast ("A human Paradox that has four arms, four legs; two human beings, but with one head"); and the Big Sea Horse ("Six feet long and made to ship in box. It is a mummified subject with a big natural horse's skeleton head and two legs with slit hoofs").

In the 1920s, Nelson was still selling mummified curiosities such as the Cigarette Fiend, Horn Lady, Ossified Man, and Four-Legged Girl, any one of them for $25. One of his newest freaks was the Wolf Girl, who had hands where her feet should have been. Another big seller was his wax two-headed baby. Nelson's ads continued in *Billboard* into the early 1930s. Among his last offered curiosities were the King Tut Mummies, six-legged Poly-Moo-Zukes, nine-foot baby whales, and his stock in trade, the devil child and mermaids.

Before rubber two-headed babies came along, the best material for making ones that would last was papier-mâché. There were plenty of masters of the art, supplying whatever showmen might need. In 1888, Fawcet Robinson of New York City advertised in the *Clipper* that he did papier-mâché work of every description. The Western Papier-mâché Co. in Chicago ran ads in the 1893 *Clipper* offering showmen a double baby. In 1904 the New York-based Turner Company was promoting its papier-mâché skills for grotto work, weird interiors, decorations for "summer resorts, exhibitions, open-air shows, fairs, and all the best and finest places in Coney Island." They also made papier-mâché dragons, skeletons, devils, monkeys, statuary, animal heads, and trick and straight properties for vaudeville. During World War I, E. Walker of New York offered showmen a papier-mâché horse for nude girl posing acts, frames for living pictures, male and female dummies, and various prop animals.

ESTABLISHED 1875
W. H. J. SHAW
MANUFACTURER OF
LIFE SIZE DYING AND BREATHING
MECHANICAL WAX FIGURES
THEY ARE A MOVING, BREATHING MARVEL OF ART
ALSO MANUFACTURER OF
ALL KINDS OF
ILLUSIONS, MARIONETTES, BLACK ART OUTFITS
And The Best Ventriloquist Figures In The World
THEY ARE THE HEIGHTH OF PERFECTION AND SUPERIOR IN FINISH AND DURABILITY TO ALL OTHERS. IN USE THE WORLD OVER.
Victoria, Mo. MAR 22 1917 19

W.H.J. Shaw's letterhead for his wax, marionette, and vent figure making business. In addition to being the main supplier of wax figures to crime showmen, Shaw was a general dealer in all kinds of used show equipment.

W.H.J. Shaw, another supplier, was born in Hamilton, Ont., in 1859. As a teenager, he owned a minstrel show he successfully toured across Canada. Around the same time, he started a company to make and sell illusions. In 1888 Shaw offered the plans and secrets to the She Cremation, Omega, and Crystal Coffin illusions. Shaw toured a magic show with a magician named Edmond while continuing to sell magical apparatus, secret photographs, and theatrical supplies. In 1891 he offered instructions for 22 fire acts and eight other stage illusions. The following year, he was in Chicago dealing in Indian and war relics, wax figures, stereopticons, illusions, spiritual effects, crystalized skeletons, finely crafted papier-mâché vent dummies, and Punch and Judy figures.

Shaw was the first sideshow supplier to advertise in *Billboard*. His August 1896 ad read: "Wax figures of McKinley Bryan, Scott Jackson, Walling, Pearl Bryan, Sitting Bull, etc. and other sideshow stuff, magic, punch figures." By World War I, he had moved to Victoria, Mo., where he manufactured life-size, breathing mechanical wax figures described as "breathing marvels of art." He continued to be one of the main suppliers of wax outlaw and crime figures for the new Law and Order walk-through shows that were then popular on midways.

In 1921 Shaw offered showmen something different — Dark Room Radium Eggs at $4 a dozen, guaranteed as a crowd-pleaser and a good bally for a pit show. All the showmen had to do was get the hen. Shaw died in 1929. In addition to his other accomplishments, he had written three books on magic and several instructional booklets including *Shaw's Book of Acts for Carnival, Sideshow, Museum and Circus*.

His wife and son moved the shop to 1804 Broadway in St. Louis and continued the wax business. They were still offering showmen wax figures of Dillinger and Jesse James billed as "20th Century Sensations." The figures could be made lying or standing, and according to their ads, "A reproduction in wax is the next best thing to a human being." Showmen thought they were even better — they didn't eat and could be carted around in a box.

In 1943, Mrs. Shaw offered the business for sale. She listed the 50-year-old enterprise as the W.H.J. Shaw Life-Size Wax Figure Business, consisting of plaster molds representing presidents, generals, characters of the West, beautiful women, and outlaws. She said it was a wonderful opportunity and that she would teach the buyer the business. B.W. Christophel, who also had a wax studio in St. Louis, likely took over Shaw's molds and his show-business customers .

Christophel billed himself as a wax sculptor and modeler specializing in figures for theater lobbies as well as complete wax shows for exhibition. He sold figures of notorious criminals of the past and present, officers of the law, scouts, Indian chiefs, actors, presidents, and other famous people. All figures were life-size, either standing or sitting, with full papier-mâché bodies and jointed wooden arms. Christophel used human hair and made the heads and hands from the best

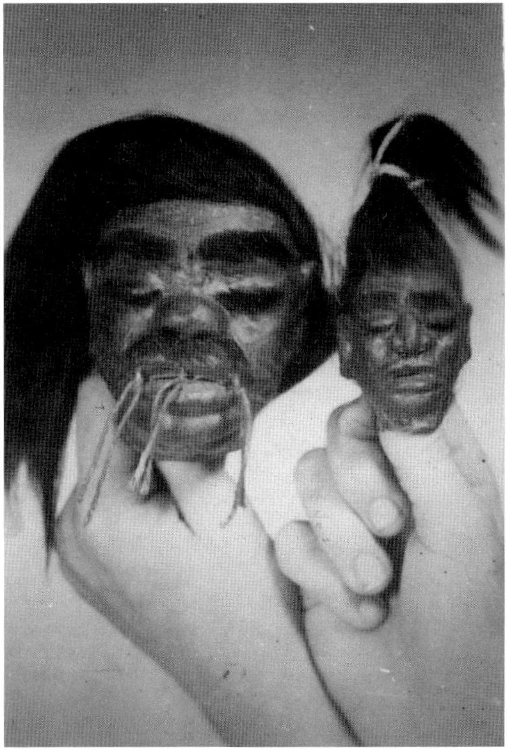

"Shrunken heads from Ecuador, best made, by Jivaro headhunters from real skin, with hair grown on. [This is] the best thing to a genuine human shrunken head." The shrunken heads were offered for sale by Harvey Lee Boswell in the 1960s for $69.50, and used to be part of his "Jungle Exhibit."

imported wax, and none were priced higher than $60, which included a descriptive placard. For crime showmen, he sold caps, striped prison suits, and electric chairs.

Christophel kept up with the trends — in 1927 he was offering Lindbergh in wax. In 1930 he wrote to a customer saying he could fill an order ten days after receiving it — the time it took the papier-mâché to properly dry. When a crime showman wanted to mount a wax figure in an electric chair on the front of his truck, Christophel advised that the figure be made of papier-mâché instead, because of exposure to the sun.

In the 1930s, Christophel's main trade was supplying figures of a hundred or so public enemies, but by the next decade he was offering shrunken heads and mummies with an ad touting: "Tiny shrunken heads that stand close inspection." In 1948 he offered complete baby shows: "Birth of a baby in wax from two months to delivery in natural colors and including one Caesarian operation, life-size in a glass. Also four heads, four hands, and one foot each mounted. Twenty-four venereal colored pictures in a frame and one wax two-headed baby in a jar." Showmen said his wax two-headed babies were first-class.

He was also making "Sitting Bull Mummies," which his ads called "a reproduction of course but looks like the real thing as it has hair, fingernails, toenails, and teeth. Full-size nude body. Will stand close inspection and not affected by weather. This is a big attraction because everyone knows Sitting Bull." In the early 1950s, Christophel made wax freak figures he called "P.T. Barnum's Freaks." Featured were Tom Thumb, Jo-Jo the Dog-Faced Boy, the Bearded Lady, and the Original Siamese Twins.

Over the decades, many "clearing houses" sold used gear to showmen. They were spread out across North America and each flourished for a few years and then disappeared. However, one shop, Weil's Curiosity Shop in Philadelphia, Pa.,

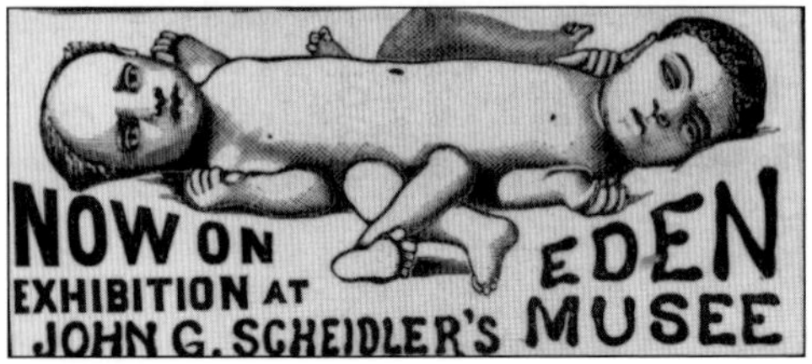

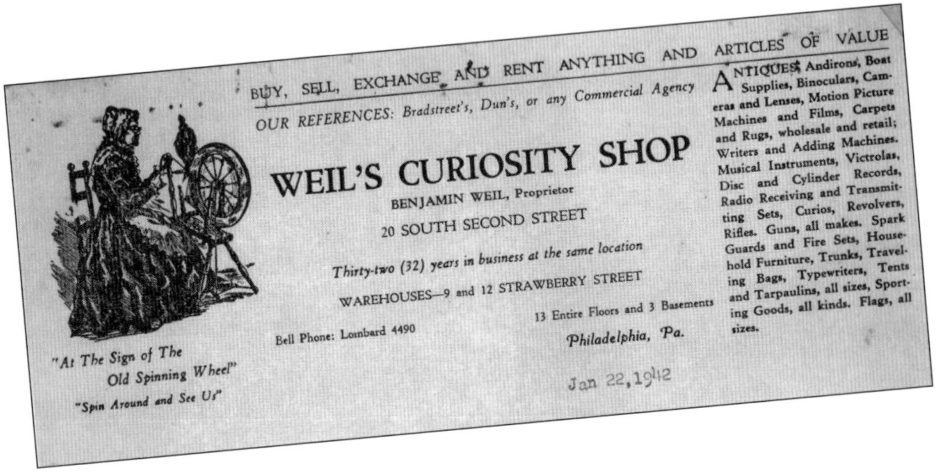

operated longer than any of them, from about 1909 until the late 1950s. In 1909 Weil's was offering showmen an eight-legged pig with two bodies, one head, and three noses. It was both male and female. Weil's bought stuff from showmen in the winter when they were broke and sold it in the spring when everyone was looking for a new attraction.

The late Harvey Boswell remembered dealing with Weil. "I remember going up to Philly to Weil's Curiosity Shop to buy a mummy," he told me in 1998. "It was a fake Hollywood prop. The place was four or five floors, wax figures, rows of pickled punks, you name it. Stuff piled everywhere, and the fire marshal was giving him a hard time. He had some wax replicas of diseased sex organs. I called them jock shows — they were for men only. I bought one. I booked it on Coleman Bros. Shows around 1956-58. All in glass cases. Very nice. I called it 'The Destruction of Mankind.'"

Weil's ran a small weekly ad in *Billboard*. One week it was a guess-your-weight scale, a concession tent, a head-on-a-sword illusion, a two-headed baby, and 23 musical glasses. The next week it was 13 unborn specimens, a set of funhouse mirrors, a wax head showing brain and blood vessels, and an Iron Boot torture subject in a nice glass case. One ad in June 1946 offered 800 pieces of wax medical subjects bought from a European museum.

A 1955 *Billboard* ad offered 16 unborn subjects plus four small goats, all in bottles, the whole lot for $185. "Will pack carefully," Weil's promised. One can only imagine his shop. Around every corner and through each doorway stood a surprise. Attractions were piled everywhere, just waiting to be turned loose on the unsuspecting showgoing public.

One art the showman — especially the peep showman — had mastered was that of making his show seem bigger than it was. The American midway was developed long after the peep-show era, but through the efforts of one man, peep-show-style attractions became a part of the American midway scene from the late teens until the 1950s. Starting in 1922, Charles T. Buell of Newark, Ohio, made peep shows for the midway and storefront showman. Buell's shows focused on current disasters, popular figures, crime waves, and war and its atrocities. He referred to his attractions as "walk-through shows." Pictures on colored glass were displayed in several rows of viewing boxes like the old peep shows. Between viewing boxes were blow-ups and mounted displays to enlarge the exhibit

These viewing boxes that Canadian back-end showman, magician, sword swallower, and knife thrower Joe Kara owned were sold in a carnival auction in Tampa, Fla., in the 1990s. They were the type of units Buell manufactured and sold for his walk-through shows, and were placed on a lumber frame or stand to make them chest high so viewers could easily look in through the lens holes.

and get you around the tent and out the exit in enough time to maybe make you think you got your money's worth.

One of Buell's earliest offerings was advertised to showmen in the March 1926 *Billboard*: "Through the Opium Dens and White Slave markets of Chinatown. The views in the peep boxes consist of the best of New York, San Francisco, and Chicago Chinatowns years ago when at their worst." For $150 you got 24 pictures on colored glass and the same number of viewing boxes, plus a 6-by-10 banner. Buell promised scenes of "opium dens, gambling dens, women in slavery, executions, Chinese funerals, poppy fields for opium, tong wars, riots . . . just one thrill after another." The whole package weighed less than 150 pounds and Buell claimed showmen could average $1,500 a week with it.

In spring 1924, Buell offered showmen The Great Battlefields of France and Americans in Action, a walk-through show made up of photos taken by Machine Gunner Buell in the war. The Great Prison Show, his 1927 season production, sold for $125 and came with "free" views of either the Plucky Lindbergh or the Mississippi Flood shows as a bonus.

Buell described his 1928 Great Underworld Show as the perfect show: it had no "nut" — slang for expenses. "Requires only 10 feet frontage by 24 feet deep and can be operated by one or two people. Put a grinder on it and it sure will get the money." Inside the 20 boxes were views of Ruth Snyder in the electric chair, child murderers, and other monstrous criminals. During the 1930s, he continued to turn out crime theme shows as well as shows based on nudism, social diseases, astrology, and "Before Birth."

This photo of the world's strangest married couple, Percilla the Monkey Girl and Emmett the Alligator Skin Man, was one of the hundreds of freak photos sold by Bernard Kobel from his home in Frankford, Ind., and later Clearwater, Fla. His 1963 *Amusement Business* ad offered 12 freak photos for $2 or 50 for $5.

When America was at war in the 1940s, Buell was right there with shows he described as "Patriotic. No nut. Two people run show. Powerful. Up to the minute. Most hair-raising." This one was also aimed at the storefront showman, who Buell

Peek-o-rama, Gasatorium, and even Squintatorium were titles put on the show fronts of these exhibits, which were nothing more than a collection of Bernard Kobel's freak photos. As one showman told me, "If the marks went into that show first, the rest of the shows on the midway suffered for it. It was a total heat score."

claimed could earn $150 to $500 a week. In 1944 he sold shows titled Jap Atrocities in March of Batan and Bouquet of Life.

The 1945 season's offering included Atomic Bomb and Jap and Nazi Atrocity Shows. The following season saw him put out another crime show featuring Boy and Girl Gangsters. Buell claimed his "no nut" shows got money where other midway shows couldn't and that the show could be transported in an automobile or checked as baggage. His were shows that didn't "eat their heads off over weekends." His ads gave no address, just a post-office box number, although he invited showmen to stop by.

THE YUCATAN WONDER
ALIVE! MONKEY GIRL
Bostock Carnival

HOOCHIE-COOCHIE DANCING BEARS

Wild Animal Shows, Zoos, and Circuses

Horses were the first animal stars of the circus. For decades they were not only the main performing animals but the circuses' main means of transportation. Into the 1930s horses still had to draw wagons in the parade and get the show wagons to and from the lot each day on the big railroad circuses. But, the new 20th-century stars in the circus ring were wild animals exhibited in circular steel arenas. From about 1910, big cage acts became a staple of American circuses. Most of the large shows of the 1920s and 1930s featured wild animal acts.

Opposite: Frank Bostock's carnival company laid out in a big circle at the 1902 Nashville, Tenn., Centennial. The third show from the right hand corner is the wild animal show with a huge organ on the front.

Earlier reports of wild animal displays included menagerie showman Isaac A. Van Amburgh going into a cage with a lion, leopard, and panther at a theater in the Bowery in 1833. The 1850 Hemmings, Cooper, and Whitby Circus advertised that the keeper of the lions would enter the cage at each show. Most

Chapter 4

Wild animal acts in steel arenas were the big draw on circuses and carnivals by WWI. But horse power was still needed to get shows on and off the lots. Here is the Greater Sheesley Shows trying to get off a flooded ball field.

acts remained simply displays of bravery until Wilhelm Hagenbeck, a German trainer, invented the circular portable exhibition cage in 1888. It was built in 24 sections and enabled animal presenters to incorporate high pyramids and wide jumps in their routines. Hagenbeck also invented the pedestals on which the animals sat. Karl Krone, another German menagerie and circus man, came up with the tunnel or steel runway that ran from the exhibition arena in the tent back out to the cage wagons outside. This prevented disruptions of the performance caused by dragging cages in and out of the tent. In 1905, Prof. Dr. Ludwig Heck invented the rope netting placed over the top of the steel arena to keep cats from jumping out. The same basic constructions are still used for wild animal acts in the circus.

Wild animal shows brought to America by English showmen Frank C. Bostock and the Ferari Brothers became the nucleus around which many of the early street-fair showmen built their midways. These shows filled the void in cat act presentations between the time Col. Edgar Daniel Boone and Miss Carlotta presented wild animal acts on the Adam Forepaugh Circus 1891 and the general return of such acts to circuses just prior to World War I. In 1892, Boone offered his services to managers of watering places, summer resorts, and fair-grounds and expositions in his *Clipper* ads: "Col. Edgar Daniel Boone and the Lion Queen Miss Carlotta in the 40-foot circular steel cage present all full-grown lions captured by Boone himself in Africa together with great German boarhounds Nero and Saxon."

Wilhelm Hagenbeck and his brother Carl first made their money in the 1870s exhibiting exotic people at European venues. They put their earnings into feeding their passion for collecting and training

The 1898 Bostock and Wombwell menagerie layout in England, with the two-wagon front and the cage wagons running down each side of it covered by a canvas tilt. Frank Bostock and Joseph and Francis Ferari introduced America to such shows.

wild animals. Americans first saw the brothers' showmanship at the 1893 Chicago World's Fair, where their Hagenbeck's Arena and World's Museum was presented in a building that could accommodate 40,000 daily viewers to their zoo and 6,000 seated spectators for performances. The performances, given three times a day, revolved around presenting animals that normally didn't get along. Acts involved a baby elephant, trained pigs, and wild boar together, as well as Shetland ponies and boarhounds, and lions riding on horses. Heinrich Mehmann, brother-in-law to the Hagenbecks, was the main presenter; his production of 12 routines included lions, tigers, panthers, leopards, boarhounds, polar bears, sloths, and Tibetan bears.

From 1894 through 1903, Carl Hagenbeck and Frank Bostock competed at Coney Island and for winter zoo locations. In 1903 Hagenbeck was averaging 8,000 visitors a day at Coney Island — about half of Bostock's crowds despite numerous sensational newspaper stories about lion

Set up in Williamsport, Pa., in 1916, this is one of the massive fronts used on the Col. Francis Ferari Shows for their wild animal acts. This front appears to have the large organ imported by the Berni Organ Co. of NYC mounted on a wagon.

escapes and a lion eating $350 that fell from the bosom of trainer Mme. Schelle's dress. But in 1904, the Carl Hagenbeck Trained Animal Show Co. played the St. Louis Exposition and reported profits of $70,000. As the fair ended, the show hired the Bothe Wagon Co. in Cincinnati, Ohio, to build 48 wagons for the launch of a new railroad circus. When the circus opened in April 1905, the big top seated 7,500 with the show presented in two rings and a slate-bottomed, rubber-lined steel arena. The performance consisted of 15 of the most exciting and humorous acts ever performed by wild beasts. Al G. Barnes and other circus showmen quickly followed; the era of the big wild animal circuses had begun.

Hagenbeck opened his German zoo in Stellingen in 1907 but continued to influence the animal business in America as one of the main exporters of animals to American showmen. British-born Bostock arrived in the United States in the summer of 1893. He set up near 5th and Flatbush avenues in Brooklyn. A colleague who saw his show wrote about his set-up in *Billboard*: "The Bostock family lived in one wagon and the other two wagons housed four monkeys, five parrots, three lions, a sheep, and a boxing kangaroo. Bostock also had a hand-carved wooden front, but no tent. The exhibition area was closed off with side wall."

In October, Bostock's lion Wallace escaped from his cage and killed a horse in the stables. The next day, trainer De Kenzo, after a long battle, got Wallace back into his cage and East Coast residents were safe again. Their fears had been fanned by stories released by Bostock's friend Tody Hamilton, the best circus press agent in the business and a long-time Barnum associate. Newspaper stories claimed Wallace weighed over 900 pounds and had killed three men in England.

In the "bounding lion act," as it was known in England, the trainer entered the animal's cage and the animal leaped around and over him or her, running past the bars

Conswela and her fighting lion act on the Bill Lynch Shows midway in the 1940s. She had been a show girl and circus performer before teaming up with Capt. Schultz to come to Canada and operate a circus and wild animal show on midways.

Consul, Bostock's chimp that he toured in the off-season, when he performed at the Follies Bergères and earned $1,000 per week.

on the cage sides. The fighting lion act went into circus sideshows and was still being featured on the 1940s Dailey Bros. railroad circus and also on the 1950s King Bros. truck circus. To American circus people, the number is still called a "Wallace act."

Dime museum and vaude theater circuits became a lucrative off-season market for these animal showmen. The Feraris — brothers Joseph and Francis — booked Big Frank, their boxing kangaroo, and Fatima the Hoochie-Coochie bear. Besides Wallace, Bostock offered Rham-a-Sama the Missing Link, and a lady animal hypnotist. But, his greatest moneymaker was the "man chimp" Consul, who wore clothes and walked erect like a human being. He also drank wine, smoked cigarettes, rode a bike, and displayed better manners than many humans.

Consul was first presented in Europe in 1903 as the pampered pet of a rich Chicago pork merchant. He arrived in first-class boat accommodations and occupied a suite of rooms at the Paris Hotel Continental. The press had a field day, and Consul's engagement at the Follies Bergères was a big success. After the summer season at Coney Island, Bostock sent Consul back to Europe. In Berlin he got sick with bronchitis and after three days of illness, he died. After his death, a London *Billboard* writer noted he'd last seen "Consul in December when he was dressed as a chauffeur and driving a car through Fleet Street, London, England, en route to one of the newspaper offices to do some publicity work for the London Hippodrome where he was appearing. I thought they were taking chances with

A gun-toting lady trainer is surrounded by four male lions in a small performance cage on this midway wild animal show. Note the painted jungle motif on the back wall and the ornate wood on the lion pedestals.

such a valuable animal having him out in the cold weather." Consul's body was embalmed and placed in a coffin, where he lay in state at Bostock's Paris Hippodrome for a week. Back in America, Bostock was booking Consul II.

Bostock often said, "Kindness is the whip used to lead dumb animals to obey." He approached people the same way and was free with his advice to those starting in the business. When animal showman George Rollins bought a wild animal show from him, Bostock advised, "Don't fool away your money on deer, armadillos, and bears, or alligators. While they are good, the public want to see good, big animals with a mouth and teeth; those which will bellow with trainers that are not afraid to make their charges talk. If the public wanted to see a goat or sheep show, they would not have spent their money with a wild animal aggregation."

One of Bostock's traits, according to fellow showmen and employees, was bravery that approached absolute fearlessness. He had been mauled and bitten many times over the years, mostly in rescuing trainers that worked for him. One of his worst maulings occurred when he saved the life of Gertrude Planka in Kansas City, after which Bostock spent four months in hospital. In 1911 he bought the Hippodrome in Blvd. Clichy in Paris. His trainer, Jack F. Gentner, billed as Capt. Jack Bonavita, lost a hand while presenting lions there. During a fundraising dinner held for Bonavita in the lion's den, the trainer was again attacked. True to form, Bostock came to his rescue.

Prominent American cities have boasted permanent zoos since the 1860s, though many of these lacked permanent buildings, pens, and yards until three decades later. The Central Park Zoo had the advantage of being where Barnum kept his animals. The great showman had no permanent winter facility to house his substantial menagerie and placed rare animals in the park until his Bridgeport, Conn., circus winter quarters were built in 1880.

Each year, Bostock and the Feraris operated winter zoos. Circus and variety acts were added to the performances and changed every second week. The winter zoo served two purposes: the animals were fed and kept performing, and the show was repaired with the receipts from the door. Bostock had zoos in Baltimore, Indianapolis, and Milwaukee in the winter of 1900. The Indianapolis zoo housed hundreds of animals inside a circular building where the exhibits were organized into categories — for example "Cat Section," "Birds of Prey," "Cud Chewers," "The Hog Family," and "Insect Eaters." The elephants, hippo, rhino, and tapir were exhibited in the section marked "Thick-Skinned." The performance consisted of 12 acts, including Bonavita and his 20 lions, and the fighting lion Sultana, plus jubilee singers and cake walkers, a dog and baboon act, a midget horse, and a Punch and Judy show. The final act, a monkey balloon ascension, was presented outdoors and served as a blow-off to clear the building of people.

A bally in progress on the Bostock Wild Animal Show at Dreamland after the Coney Island fire. The dark-skinned man standing on the elevated stage is Ferdinand Frothingham, a.k.a. Bamboula the Ballyhoo Man. He rarely spoke or responded to English, and spent his time with wild animals and snakes.

With the Ferari Brothers, Bostock launched the street-fair business in America and between them they operated midway companies for several seasons. Francis and Joseph Ferari, both born in the 1860s, were sons of Italian-born English showman James Ferari. Francis first toured with a novelty show and then exhibited giants, midgets, and other freaks. In Britain, he toured a tribe of South African Zulus, members of the Impi, who had annihilated a British Regiment at the massacre of Isandlwana. Ferari became famous overnight. In 1892 he purchased Biddle's French Menagerie and renamed it Noah's Ark. After touring fairs in England and Scotland, he partnered with Frank C. Bostock, arriving in America with his own show in spring 1894 along with his younger brother Joseph Ferari, also an animal trainer. By 1896 they were featuring a lion riding on a horse and jumping over banners and through hoops; Mlle. Adgie Castello doing the Spanish dance in the den of lions and tigers; and Herr Conor in the den with lions, wolves, bears, and boarhounds. Other acts included a wrestling lion and boxing kangaroos.

Frank Bostock posing with part of his lion troupe in a 1905 souvenir postcard.

The same year they partnered with Bostock to present the Olde English Fair Carnival Co., credited with starting the street-fair business in the U.S. Their midway featured their animal show plus a dozen or more attractions, including the $50,000 Venetian gondola ride, Chiquita the Midget, the Streets of Cairo show, several other girl-oriented productions and illusion-based shows, the new Crystal Maze, a Gypsy Village, and a trip through the Opium Dens. An aerial flying act and balloon ascensions were the free acts carried. Camels, elephants, and burros gave rides to the public.

Bostock dropped out in 1903, and died in England nine years later at the age of 46. The Feraris operated together until 1905, then ran separate shows until the end of their careers. Francis died at the end of his 1914 season, and his wife carried on the show until the end of the decade. Joseph retired in 1920 to Mariners Harbor, Staten Island, where the show had its winter quarters. He made and repaired carousels, imported organs, and sold used show equipment. He died in 1953.

A study of the month-to-month operations of wild animal showmen Frank Bostock and the Ferari Brothers is almost impossible. They randomly operated together and separately in various locations as their business interests warranted. But, one thing that remained the same was their formula for touring wild animal shows on midways. Their shows had elaborate fronts, some built on two or three wagons, and all sported band organs in the entranceways. Inside the tent were several cages, including an arena for the performing animals.

Col. Francis Ferari and his leopards in 1909. Both he and his brother Joseph were wild animal trainers like Frank Bostock, and all had their own touring menagerie shows in England before coming to the U.S.A.

Each show had a core of four or five trainers who also presented the animals. There was always a lion act, a fighting lion act, and a mixed act of leopards and panthers worked by a lady trainer. Often, the boxing kangaroo act opened the show and the hoochie-coochie bear closed it. The Joseph G. Ferari-operated Ferari Anglo-American Trained Animal Show, opening at Corning, N.Y., in spring 1900, traveled on its own rail cars and was set up behind a $10,000 illuminated front. It contained eight cages of wild animals, including 18 lions. The performance was directed by T.J. Hurd as lecturer, and announcer Captain Grant presented a talking horse followed by Joe Karmo's presentation of the Lion Hunt, Chase and Capture with two lions named Brutus and Spitfire. Next, Mme. Louise presented five pyramid lions, and Mlle. Almetta the Reptile Queen and Baby Boots the Snake Enchantress did their acts. Colonel Woods put more lions through their paces and Peter De Geith closed the show with his performing bear Big Frank.

Midway showmen quickly learned that more publicity could be obtained with wild animal features than with any other attraction on these early midways. Animals appealed to young and old and combined the strong elements of fear and curiosity.

The bally on the Joseph G. Ferari Wild Animal Show. This show front is a combination of carved wooden sections and canvas banners. Note the hoochie coochie bear beside the lady in the white dress.

In America, a tent replaced this British system of poles and ridge lumber pieces over which a canvas roof was draped and secured to the cage wagons on each side.

By the early 1920s there were a dozen large railroad carnivals competing for the best fair dates in North America. The wild animal show blossomed into mini-circuses. These high quality shows with beautiful carved and painted fronts, along with the big girl revues, were used to snag fair contracts. This show on the Johnny J. Jones Shows features elephants, ponies, dogs, and "Captain," the only mind-reading horse.

One way of getting free newspaper space and the rapt attention of the locals was a wedding staged in the lion cage of the show's wild animal exhibit. The promoter or carnival press agent would find a young couple that were to be married and offered them money to do so in the steel arena with the lions, the trainer, and a minister. Often the hardest part was finding a minister.

George Rollins once said that the key to the operation of a successful wild animal presentation on the midway was to keep it working whether there were ten people or a thousand inside the tent. As long as there was activity, the animals were active too and their cries and roars attracted more paying customers. Other showmen noticed the roar of the big cats drew people. Someone came up with what carnies called a "groan box." The easiest way to make one was to get a pair of rawhide shoelaces from a shoemaker, punch a hole in the bottom of a gallon can, tie a knot in one of the shoelaces, and shove the loose end of the shoelace through the hole and into the can. Then wet your hand and place the can under your arm. Grip the lace and pull it, and out comes a deep roaring sound.

While animal shows in England covered the tops of their cage wagons with canvas laid over wooden rafter pieces, North

The bally of Mettler Bros. miniature circus and menagerie on the Beckmann and Gerety Shows in the 1930s.

American showmen used a tent behind the front. Cage wagons were lined up along the sides with the performing arena placed in the back end of the tent, in front of painted wooden or canvas backdrops. The tent accommodated several hundred people, and at first there were no seats. The smell played an important part in turning the crowd over, and tickets were priced higher at feeding times. A cage boy "dragged the midway" — he walked through with a big piece of meat on a fork, and people

The large show front that the Johnny J. Jones Shows used for the Clyde Beatty Circus in 1942. It was the only time famed lion trainer Beatty worked a full season on a carnival. Appearances in several jungle movies made his name a good midway draw.

followed him back to the show, thinking they would see the animals being fed.

Manageable animals were also brought out onto the bally to draw crowds. During the winter of 1900, street-fair promoter Frank White wrote *Billboard* about the previous southern fall fairs: "At Savannah, Frank Ferari had fired the trainer for Fatima the Hoochie-Coochie bear. All went well with the new 'Captain' whatever until he brought the bear out onto the bally and the band started playing 'She Never Saw the Streets of Cairo.' The keeper started the bear dancing, but when he told her to stop she wouldn't. She kept wiggling. The bear finally got angry with the keeper's attempts to stop her dance and hit him on the side of the head, knocking him down. Then the bear knocked down a woman and took off down the midway. Roustabouts cornered her in the Streets of Cairo tent and returned her to Ferari's show."

Carnival booking agents dealing with a town or fair committee looking to bring in a midway company touted the "educational" value of the wild animal show. The operators of the J.L. Edwards Animal Show claimed in 1908 to "carry a scientific lecturer which makes the exhibit very instructive for the better classes." In the early years of the carnival business, when it was being attacked by the churches and street fair committees for the grift and nudity associated with midways, Frank Bostock and the Ferari Brothers were just the showmen the business and the public needed after so many years of Barnum's hoaxes.

Carnival owners James Patterson, Johnny J. Jones, C.A. Wortham, and Rubin and Cherry built first-class wild-animal shows to anchor their midway companies and snag lucrative fair dates. In 1922 Jones sold his animals to the Howes Great London Circus, telling *Billboard*: "People liked the show but it was the same thing each season." Carnival companies now had thousands of dollars tied up in rides, show fronts, tents, wagons, trucks, and rail cars. New back-end shows had to be framed on an annual basis to hold contracts at the big fairs.

One show that resembled a circus on early carnival companies was the "stadium show," an idea that sprang from the free acts that street fairs employed. Showmen saw how much excitement such acts created and how the crowds turned out to see them. The next step was to enclose them and charge admission.

The major circuses with their large tents had been featuring some of these high-thrill acts in their programs. Aerial acts like high dives and loop-the-loops needed height, and carnival tents were not big, so many of the stadium shows had canvas side walls. However, an early photo

Terrell Jacobs, seen here as one of his lions walks over him on two ropes, was one of the unique trainers of wild animals from the 1930s to the early '50s. His career was spent on most of the major tent circuses of the era and also with his own wild animal circus that he booked on to various carnivals.

When the Canadian National Exhibition grounds in Toronto were taken over in the 1940s for the war effort, Patty Conklin moved the "Ex" to Riverdale Park. He bought the Tom Mix big top and hired Terrell Jacobs to put on a show. Here we see an elephant doing a hind leg stand as part of the bally.

of C.A. Wortham's stadium show indicates that it was presented in a small round-end tent of perhaps 60 feet with two 30-foot middles. At one end, the side wall extends from the tent in a huge semi-circle to enclose the high-dive ladder, its tank, and various other rigging. Midway gawkers could see the high diver jump, but couldn't see the landing unless they paid.

The 1921 Great Patterson Shows' wild animal show was more like a big-time circus, with lots of good acts including a 12-pony drill, high-school horses, an unrideable mule, riding monkeys, three performing elephants, and a five-lion act, plus musical acts, trapeze, and acrobatic numbers.

In the 1940s, noted circus wild animal trainers appeared on large rail carnivals. Clyde Beatty spent the 1942 season on the back end of the Johnny J. Jones Shows. Beatty's show seated 2,500 people placed in a 100-by-180-foot big top behind a 90-foot show front. The program featured chimpanzees Minnie and Mickey, Harriet Beatty with two Bengal tigers riding on an elephant, Jean Evans' aerial and web acts, and three clowns. The show closed with Clyde Beatty's battling cage act of 30 wild animals.

Another big-time animal trainer who spent even more time around carnival back ends was Terrell Jacobs. At the age of 13 Jacobs left his home in Peru, Ind. — a small city that had been the winter home to many large circuses over the years — to join the Hagenbeck-Wallace Circus. He worked the fighting lion act in the sideshow of the Sells-Floto Circus in his animal apprenticeship. From 1929 to 1939, Jacobs was the feature wild animal presenter on four large tent circuses, including Ringling Bros. Barnum and Bailey. He played the San Francisco World's Fair with his animal acts and then worked independently on several rail circuses.

Patty Conklin called on him to furnish a large circus in 1942. Conklin had been awarded the coveted Canadian National Exhibition (C.N.E.) contract in 1937 and was building a wonderful midway operation when World War II broke out. The fair was canceled and the grounds taken over by the military. Conklin hustled up a cause titled the Fair for Britain and secured Riverdale

Park for a location. He built a pipe frame and plywood front for Jacobs' show that Jacobs later used on several of his carnival adventures, including stints on the 1947 World of Mirth Shows and the 1949 Royal American Shows.

From 1941 through 1951, Jacobs played the annual spring circus at the Chicago Stadium. In 1952 he was on the James E. Strates Shows. *Billboard* reported the show was sending the locals away happy and eight out of ten people coming through the front gate of the carnival were hitting the midway with their eyes toward the circus. The zoo part of the show consisted of three working dens of lions and tigers, a bear cage, llamas, and Baby Jean, a two-and-a-half-year-old elephant. Louis Reed presented her in the performance that took place in one ring and the big cage, while Jacobs worked his mixed cage act featuring Sheba the lion. Trapeze, clown, and dog and pony numbers rounded out the 35-minute show. Patrons paid a quarter to get in and an extra 20 cents for chair seating.

In 1955, Jacobs toured his show on Jimmy Sullivan's World's Finest Shows in Canada. The next season he was on the Kelly-Miller Circus. His last working tour was on Paul A. Miller's combined carnival and circus. Jacobs died in 1957.

Jay Gould poses in front of his bandwagon semi-trailer on his Jay Gould "Million Dollar" Circus. Gould was one of the early showmen to successfully combine a free circus performance with a full carnival operation.

One idea showmen tried was running a free circus surrounded by midway rides and joints. Perhaps one of the earliest showmen to present such an operation was Jay Gould. As the Depression came along, he had bought a merry-go-round and put out a combination carnival and circus. In 1938 he ran a one-night-stand circus unit called the Jay Gould Revue and Circus. But the circus business was not good for him and his 1943 unit closed early. A few months later, Gould took a friend's suggestion to try the combination carnival and circus again. This formula clicked and he successfully operated it with few changes until the 1960s.

The Jay Gould Circus with carnival rides first worked on city streets with the local auspices guaranteeing the cost of the circus acts. Gould carried a thousand chairs, but soon found that too many people couldn't see the show. He quickly

Bert Pettus with the three ex-King Bros. Circus elephants in front of the zoo show on the James E. Strates Shows midway in 1957. The elephants were used in parades, fair grandstand shows, and outings to car dealerships and car washes for promotions.

reduced the number of chairs to a couple of hundred and rented them for 25 cents each. If you wanted to stand, though, the show was free. In the 1950s Gould bought newer rides and added concessions to his operation. He started playing regular carnival lots and fairs. On the lot, his show looked like a carnival, but its drawing power was based in the free circus shows given at 2 and 8 p.m. each day.

Paul A. Miller's Free Circus and Carnival, started in 1957, was another successful circus-carnival combination consisting of eight major rides, eight kiddie rides, two shows, a fun house, a glass house, and 30 concessions. Miller booked circus acts to work on a semi-trailer stage with a ring and an animal arena on the ground in front of it. Another profitable operation was Siebrand Bros. Carnival and Circus, which started as a gilly carnival in Phoenix, Ariz., in 1916. In 1932, they switched to trucks and a few years later added the circus to draw more people. In 1951, patrons paying the 14-cent gate admission on "still dates" saw the one-hour circus free while patrons on fairs paid a dollar to see it. The Siebrands' competition came from Arizona showman H.N. "Doc" Capell's Shop-o-Rama Free Circus and Carnival, which stayed out all year playing plazas.

In the 1950s, the breakup of several large truck circuses resulted in big menageries going onto carnivals. In 1952, Frank Bergen hired what remained of Cole Bros. Circus, now retitled Barnes Bros. Circus, for a summer tour on Bergen's World of Mirth Shows. The elephants proved a great asset in getting publicity. In 1953, animal collector Tony Diano and Ben Davenport's Diano Bros. Circus broke up mid-season, and the next year Bergen hired

Diano's large menagerie — ten elephants, a giraffe, a zebra, a rhinoceros, a hippopotamus, chimps, monkeys, and several species of cats. Diano's menagerie was featured in 1955 and again in 1957 on the World of Mirth Shows midway.

In 1956, Arnold Maley and Floyd King put out two units of their King Bros. Circus, but business was so bad that within weeks they were abandoning animals and equipment. By June, both units were closed. By late fall, E.J. Brady, a Macon, Ga., investor in the show, freed up some of the animals and sold them to James E. Strates Shows. For $17,000, Strates bought three elephants — Mona, Alice, and Marge — plus Friendly George the Hippo, a polar bear, a leopard, two lions, and a black bear. The carnival was in Shelby, N.C., when the animals arrived, and Strates put them under a tent formerly used to house the Dancing Waters show. The elephants finished the season moving by truck, but next year Strates added a circus stock car to the train for them. In February 1958, the show purchased three more elephants from Pollock Bros. Circus. The zoo worked as a regular back-end show until 1969, but the show kept the elephants for publicity purposes. To pay their keep, a 10-cent midway grind show titled Tarzan's Elephants featured the elephants for several more seasons, until they were sold.

Today there are still circuses and wild animal shows at fairs, but not on carnival midways. People come out to the fair to be entertained, and for 80-odd years shows on carnival back ends did just that. However, when the fair board raised carnival percentages, leaving shows with a smaller cut of the gross, all the back-end shows disappeared. Fairs now pay hundreds of thousands of dollars to put the same shows back on the fairgrounds. In the past they didn't have to pay for them, and they received 20 to 30 percent of their gross. As the touring circus business shrinks, this is welcome work for both acts and circus owners.

ELECTRIC PALACE
ENTRANCE
TICKET
OFFICE
TICKET
OFFICE
ORIE
LORI

WHAT DO YOU EXPECT FOR A DIME?

Midway Movies and More

Over the years, showmen went from exhibiting drawings and paintings, peep shows, panoramas, and lantern slides to showing moving pictures. In 1895 a variety of cameras and projectors were introduced in Europe and the United States. Kinetoscope and Bioscope film projectors were quickly adopted by the traveling showman. Inventors created the moving image, but it was the showmen, under midway black canvas theaters or in storefronts and rented halls, who turned movies into a spectacle and made them popular. Northern folks eventually saw movies in vaudeville, but in the South, where vaudeville was not big, many people saw movies in showmen's tents.

Opposite: The Electric Palace show at an Indiana town street fair in the early 1900s. Movies were combined with various other vaudeville acts as well as Lorie the Butterfly and skirt dancer.

Magic lanterns and stereopticons were ideal for showmen as they were not expensive and the show could be run by one person. Thomas Walgensten, a teacher and lens

Chapter 5

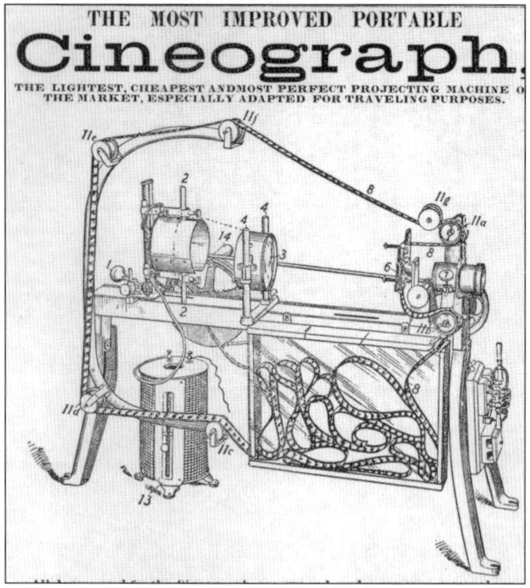

The cineograph, an early projector from 1897.

Early tent movie shows were very basic affairs. This one, however, has low wooden girl show-style seats, a curtained off proscenium at one end of the tent for the screen, and a phonograph for music.

grinder living in Paris, developed the magic lantern and gave local exhibitions by 1664. He exhibited in other European cities and sold lanterns to showmen for shows at fairs. In the 1740s, Americans saw lantern shows in homes and coffee houses. Americans first saw Phantasmagoria shows in 1803 at the Mt. Vernon Garden in New York City. The audience saw startling images projected onto a screen. Behind the screen, large stationary lanterns projected backgrounds and smaller moving lanterns projected figures into the mix.

In the 1830s, Englishman Henry Longdon Childe perfected dissolving views. By the next decade, William and Frederick Langenheims introduced the stereoscope to Americans. Stereo views were sold for use in lantern slides; the lantern showmen simply cut the double image in half and projected the single slide in their lanterns. Slides changed from those painted on glass to actual photographs in the 1860s, and in 1863 Barnum presented the Great English Stereopticon at his American Museum.

The optical business in America was first centered in Philadelphia. John McAllister was the first major dealer setting up shop in 1779. But, it was not until a century later that *Clipper* ads for stereopticons began to appear. In 1885, the McAllister Manufacturing Optical Co. in New York — run by McAllister's grandsons — was offering magic lanterns and stereopticons for sale to traveling shows, street advertising companies, and public exhibitions. James Lee of Staten Island offered showmen the new patented revolving stereopticon with two or four lenses that showed from 24 to 43 views. For an investment of $75, he claimed, showmen could make $10 a day. That same year, the New York Calcium Light Co. offered a pair of stereopticon lanterns, blow pipes, hose, couplings, and packing cases plus a lecture script for $100. Many showmen went from town to town with such a show while others formed small circuits around where they lived.

Billboard reported in December 1900 that J.R. Bonheur of the Bonheur Carnival Shows was the real originator of the moving-picture device embodied in the first animated picture machine built by T.A. Edison. "Bonheur had perfected a machine with a mechanical dissolver that renders possible the perfect dissolving of slides and film with the elimination of darkness between the still views and the animated film," *Billboard* stated. "No such device has been duplicated in the world as yet and it makes his picture shows on Bonheur Bros. Shows so very popular. These are a huge drawing card in public exhibitions."

A.M. Whaylen, better known as "Piano Bill," was another pioneer movie showman. He started out in 1898 with Whaylen's Mechanical Opera Co., consisting of an old Lubin moving-picture outfit, 300 feet of film, 50 Cuban war slides, 30 comic slides, and one illustrated song. The show traveled in one wagon in which the crew also slept and cooked. The next year they added a wagon and toured four states. Piano Bill did fancy trick shooting around each show town during the daytime to advertise the show. By 1901 he was the first showman to carry a "light plant" — or generator — to show movies, changed the show title to Whaylen's Wild West on Canvas, and showed Western films. In 1903 he added a two-cylinder automobile and put the dynamo on the rear end and belted it up to the fly wheel on the auto engine. Crowds were just as interested in how Whaylen made the electricity as they were in the two hours of films he showed.

The first carnival company in America was started by Otto Schmidt, who was employed at the Hopskins Theater in Chicago as a scenic artist. Seeing the 1893 World's Fair gave him the idea to launch the first midway company in 1894. A fellow employee of the Hopskins Theater came along as a young showman. He had procured a crude moving-picture machine and a reel of film. He tried showing the film in a white tent without success. He then blackened the inside of his tent, but the material rubbed off on the clothes of the patrons. Moreover, only a few people could be accommodated inside the tent, and those who went inside could stay only a few minutes because of the heat given off

MUSICAL MOTION PICTURES

150 FILMS. SONGS, DANCES. SKETCHES, NEGRO NUMBERS, ETC., ETC.
No singer required. The phonograph does the work by a simple attachment to the picture machine. Can be operated by anybody. Simple and efficient. The biggest money making attraction ever offered for fairs, circuses, touring shows, etc., etc. Write or wire for list of films and prices. RENFAX FILM CO., INC., 110 West 40th Street, New York City.

by the machine. Still, this shaky start led to movies enjoying a very successful time on future showgrounds.

Itinerant movie tent showmen were like drive-in owners — they had to wait until dusk to begin their show. A year or so after movies hit the showgrounds, show tent companies were listening to the needs of their customers and offering movie showmen "black tents," with double sun curtains at the eaves and sod cloth at the bottom of the walls to make the inside darker than night. As movie shows on midways grew into combined movie, special effects, dancing, illusion, and musical comedy shows, the dark tents grew to accommodate bigger seated audiences.

The filmed prize fight between Bob Fitzsimmons and James Corbett, made by the Kinetoscope Exhibition Co., was the first big movie success on the fairgrounds. Prize fighting was illegal in most states and the company was instrumental in convincing Nevada officials that the filming of the fight in that state would stimulate economic and population growth there. The fight was held at Carson City in the spring of 1897, and the film released on May 22 at the Academy of Music in New York City. Both fighters were to receive 15 percent of the film's grosses. Fitzsimmons quickly formed a vaudeville company and played theaters.

By the fall, there were 11 exhibition companies touring the film, which showed Corbett being fouled — an incident the referee hadn't seen during the match. The controversy certainly helped attendance, and although women didn't attend fights, the movie, which eliminated the actual fight environment, enjoyed moderate female patronage. It was a big success at Coney Island.

Moviemaker Sigmund Lubin didn't wait around for the real thing to come out. He hired two Pennsylvania Railway freight handlers as fighters and shot a reenactment of the fight on his rooftop studio. This film, known as *Lubin's Reproduction of the Corbett-Fitzsimmons Fight*, was shown in a black tent on the 1897 Ringling Bros. Circus midway. The film was terrible, and beefs to the showmen running it were countered with, "What do you expect for a dime!"

The Great Train Robbery by Edwin S. Porter, released in 1903, became an instant fairground hit. The film broke with stage forms and techniques previously used by filmmakers, and demonstrated for the first time the power of the "cut" in delivering a story on the screen. The eight-minute film had scenes of a train robbery, the formation of a posse, and chase of the bad guys, all patterned after acts presented on touring Wild West shows. One scene had a cowboy firing a gun directly at the camera, with Edison's catalog suggesting the scene could be used at the beginning or end of the movie. At that time, showmen selected moving picture scenes and stereopticon views from various film companies and arranged them in the order and length of time they needed, adding their own narration and music.

Edward Amet, from Waukegon, Ill., was not only a fairground movie pioneer but also a filmmaker. His films and Magniscope projector were sold through two of the biggest optical dealers at the time, the Keine Optical Co. in Chicago and the McAllister firm in New York. His midway picture show in 1898 played behind a five-banner front. The novelty of movies and the potential profits from their exhibition prompted one major carnival company to convert a large

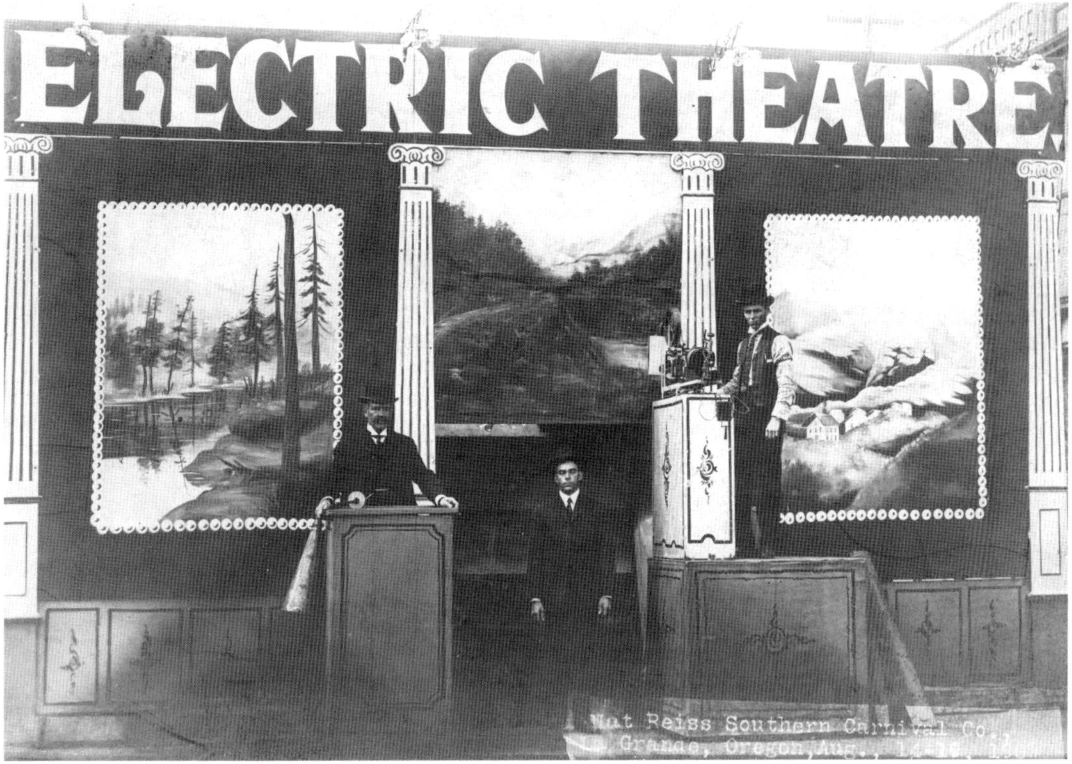

These showmen in front of their movie show on the 1905 Nat Reiss Shows are ready for the crowds. Before people traveled, movies showing scenery and various natural wonders like Niagara Falls and the Grand Canyon drew patrons. Note the projector on its stand on the small bally platform.

two-wagon carved front from their wild animal show to one showing Edison's latest productions using his Phantoscope. Movies shown included *Roosevelt Christening the Meteor*, *Eruptions of Mt. Pelee*, *McKinley's Last Speech*, and *Glorious Cinderella*.

For the first few seasons, movies did well on midways as a novelty. Audiences were entertained by them regardless of their quality and brevity, because these films gave life to events they had only been able to read about. But movies didn't represent a whole performance, like a minstrel show, a circus, or vaudeville. In fact, vaudeville theaters put movies last on the bill and used them as "chasers." Carnival operators took a similar approach by blending movies in with other acts and illustrated songs. Panta's Palace of Illusions on the 1902 Monk Bros. Combined Carnival Co. offered the public magician Willie Walker, serpentine dancer Grace Kendall, vocalist Fred Boggs, the illusions of Rotain, and the films *Mt. Pelee in Eruption* and *McKinley's Funeral*. On the 1909 Robinson Am. Co. midway, the Talking Moving Picture Show featured *The Life and Death of Jesse James* and a bally in which a young lady did

Hale's Tours were a real novelty on the fairgrounds and in amusement parks. A movie was shown in the end of a railroad coach that was rocked side to side by a motor while train sounds and wind were piped inside to simulate an actual train ride. This elaborate front was manufactured by C.W. Parker and sold to showmen.

juggling feats on a rolling globe.

George C. Hale gave moviegoing a new twist. As fire chief of Kansas City, he had represented America with a fire-drill team at the Paris Exposition of 1900 and it was there that he got his taste for the showman's life. In 1905 he opened his Hale's Tours at Kansas City's Electric Park. Hale's theater looked like a railway car from the outside — patrons boarded, paid the conductor a dime, and sat in a theater resembling a railroad coach interior. The window in the door at the front of the car was the movie screen, while the movie, shown by a rear-screen projector, made the spectators feel they were watching scenery from inside a real train. To make the trip even more convincing, the cars were gently rocked to simulate the motion of the train and train sounds were piped into the car. Within a couple of months, Hale's production was being presented as an attraction at Coney Island, and soon every park had a Hale's Tour or an imitation.

Fighting the Flames was another film featured on midways. In 1906 the Fighting the Flames Co. in Indianapolis, Ind., wrote

By the 1940s, movies on carnival midways were restricted to short clips shown inside "unborn" and crime shows, or as sideshow blow-offs. This Birth of a Baby movie show behind a panel front on Convention Shows in 1940 was an exception.

to the Parker Am. Co. regarding the purchase of the film for use on their midway. The film sold for $160 with copyright. The writer pointed out: "The average film sells for 12 cents a foot so that you are only paying about $40 for the exclusive rights. The film is a whole show on the midway."

The arrival of film censorship helped to end the showing of movies on carnivals. By World War I, exploitation and censorship were evident on the showgrounds. The 1914 *Horrors of the White Slave Traffic* film shown in the movie show on the Parker and Kennedy Shows was pitched to showmen in *Billboard* ads that read, "The exposure of the white slave trade in four parts. Only picture dealing with the subject that has not been interfered with by police or censors."

Fairground movie showmen were up against strong competition by 1909 from storefront picture showmen. There were often a dozen in town at the same time as the carnival, each charging only a nickel. As film production and projection methods rapidly improved, the movies moved from storefronts to nickelodeons and from novelty feature added to an established entertainment form to being presented in theaters as a stand-alone attraction. Movies were soon a dead business on carnivals.

Still, movies, like many other attractions, came and went from the fairgrounds. Gangster movies of the 1930s were described by film historians as a breath of fresh air — full of action, with racy language and stories that came from current headlines. Midway crime showmen ran newsreel coverage of a gangster's funeral, court case, police raids, and murder scenes. Unborn shows added childbirth films. Sideshow operators used short films on double-sex oddities in their blow-offs. In 1948, Strates had a film shot while the show played Washington; edited to a small trailer, it was shown in each sit-down show to advertise the other attractions on the midway. Besides increasing business for the other shows, the trailer entertained the

Scenic theaters were soon found on midways. Inside, miniature scenes of various disasters were enhanced by stereopticon slides and theatrical lighting that created various weather effects and mood changes. This Mt. Pelee Eruption show built by C.W. Parker in the early 1900s used simulated fire effects to recreate the volcanic eruption in miniature.

crowd while the talker filled the tent.

Walter Gettinger, owner of the Howard Theater in Baltimore, and road showman Theodor Magaarden put stripper Zorita, star of the film *I Married a Savage*, on the World of Mirth midway in 1950. The show consisted of Zorita dancing with a snake and clips from her movie. It grossed $82,000. Next year they put a combination film and Hawaiian show on the James E. Strates midway.

The 20th century was the "electric century." Buffalo called itself the "Electric City" and its 1901 Pan-American Expo was lit with millions of bulbs outlining the shapes of the fair buildings. "Electric parks" built by trolley-car companies flourished. The March 1903 *Billboard* reported the Brundage and Fisher Shows had the only electricity-driven merry-go-round on tour, using their own dynamo and motor. They also claimed to have an electric theater that used electricity to cool the air. For the carnivals, electricity added not only inexpensive and safe light, it led to new types of attractions.

The first electric scenic theaters — combinations of miniature scenes with special effects — were seen by Americans at the 1893 Chicago World's Fair. Both were titled A Day in The Alps. The German-made one was in the Midway Plaisance and the American one in the Electrical Building. The American-made attraction had scenery built and painted by the great Chicago scenic studio of Sosman and Landis. This show went to the California Mid-Winter Fair in San Francisco and then disappeared. The German show vanished after the Chicago fair. The opening of the Chicago Masonic Temple Rooftop Garden in 1894 also featured two scenic theaters. One, a smaller but finer version of A Day in the Alps, played the 1895 Cotton States Carnival in Atlanta, Ga., the Texas State Fair, the 1897 Nashville Centennial, the 1898 Milwaukee Exposition, and the 1900–01 Pittsburgh Expo. During the winter of

1903–04, Sosman and Landis built another scenic alps theater supervised by Thomas G. Moses, who had painted the first one and kept the original drawings. It played Philadelphia with the World's Fair Midway Shows, Madison Square Garden in New York City, and Boston, and closed at the St. Louis Indoor Exposition that fall.

A Day in the Alps depicted an entire day in the life of a Swiss town. It started with a darkened room, where patrons saw a beautiful sunrise that brightened as the village awakened. Villagers were seen crossing a bridge over a flowing river. Distant music caused them to stop and watch a circus parade go by. Dark clouds appeared and the people scurried for shelter. Flashes of lightning and thunder then brought on the storm scenes, which ended with a rainbow over the village and the swollen river. As the light faded and night drew in, the scene was highlighted by the glow of the mountaintops. The show ended as the church bell tolled and a moon rose over the village.

E.J. Austin's Johnstown Flood, built for the 1901 Pan-American Exposition, depicted scenes of the notorious flood that destroyed this small Pennsylvania city on Memorial Day 1899, killing 2,209 people. The biggest money earner at the fair, it became a seasonal attraction at Coney Island. Austin also created

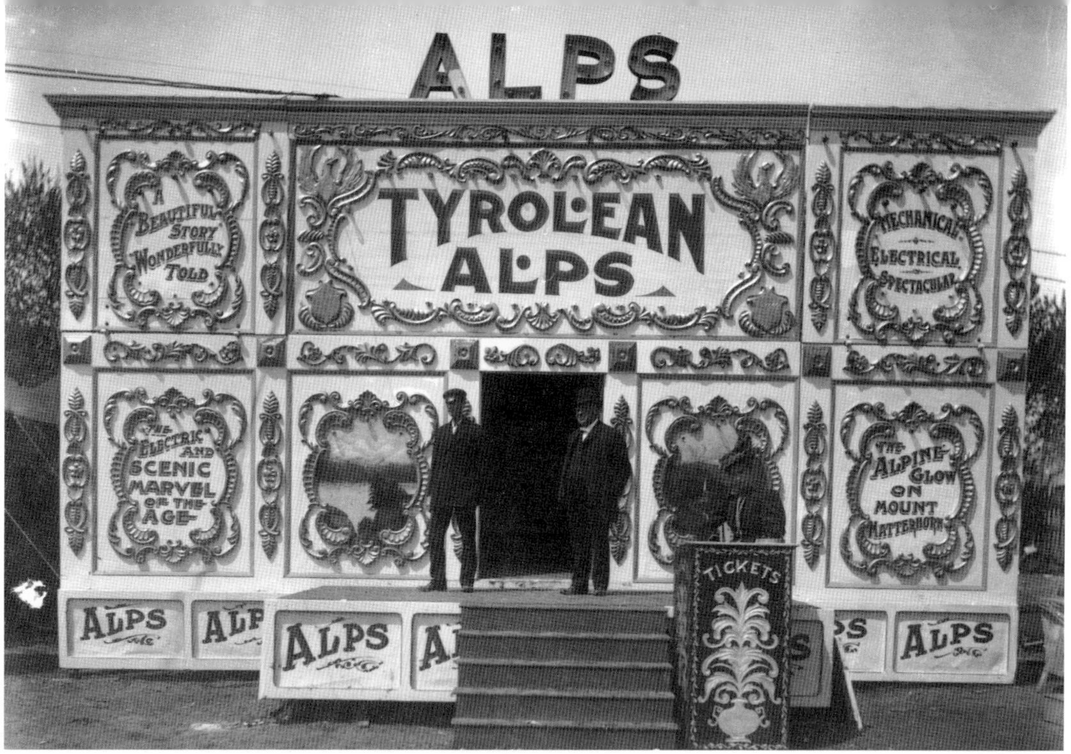

A beautiful one-wagon front built by C.W. Parker for the "Alps" scenic theater shows he made and sold to showmen.

The miniature Swiss town where all the action takes place in one of Parker's "Tyrolean Alps" scenic theaters. This one is mounted on a wagon with crude farm machinery-type wheels. Note the frame built around the village to create the effect you are looking at a painting.

Inside the "Alps" show on the 1906 Con. T. Kennedy Shows. Note the people and horse-drawn vehicles crossing the bridge and going along the town's main street. During the show, a train will pass on the railroad bridge in the background, and real water will turn the waterwheel and run in the river.

a scenic show based on the Galveston Flood for the 1904 Louisiana Purchase Exposition at St. Louis. While the first scenic theaters at the Chicago fair had a proscenium opening eight feet wide and six feet high, Austin's were 80 feet by 25 feet.

By 1903, a Sosman and Landis version of A Day in the Alps was doing big business on the Wright Carnival Co., and other showmen were quick to place these scenic theaters on their midways. C.W. Parker started building them for carnivals, as did A.T. Wright, who offered showmen a live Mt. Pelee that threw hot lava, smoke, and fire, and burned a real city before your eyes inside the tent. The Joseph Menohorn Manufacturing Co. on Broadway made a prismatic rainbow for the Johnstown Flood shows at Coney Island and Revere Beach besides offering showmen moving clouds, lightning, and fire photographed from nature. Kliegl Bros., another fine New York stage lighting company, made the latest scenic and stereopticon equipment, including effects for Last Day of the World, Creation, and Galveston Flood, plus special slides for the Loie Fuller act that included devouring-flame effects, astronomical illusions, fluttering butterflies, silver rain, and electric fountain effects.

Scenic theaters held the same problems as any attraction that could not be altered. Showmen had to continually change their routes or build new productions — but some added a twist to these shows: they combined them with live performers. One of these new acts was "transformation dancing." Dancer Loie Fuller is credited with stumbling upon the idea of having a pattern projected onto a dancer while she danced in a billowing white costume. The *Clipper* mentions performances in which dancers combine dances and orchestrations of light as early as 1870. The stereopticon allowed fairground showmen to exploit this technique in a big way. By the 1900s, several companies were selling serpentine and cloak slides for a dollar each.

George La Rose started presenting La

Rose's Electric Fountain show on midways in 1899. His letterhead describes it as "a bewildering combination of Art, Beauty, and Science. The show is the only one in existence equipped with a large revolving stage that rises from the interior of a fountain. In the rolling mass of water are a number of selected lady artists that do statuary groupings, illuminated dances, picture dances, and living facsimile reproductions of only the most refined subjects." The show also featured scenic and motion-picture effects and closed with the eruption of Mt. Pelee. It combined fire, water, electricity, pyrotechnics, and human performances and was still going strong in 1915 on the Rutherford Greater Shows.

Showman George Andrews presented Mamie, a fire and serpentine dancer, to packed crowds in his Electric Theater show on the 1903 Fish's Syndicate Shows. Next season, Francis Ferari Shows' Grand Electric Palace featured Mlle. Mamie, the Terpsichorean Queen of Spectacle, in her latest French novelty fire, water, and snow dances. She wore a lighted dress valued at over $10,000 while performing numbers advertised as The Electric Fountain, The Electric Forest, The Waterfalls of Fire, The Magic Lake, and Electric Dante's Inferno. George Loos' 1909 Mamie show included

The ornate front on a C.W. Parker Johnstown Flood Show.

Sketch of a stereopticon.

Electric dances and fountain acts.

Movie shows that were combined with skirt dancing and other electrical effects gradually developed into full-blown girl revue shows. By the 1920s many of these shows, like this one in Winnipeg, Manitoba, were quite elaborate with carved fronts and first-class stage settings.

the flying-lady illusion, black art feats, moving pictures, and a marionette act. Parker Amusement Co. titled their feature show Superba — here, Etta Louise Blake, along with three girls and the Rosays novelty act, performed a 40-minute show of color dances, illustrated vocal selections, Parisian poses, and the Galatea illusion to piano music. Among showmen, these shows were known as the "comeback shows" that season, as they took several worn-out midway attractions and gave new life to them in a fresh production.

These scenic effects shows, combining illusions and specialty dances, continued on the big carnivals well into the 1920s. Like wild animal shows earlier in the century, they were used to secure the better fair contracts. Showmen strove to keep their shows new. Change came with the introduction of popular dances and musical comedy. The old scenic theaters were changed into larger shows seating four or five hundred patrons with more elaborate stage sets. Small orchestras were added along with eight- and ten-girl chorus lines. New shows bore titles like Tango Girls, Fox Trot Girls, and Tipperary Maids. These shows, first presented as musical comedy, tab, and variety shows, quickly evolved into the girl revues of the 1930s, continuing as the feature midway shows on major carnivals into the 1970s.

Movies were on carnivals in the beginning and they were on carnivals as back-end shows faded away. In fall 1961, crowds filled a 3,000-seat inflated Cinerama theater with a rubber screen in Mantes la Jolie, France. Cinema 180s came to the fairgrounds in the mid-1970s. Operators referred to these vinyl domes as "the bubble," while carnies called the attraction a "bubble show." An electric motor drove a fan that pushed air inside to keep the dome inflated. The dome was fastened to a metal ground ring that encircled it. Patrons entered through a set of revolving doors and stood in the middle to watch the movie projected 180 degrees in front of them on the inner vinyl surface. The movie started about seven feet off the ground and the area it was projected on was painted white or silver. The rest of the dome was black.

Dick Marchant Jr. — whose late father, Richard Edward Marchant, a New England carny, was one of the early developers of the Cinema 180 — recalled that at some fairs their family played, in the 1960s, Chevrolet had a dome show promoting their products set up on the independent midway. The Chev's 180-degree movie was mainly about riding around in the company's cars and trucks, with just a little action and minimal narration. Dick didn't remember if this inspired his dad to build a Cinema 180 or if his father was inspired by a show called Thrillsphere that a German showman had on tour in America. He does remember his dad's words after seeing it: "I could sell this to every carnival in the country." Marchant Sr. worked out the details but didn't have the money to build the dome himself. He approached ride manufacturer Fred Hollingsworth and they became partners. With Fred as president, they formed Omnivision to manufacture the Cinema 180s. Dick's dad sold and toured "the bubble."

In their first season, 1976, they had two silver domes out. Neither had a front, just the door boxes and fire exits, and there was no talker, only a grind tape. In one dome,

Electrical dances combined with the film *Horrors of the White Slave Traffic* on the Parker and Kennedy Shows midway, 1914.

the projector was in a square wooden booth they rolled out from a truck. The second dome's projector was built into a Wells Cargo trailer, which had to be jacked up high. Eventually the prototype was reworked so that each Cinema 180 had a nice flashy front painted by show painter Bill Browning and was built on a semi-trailer. The projection booth slid out of the back of the trailer and snugged up against the side of the dome. A plastic window allowed the film to be projected inside.

Cinema 180 had a rocky start. "It was not a self-selling show," explains Dick. "The new crowd had to wait 15 minutes until the old crowd was out and we started the film again. It was very hard to hold them." That all changed when veteran talker Bill Thompson came along. Bill was one of the best girl-show talkers in the business. "Bill Thompson showed us how to sell it and he made people comfortable while waiting," remembers Dick. "One line he used I will never forget; people would be in line and Bill would turn and look right at them and say, 'I don't care if you are a mama, a papa, a child, or a chicken. When you come out and I ask you how you liked the show, you are going to say, "Uh-huh."' He would time this so that the crowd inside was just coming out. He would ask them how they liked the show. They would say, 'Uh-huh,' and the new tip would just crack up laughing.

"The funniest incident was this day I was running the projector, and in the film there is this scene where a catamaran is whipping through the water with all this spray flying. I see drops of water on the lens. I look out at the audience in the drome and they are wiping water off themselves. I told Bill to look around outside and see if there was a leak in the dome skin, and he comes across this drunk pissing in the outside blower. Coming out, Bill asked the crowd how they liked the show, and no 'Uh-huh' this time. Most said, 'That's neat,' like it was a special effect in the show."

The films ran about 12 minutes, and there was an art to getting the new tip in. Dick explains, "We never cleaned the theater of people. Usually the new people crowded the last crowd out, but if someone

THE COOKS

Present a marvelous **Pantomime Act** in

BLACK ART Introducing

THE DECAPITATION
FLYING JAP.·.·.

And a host of Startling and Amusing Tricks

DECAPITATION

The FLYING JAP

We have an Up-to-date **Moving Picture Machine** *and* **Stereopticon Combined** and a carefully selected lot of Moving Pictures.

.·. **BUTTERFLY DANCE** .·.

Consists of beautiful colored slides being shown on the dancer in connection with colored lights.

Here are 3 GOOD NOVELTY ACTS

We carry paraphernalia and operate the same.

Please state whether you have electricity *and* what voltage

IF NOT I USE CALCIUM

Permanent Address: N. Y. Clipper......

Above: Letterhead from the Cooks providing three good novelty acts, including the Butterfly Dance. Note their permanent address: N.Y. Clipper, the theatrical magazine.

In the late 1960s, movies were revived as a show on carnival midways with the development of Cinema 180s, where action films were shown on the surface of a large vinyl bubble kept inflated by a constant air flow. Viewers felt as though they were riding in a plane, boat, or roller coaster.

When Cinema 180 business waned in the 1980s showmen tried laser shows inside the vinyl bubbles. These shows had an even shorter midway life than did the film shows.

The great sideshow talker Paul "Mush" Wonder and famed girl-show talker Bill Thompson hold up a half boy on the 1960 Royal American Shows' 10-in-1. These two gentlemen could talk you into anything! Bill Thompson came up with the patter that lured customers into the first cinema 180s.

wanted to stay it was okay with us. The dome held 100 to 150, so if you wanted to make money you had to run as many shows as possible each day. Back then the ticket price was $1.50 and we would run it for two or three people when grinding rather than take a chance of losing them waiting in line."

By the end of the 1980s, Cinema 180s were being replaced by laser shows and simulator units. One enterprising carny did good business by painting his old Scrambler ride black and putting it inside his dome, accompanied by black-light effects and a powerful soundtrack.

TORTURERS
AND FIENDISH
KILLERS
IN ACTION
HEAR THEIR MOANS AND GROANS
SEE THEIR VICTIMS
SEE THIS
SEE THIS.
MUSEUM of THE DOOMED
The IRON MAIDEN
SEE THIS
HINDU SKELETON
SEE THIS
SCIENCE vs. IGNORANCE
20th CENTURY
16th CENTURY
DEMONSTRATION
The TORTURE OF A WITCH
The GARROTE
SEE THIS
20
UNUSUAL

HEAR THEM MOAN! SEE THEM SUFFER!

Torture Victims and Opium Eaters

Chapter 6

War has provided a rewarding attraction for those in show business. When panorama shows started to wane in the early 1860s, the Civil War saved many showmen. Even before the war ended, panorama men were displaying its battles on miles of canvas. Many in their audiences had known people who fought in the front lines and they were painfully interested in the painted tale scrolling by before them. After the Civil War, photos and relics appeared in dime museums and in the tents of touring showmen.

Opposite: In the late 1950s Ray and Mary Chambers operated this torture show on the World of Mirth Shows midway, which was framed by Noel Lester. The banner in the lower right was deemed offensive by the Indian consulate during the show's exhibit at the Ottawa, Ontario, fair, so Ray had to cover up the lettering.

Most of the war shows on organized carnival companies after the Chicago World's Fair were either miniature mechanical shows or those showing stereopticon views or movies. J.H.W. Brady's June 1903 *Billboard* ad seeking bookings for his new Brady's War Museum offered to provide a moving-picture

World War I relics show in a small top. One of the items displayed out front is a trench motor gun.

machine, operator, and lecturer to any fair manager for $250 a week or on percentage to any carnival owner who supplied a black tent, a front, and moved the show. The show consisted of views of Gettysburg, 1863 battlefields, regiments, trenches, camps, charges, prisons, wounded soldiers, and burial of the dead from 1861 through 1865, all made from 40-year-old Washington War Department negatives. Fourteen years later, Brady's Scenes of the Civil War was still going strong on midways.

The carnival business was well-established by the time of America's next big war. Midway war shows depicted the horrors of the trenches, rats, and poisonous gases. Louis Selzie's Automatic City and Panopticon on the 1915 Sheesley Midway Shows featured "lifelike" action and actual-size reproductions of the German and Allied forces at war. In 1917, a war show on the Rutherford Carnival Co. was called The War of Today; it claimed to be the only attraction under canvas depicting the most terrible scenes of battle with Zeppelins bombing cities and airplanes shooting poisonous gases. Up in Boston, freak builder William Nelson offered to "Showmen Only: REAL, Montezala Alkified Bodies from the Battle Fields of Europe."

Lieut. Col. C.H. Ackerman of Peterborough, Ont., was one of the first persons to have a Trench Warfare Exhibition on midways. The show featured trench mines, hand grenades, gas masks, real dugouts and tunnels, wounded soldiers, trophies of the battlefields, wire entanglements, and wireless and telegraph communications posts. His 1918 *Billboard* ad read: "Canadian Wounded Soldier's Trench Exhibit . . . A party of returned wounded soldiers honorably discharged from the service carry with them hundreds of souvenirs from the battlefields of France. They explain the souvenirs and the constructions of the trenches. A bona fide exhibition." Showman Sgt. G. Norman Shields was inspired by Ackerman and built similar shows, becoming one of the leading war showmen of the time with units on carnival midways and in storefronts. Incidents of live ammunition and gas canisters exploding on touring war shows and casual exhibits by Legions and veterans groups prompted the government to issue rules on how these artifacts could be secured and displayed. Helmets, uniforms, and guns could be shown, but no live shells or full gas cylinders.

War shows lasted long enough for another conflict to come along and give them a further bouquet of freshness. World War II fostered new horrors and villains: midway war shows featured Hitler, Mussolini, and Tojo. Homer Tate stopped making Wolf Boys and began turning out "Shrunken Jap Soldiers" for showmen. Ball

A Hitler wax figure on display in the World of Mirth war show. On the right is veteran press agent Raymond Cox.

"Through the Trenches" show, made by Modern Showbuilding Co. in 1918, consisted of trenches with dugouts, a machine gun pit, crevices, periscopes, and tunnels.

games like Hit the Jap and Knock off Hitler's Head allowed homebound patriots to vent their frustrations and win chalk figurines of flag-carrying enlisted women and men. Carnival companies ran war drives, and after the war bought surplus searchlights, generators and trucks, giving their equipment a military look. Communism was a hot seller, and show fronts shouted: "RED KOREA WAR ATROCITIES" and "BRUTAL COMMUNIST AGGRESSION." In these shows, veteran showmen made good money pitching war booklets. Over on Conklin, the war show was the ideal location for one of the show's Skill-o joints. In the back of the war show, men found out what losses were really about as an old beret-wearing agent nicknamed Soldier Smitty worked them over.

Seasonally, Chas. T. Buell turned out three or four new shows to keep pace with wars, crimes, and other sensational occurrences. During World War II he offered shows titled The Great Atomic Bomb, Jap and Nazi Atrocities, Jap Atrocities in the March of Bataan, and The Great Lightning War. His 1940 ad in *Billboard* gave this description: "Nothing like it ever shown since the beginning of time. Uncensored scenes direct from the front that wring people's hearts. Tanks, bombers, liquid fire, new weapons, all crashing down on humanity with men, women, and little children the fallen victims."

Above: A walk-through war show on the 1952 World of Mirth Shows midway.

Inside the war show "Hitler and His Henchmen after Death." Wax figures on the right lie in coffin-like boxes, and display boards on the opposite side are used as stalls to slow down the crowd and lengthen their visit. Notice the "sucker netting" attached to the side poles along the wall of the tent to keep people from sneaking in.

War shows hung around on the midways into the early '50s and then slowly faded away as the "make love not war" '60s rolled in. But peace was shortlived — when the war in Vietnam started up, Larry Friedman's Viet Cong Booby Trap show made its owner a decent living. Those Giant Rats had changed locale too — they were no longer from the Sewers of Paris or even the Dungeons of Russia: they were Giant Blood-Sucking Secret Viet Cong Killers!

At the end of World War II, a whole slew of Mercedes cars came over from Europe, several of which were billed as Hitler's personal limousine and exhibited on midways. One Hitler car, owned by Christopher Janus, an importer-exporter living in Winnetka, Ill., was first exhibited in 1948. It drew big crowds while on view at the New York Museum of Science and Industry in Radio City. Amusement Corp. of America hired the attraction and it started playing their fairs that summer in Springfield, Ill., under the supervision of veteran back-end presenter Cliff Wilson. For its trip to the Springfield fairgrounds, the car was driven rather than shipped. A Chicago newspaper reporter rode along with it and the publicity created crowds of more than 5,000 daily. Adults paid 50 cents and children, a quarter, to see the former house-painter's car.

One of the Hitler cars on display inside an exhibit trailer in France.

Along with the car came a photo showing Hitler in Berlin in 1941 riding in the vehicle. A postcard description reads: "All the glass in the vehicle is an inch and a half thick. On the right side front door is a built-in case that holds a Luger pistol. Behind the rear seat is a leather covered sheet of armor that cranks up manually. The car has a 153-inch wheel base, making it a long car. It is also heavy, weighing 9,500 pounds. It has an eight-cylinder overhead valve motor capable of developing 230 horsepower. The transmission consists of five speeds forward and one reverse plus an overdrive that can be used at speeds up to 125 mph. The large gas tank holds 60 gallons."

In April 1949, the car opened its exhibition tour at Little Rock, Ark., on the Hennies Bros. Shows midway, then disappeared from mention in *Billboard*. The December 29, 1972, *Miami Herald* reported that a Hitler car described as a 770 K Mercedes was to be auctioned in Scottsdale, Ariz., the following week: "This was a car that Hitler, Mussolini, and Mannerheim had ridden in on state occasions. Mannerheim had later shipped it from Finland to Sweden so the Russians wouldn't capture it. It was seized by the Swedish government and traded to an American firm that made ball bearings."

After WWI, Chinese themed walk-through shows became a popular attraction spurred on by movies of the same subject. One manufacturer was C.W. Parker of Leavenworth, Kansas. Here is one of his 1918 displays titled "Sin Toy's Opium Den," which consisted of five to eight rooms in which wax figures portrayed scenes of prostitution, gambling, and dope in the Chinatowns of large American cities.

Janus' Hitler car was not the only one in America. A November 1949 *Billboard* ad boasted: "Adolph Hitler's Genuine Personal Armored Limousine" and, in parentheses, "Not One That He Just Rode In." The limo was allegedly captured by Free French Forces at Berchtesgaden. Mounted in a semi-trailer, it had attracted 220,000 paid admissions at one exhibition. While the car was on tour in Texas in 1957, the Prospect Association — its owner — advertised it for sale for the best offer over $3,500. It was on tour at the same time Pennsylvania back-end showman Pete Sevich had a Hitler car on World of Mirth shows.

A January 1955 *Billboard* reported that Jack W. Burke of Baldwin, N.Y., had hired Carl Hauptmann to be the advance agent for his Hitler Mercedes-Benz car exhibit. Both had been field managers for units of Ripley's Believe It or Not tours. In 1954 the Hitler car had been on tour for a solid year and closed Christmas Eve in Chattanooga, Tenn. Burke continued to show it for several seasons. Sevich billed his exhibit on the 1957 World of Mirth Shows midway as "Hitler's $35,000 Armored Limousine." Sevich was still booking his car as late as 1966. Bill Hall, a carnival showman, collector, and band organ restorer, later bought the semi it was displayed on. It had a 28-foot display area for the car with an eight-foot living area over the fifth wheel. Hall used it to display his model of the World of Mirth Shows on various carnival midways. He says the car proved to be a fraud and was taken off exhibition and sold for $30,000.

The Canadian War Museum, which has a real Hitler car, reports that only two Mercedes vehicles in North America were actually used by Hitler. Their car first came to the United States where it was used in various bond drives to pay off the war debt. In 1956 it was sold to a Canadian, and 14 years later the museum acquired it after it was shown at the Montreal exhibition Man and His World. The only other authentic Hitler car is at a Las Vegas casino.

During Christmas week of 1888, Austin and Stone's Nickelodeon and Dime Museum in Boston presented a pair of opium eaters. Even with an innocent wood-chopping contest on the same bill, the *Clipper* reported it to be the vilest act seen in Boston in a long time and questioned if such an act was of any value. The public answered with turn-away box office.

Drugs were not new to showmen — weekly *Clipper* ads offered cures for various addictions. Drugs, white slavery, and devious foreigners, however, provided a combination few showmen could pass up. The 1899 Bostock midway, for example, featured a Chinatown Opium Den show, and after World War I, New York Film Corps released *Chinatown*, touted as approved by New York censors and depicting Chinese opium dens and the dope fiends at work. The lobby display was a real Chinese opium den, complete with a mechanical moving figure of a girl and a Chinese man behind bars.

In 1917, the C.W. Parker Co. in Leavenworth, Kan., claimed to be the first to build a portable Underground Chinatown walk-through show for midway showmen. Within a couple of years they could hardly keep up with the orders from carnival showmen, amusement parks, and store show operators — at one point, they had five complete outfits going through the factories. One contained 22 wax characters, seven complete rooms or scenes, and a nine-section front for $1,500, while the bigger version, featuring an extra room and eight additional characters, sold for $2,250. The figures were finely costumed with artificial human glass eyes, planted hair, and eyebrows and eyelashes. All heads, hands, and visible feet were of finely sculptured, reinforced wax.

The Modern Show Building Co.'s 1920s walk-through Chinatown shows were promoted as a true reproduction of San Francisco's Chinatown, complete with shrines, opium dens, gambling holes, secret tunnels, and slave girls. But for showmen not wanting to lug around wax figures or mannequins, Chas. Buell had the solution with his peep boxes and enlarged photos. His 1926 "masterpiece," Opium

Front of the Parker Underground Chinatown Shows.

Dens and White Slave Markets of Chinatown, contained views of New York, San Francisco, and Chicago Chinatowns, depicting opium dens, gambling joints, women in slavery, executions, Chinese funerals, poppy fields, and tong wars — just one thrill after another.

Torture scenes have been not only the bread and butter of every wax museum, they were also important to traveling wax shows and many midway shows. P.N. Hausen called his 1890 wax show the finest museum show ever brought to America. It had traveled throughout Europe and the U.S. as Dr. Heidman's Great Museum of Anatomy, Ethnology, and

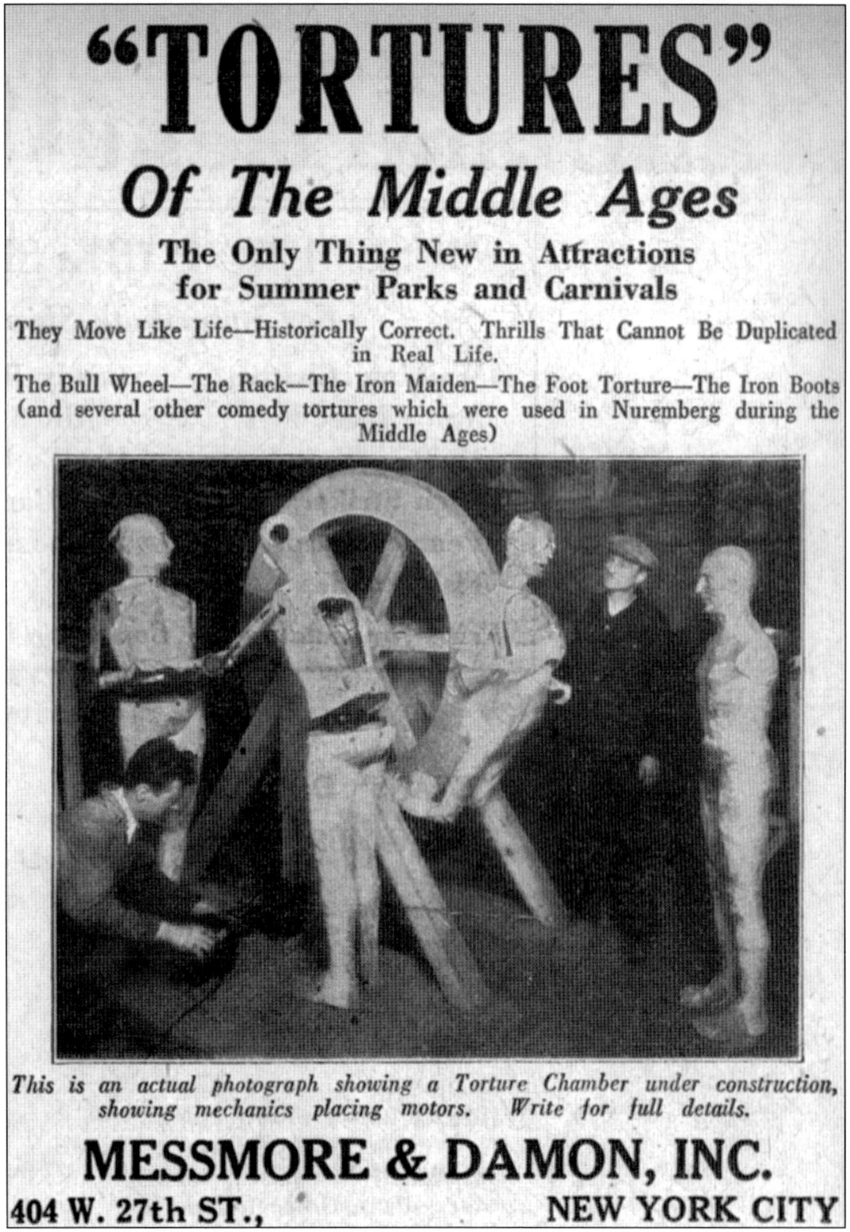

Messmore & Damon, Inc., *Billboard* ad (March 28, 1931) showing mechanics placing motors in their "Tortures of the Middle Ages" show.

Pathology, combined with an exclusive collection of mechanical and other figures depicting scenes of tortures as performed during the Spanish Inquisition. Torture displays were popular in dime museums and wax storefront shows, but didn't get onto the midway until the late 1930s. Showmen may have felt the public had been tortured enough by the Depression.

The display and figure company of Messmore and Damon put out a show in 1935 that would be a prototype for future midway torture shows. Detroit-born George Messmore worked in his father's carpentry shop but preferred the theater. At age 16, he hopped a freight to New York City, where he worked at various jobs, including pasting posters on walls and ash cans, trimming windows, building display floats, and selling beer at Coney Island. Messmore got into the display business by putting midgets out of work. At the time, midgets dressed in penguin suits and holding advertising signs were the hottest urban billboards. But midgets were hard to find and expensive, so George invented a mechanical penguin that ran by clockwork, then added a mechanical monkey and seal. Department stores wanted them faster than he could make them, so in 1919 he partnered up with a fine artist named Joe

Damon. Damon built the clay replicas for whatever figure they were making and remained with Messmore for more than two decades.

Messmore created the World a Million Years Ago walk-through show that scored big financially at the 1933 Century of Progress Fair in Chicago and the Flash Gordon in the World of Tomorrow show at the 1939 New York World's Fair. Another Messmore invention was a two-dimensional "panorama" girlie show consisting of life-size color nudes that were blown-up photographs transposed to acetate. The illusion of motion was created by constantly changing lights. George often told the story about these girls looking so real that one talker would smear a streak of tobacco juice across the model's eyes because he felt she was staring at him while he worked.

Messmore and Damon's first adventure in torture shows started in 1935 with a Coney Island horror show called the Torture Chamber. Six chambers of horrors with animated figures that talked and moved recreated gruesome practices such as the Iron Boots, the Iron Maiden, and the Chinese Rat Torture, also known as the Seven Gates to Heaven. Another section of the show featured a series of paintings highlighted by Marie Antoinette's death by guillotine.

Mickey Burns and her husband, G.N. (in the ticket box), toured this torture show on American midways in the 1950s and '60s. It had one of the most colorful bannerlines in the business. Signs proclaimed: "Hear them moan" — quite a feat for wax mannequins. One lady persisted in asking Mickey how long it took to see them die!

Messmore took the show on the road, and to increase its drawing power, added a live girl attraction he called the Crusader's Bride, in which the bride wore only a chastity belt. Fair officials told him the girl's bosom must be covered or they would close him down — but he could use any opaque material. Messmore made a plaster cast of the girl's bust and then a mold. When officials came back to see the show, they were shocked to see the girl's bosom still nude. But Messmore pointed out that the young lady was wearing an opaque, flesh-colored thin latex brassiere. She just looked nude under a spotlight from the spectators' viewing distance. Fellow showmen offered Messmore thousands of dollars for his opaque-bra formula, but he never gave out the secret.

Sideshow and illusion showmen the

Lorow brothers were among the first to cash in on Messmore's formula. They put a torture show on Hennies Bros. Shows in 1938. Ray and Mary Chambers had a similar show on World of Mirth in the late '50s and early '60s. At the same time, Bob Edwards operated his torture show on Cetlin and Wilson Shows and later Olson Shows. Inside were nine complete tortures illustrated with life-size mechanical figures. Showman Eddie Keck, a former Ringling Bros. and Barnum and Bailey circus paymaster, had various back-end shows out on the Strates Shows — his 1964 Graveyard Ridge torture show, billed as "the Greatest Scariest Show on Earth," had the usual torture and Hollywood monster figures inside, including a corpse in a coffin that jumped out at viewers.

"The sweetest show of all for roping the suckers" was how an old-time showman described a riverboat show he saw at the turn of the century. "Word of mouth advertised it and anyone seeing it surely sent others," he recalled. On the showboat, a woman dressed in a medieval costume with a high gold-lace collar stood in front of a curtain beside a girl covered in a velvet drape. The woman pitched the display as a return to the times when knighthood was in flower. Onlookers were told knights going off to war had their armorers build devices to ensure their wives' chastity: "If you went to Europe today, you could see these devices in museums, but you don't have to travel there. One of the museums has lent us one and the young woman beside me is wearing it."

The girl then removed her cape and stood naked except for the metal belt surrounding her waist, secured by a padlock. A band of metal two inches wide extended downward from the belt. It was wider and ornately designed over the pubic area; it tapered between her legs and rose up back to the belt. The girl posed and walked around in this snug belt. The men watching were silent — they made no wisecracks, as the model was a handsome, stately girl who carried it off well. Four decades later, torture showmen were still using a similar act as a blow-off feature in their show.

The canned spiel for Jimmy Dixon's

1973 torture show on the Royal American Shows midway invited crowds to "see the mutilation of a beautiful girl. . . . See a man buried up to his neck in honey, and left for ants to drive him to insanity as he slowly dies. . . . See a beautiful girl, her clothes torn away as a gigantic rip saw slices through her body." The torture show, priced at 50 cents for adults and 35 cents for children, drew *Calgary Herald* reporter Carol Hogg's rage, especially the lurid artwork on the front. In her article "Midway Gore, Torture, Do We Need It?" she wrote, "It's not a pretty picture. A woman is being tortured by two men. Her wrists drip blood where her hands have been lopped off. One man is plunging a red-hot poker down her throat, while his buddy beats her with a spiked ball and chain."

Hogg wrote that she and 26 kids waited 17 minutes for the show to start; they passed the time staring at two exhibits on either side of a stage curtain. When the show started, "a fat, dumpy dressed man walked onstage. 'Good afternoon, ladies and gentlemen. Er, uh . . . boys and girls. Welcome to the Dungeon of Torture,' he said. He explained that the exhibits were not intended to be accurate, but only to amuse the audience while waiting for the show to begin. It was a relief to know that the displays were not intended to be accurate, because I had been disturbed about a number of incongruities, notably the Japanese fishing boats in what was a Spanish Inquisition scene. The young audience snapped to attention as a man onstage proceeded to lower a rip saw through the midriff of a supine woman. But her clothes were not 'torn away' as the blurb had promised. Rather, they were gently folded to one side, as the blade whined into what was obviously a plaster cast. After the long wait, the entire show was over in less than a minute."

Hogg was further outraged by the blow-off: "The fat man offered to let the members of the audience file past the girl onstage to see how the trick was done. 'Just line up on the stage here, boys and girls,' he invited. Almost all complied. However, as they went to pass, he told them they would each have to pay an additional quarter to see how the trick was done. I gave the man a quarter and talked briefly with the girl who confirmed what was already obvious! She was lying in a depression in the couch, and the blade ripped through a plaster cast above her body. 'Does this kind of work bother you?' 'No . . . the work doesn't bother me. Just the hours. I work 17 hours a day!' As they left the show, one of the kids

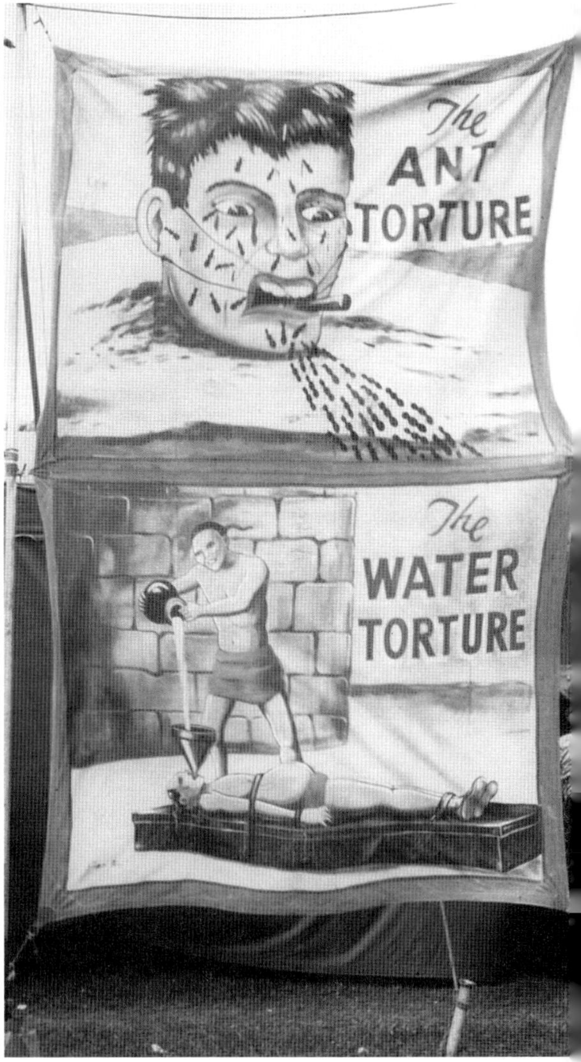

A banner on the Journey Into Fear torture show on the Strates Shows midway in the late 1970s.

remarked: 'We never did see the man buried in honey and driven to insanity by the ants as he slowly dies.'"

From the early 1800s, small anatomical displays toured America. While medical practitioners ran theirs on moral principles and included lectures on the body sciences, those operated by showmen were often limited to "men only" and their sole attraction was the naked wax female body. Fine arts, tableaux vivants, and anatomy displays were the only glimpses of the female body available to public audiences at this time. Often admission to the showmen's anatomical shows was free; his income came from the sale of medical booklets and $5 doctor's consultation fees from patrons who feared for their health after walking past wax displays of venereal diseases.

In December 1888, Dr. E.A. Bassett was selling his Gallery of Anatomy on Adams St. in Chicago. He said it came with an office and presented a rare opportunity for a good, reliable physician. In 1892, Dr. Will Baker of Baltimore was manufacturing his new 70-piece male and female disease show for showmen or medicine companies; it sold for $600. Three years later, Dr. Robert Hochmuth of New York City was supplying showmen anatomical specimens of wax made to order at short notice. And in 1897, freak maker Ernest Bruggemann's ads directed at sideshow managers said he was making anatomical models based on Dr. Hochmuth's system.

Perhaps the dean of American wax modelers was naturalist and anatomical sculptor John Michael Schliesser. His 1915 *Billboard* ads offered all sorts of anatomical waxworks plus papier-mâché objects, mummies for exhibition purposes, and "Alcohol Curiosities" for sale. During the 1930s, his studio was on Park Ave. in New York City, where he specialized in work for showmen. He claimed to be the originator of "Embryological Exhibits" in the U.S. He provided preserved specimens of all subjects, anatomical models or organs, complete entomology collections, natural and imitation mummies, wax models of any character, and mechanical models human or animal. In his words: "Always something new."

The wax anatomical show was ideal for the early carnival companies, which were mostly gilly outfits, traveling in railroad baggage cars. Typical of such shows was that on F.L. Flack's Great Northwestern Shows out of Detroit, Mich. Through the teens and early '20s he carried an anatomy show in two chests with a small tent and a single 12-by-18-foot doorway banner. The show occupied little lot space, could be run by one man, and turned a good profit each day.

Anatomical shows faded from midways by the Depression years, but the wax specimens continued to be exhibited along with real freak babies in Life and Unborn shows. Throughout the 1930s and into the 1950s, whole anatomy shows and various medical specimens, including diseased sex organ collections, were listed for sale by Weil's Curiosity Shop in Philadelphia. The odd anatomical piece can be seen among

the mummified subjects, Fiji mermaids, Tate figures, pickled specimens, and stuffed freak animals on the last museum shows still on carnivals.

The showing of ceroplastic art or "wax figures" has been popular with showmen in Europe and North America. In *Memoirs of Bartholomew Fair*, author Henry Morley mentions a waxwork show called The Temple of Diana, located opposite London's Hospital Gate, in 1699. By the 1870s, wax shows rivaled the touring menageries on the English roads. Rowland's 1875 Colossal Exhibition of Automatic Wax Figures played one-day stands or longer, exhibiting 500 lifelike models including Queen Victoria, Napoleon, President Lincoln, the Turkish Slave Market, and Lincoln assassin John Wilkes Booth. The show traveled in eight caravans and was pulled by 20 horses.

The most famous permanent exhibitions were created by Madame Tussaud. She was the niece of physician John Christopher Curtius, who in 1757 was modeling anatomical displays in Berne, Switzerland. Curtius moved to Paris, where he opened a museum at the Hotel d'Aligre in 1762, modeling only anatomical displays. Eight years later, he opened a second museum on Blvd. du Temple, where he taught his niece Marie Gresholtz the wax art. Wax sculpturing became a fad among the upper classes, and she gave them lessons. During the French Revolution, many of the decapitated heads brought to her studio to be modeled in wax were those of her aristocratic students. After Curtius died in 1795, Marie married François Tussaud, and seven years later they moved to London to open a museum. Madame Tussaud died in 1850, but her descendents carried on as museum owners and wax modelers. During the 1960s, Canadian Arthur L. Batty got approval from Josephine Tussaud to use the famous name to build museums in Victoria, B.C.; St. Petersburg, Fla.; Scottsdale, Ariz.; Banff, Alta.; and San Francisco. Recently a Tussaud's was opened in the newly "cleansed" Times Square in New York City.

In the late 1800s, most dime museums and touring storefront showmen had wax collections ranging from anatomical specimens and several wax figures of current

Carnival general agent Bob Lohmar built this wax show along patriotic lines. It was on the Morris and Castle Shows midway in the 1920s but didn't do much business. In 1954 the show resurfaced under the title "The Hall of Presidents," and enjoyed good patronage in department stores and on fairgrounds.

subjects to large groupings depicting crime and historical scenes. Such a show listed for sale in the May 1893 *Clipper* describes the wax exhibit as consisting of 20 pieces with elegant brocade and lace for the front of the store and large, framed photos for the window. Also included in the sale was a wax figure of Cleopatra dressed in silk for a free window show, and a den of snakes. The snakes seem out of place with wax figures but storefront shows of all kinds often used snakes for bally purposes. They were alive, a good attention-getter, and never complained about the long hours behind the window glass.

The first circus sideshow in the 1850s was a "wax figger" show. The April 19, 1873, *Clipper* review of circuses touring that season described several wax shows. On the Van Amburgh and Co. Circus, one of J.W. Orr's sideshows featured waxwork figures of Queen Victoria and her children; Napoleon, his wife, and son; the Emperor of Germany; King Victor Emmanuel of Italy; some prominent Americans; and several notorious English criminals. All the figures were copied from those in Madame Tussaud's museum in London. "Added at considerable cost," the *Clipper* observed, "is a correct full-length model of the late Siamese Twins so true are they to nature that many visitors upon approaching them have offered to shake their hands. The medical profession have spoken in highest praise of them."

At least one showman was skeptical about the wax figures. In his full-page ad in a spring 1873 *Clipper*, L.B. Lent claimed his colossal 60-railcar circus would contain no "wax heads, stuffed animals, corpses, and no HUMBUG," only "All living wonders and live attractions." But wax figures would be on showgrounds for another hundred years.

By 1892, W.H.J. Shaw was offering showmen wax figures including William Kemmler, the first man to be executed in an electric chair. The figure, seated in the electric chair, came with an 8-by-10-foot painting, all for $50. Shaw also advertised Cleopatra, "dressed fine," with painting. In 1918, Shaw's latest was a mechanical sleeping-beauty wax figure he claimed was good "for the Johnnies" — criminal slang for gullible people. A sleeping beauty without clothes was especially popular among males on early fairgrounds.

In 1927, Shaw's son turned out the Missing Link, made half of wax and half of hair. Like his father, he also became a dependable supplier of two-headed wax babies. By the 1930s, his big sellers were John Dillinger, Baby Face Nelson, and Pretty Boy Floyd.

From the 1920s to the 1950s, B.W. Christophel made wax figures and very fine wax babies for showmen. Christophel's 1934 *Billboard* ad for his Dillinger figure read: "Dillinger in wax. Lying in state. Same as the body left Chicago. Absolutely true to life. Properly dressed." Replying to a customer's request in 1931, Christophel wrote, "My figures have full papier-mâché bodies with jointed wooden arms. Heads and hands of the best imported wax and natural human hair used." By 1944, showmen could buy his life-size "Caesarian operation" in a glass case, tiny shrunken heads, Indian mummies, and two-headed babies in large jars. An April 1959 *Billboard* ad placed by Krewson Wax Figure Studio in St. Louis stated it was formerly Christophel's business and continued to offer wax figures to showmen.

In the late 1930s, Animated Displays Inc. in Hollywood, Calif., and Leopold

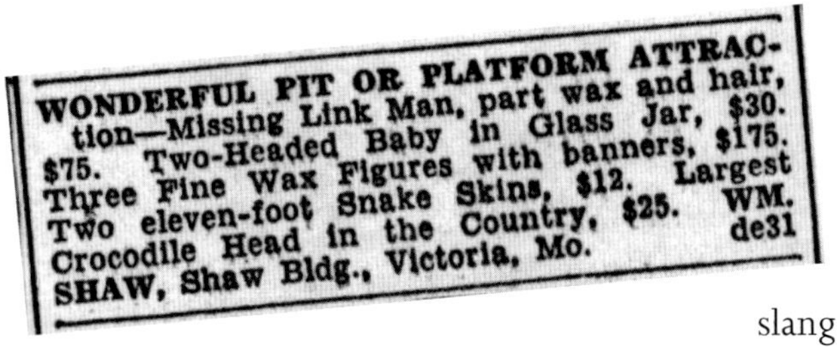
WONDERFUL PIT OR PLATFORM ATTRACtion—Missing Link Man, part wax and hair, $75. Two-Headed Baby in Glass Jar, $30. Three Fine Wax Figures with banners, $175. Two eleven-foot Snake Skins, $12. Largest Crocodile Head in the Country, $25. WM. SHAW, Shaw Bldg., Victoria, Mo. de31

Schmidt in Jersey City, N.J., were Shaw's and Christophel's main competitors. Although there were only a handful of wax sculptors making figures for showmen and museums, there was a never-ending supply of subjects — new presidents, dead presidents, old-time outlaws, and recent murderers and their victims.

Historian George C.D. Odell, in his *Annals of the New York Stage*, states that New York did not have a museum totally devoted to wax figures until the Eden Musee was built in 1884 at 23rd St. near Sixth. Run by the Eden Musee American Co., it slowly became a combination wax and dime museum, cited as one of the early places in the city where motion pictures were first shown. The museum lasted until 1914, and was then auctioned off; Coney Island show promoter Sam Gumperts bought most of the wax figures. He renamed the exhibit World in Wax and set it up next to his 20-in-1 show at Dreamland.

By 1948, the World in Wax had been a Coney Island fixture for 27 years. It was a serious trap, with entrances on the Bowery, Stillwell, and Henderson's Walk. Sam Santangelo was owner and manager, and three talkers brought the crowd in, while Madame Grace dinged with a horoscope pitch. In the '50s, Santangelo had competition from the Eden Musee at Surf and West 8th owned by Sam Bellig. After Santangelo's death, his wife Lillie kept the show open until 1984. In November 1986, the contents of the museum were auctioned by Guernsey's under the Big Apple Circus big top at Lincoln Center.

By World War I, numerous carnival companies had wax shows on their midways. The World Wonders in Wax, presenting "living breathing famous people," was on the midway of Rutherford's Greater Shows in 1917. The same season, Frank C. Byers had his wax museum on carnivals with Buckskin Ben's Wild West unit, and in the winter he played stores. Goetz's Wax Works and Eden Musee worked on carnival midways during the 1921 season. Straight waxwork shows were outnumbered by the more popular crime wax shows, and sex and crime became the only way to sell wax attractions on the midway. Perhaps people were waxed out, as many cities had permanent wax museums, and mechanical wax figures were popular department-store window displays at Christmas.

In 1930, wax makers Schmidt and Sons offered showmen Ubangi Disc-lipped Savages described as "The Wax Sensation, the only thing new in wax." Ubangi had been featured on several tented circuses, scoring a lot of media attention. Similarly in the mid-1930s, W.H.J. Shaw was offering showmen "giraffe-necked women," another circus sideshow import of the time. A 1959 *Billboard*

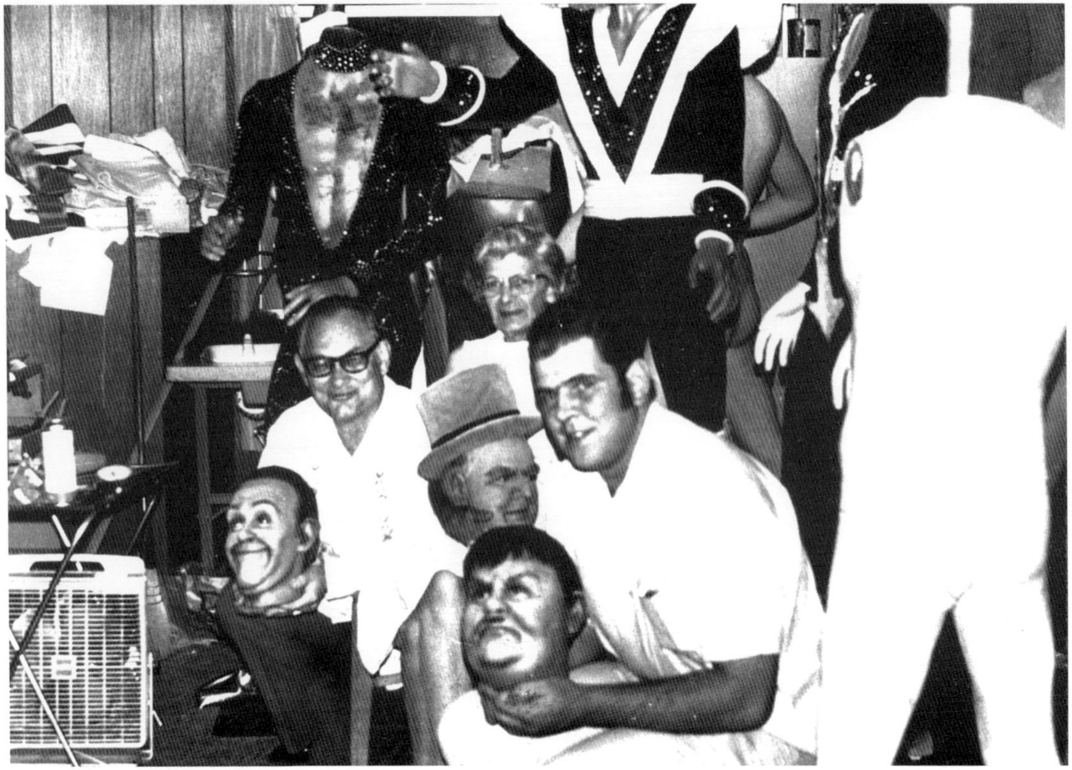

An employee named Marge Porter helps Ward Hall and Chris Christ dress the figures for their 20th Century Wax Museum show at Seaside Heights, N.J.

carried ads by sideshowman Dave Rosen selling wax freaks from his Coney Island show. He described them as life-size reproductions in wax of "the world's strangest and most sensational freaks" including a double-bodied four-legged girl, Siamese twins joined at the head, and a Mexican two-headed man. The collection came with banners for each figure.

At the same time, Snap Wyatt was making papier-mâché freaks at his Tampa banner shop. Several showmen bought these figures and framed Barnum's Museum shows to quickly find out they were total "heat scores" — they created nothing but complaints. The banners portrayed all the famous freaks of the past as if they were inside alive, which was the only way to sell the show. However, the dozen or so papier-mâché or wax figures were a great disappointment to the midway customer expecting to shake hands with Tom Thumb or see Francesco Lentini's third leg kick a soccer ball across the tent.

In the '60s and '70s, wax shows on midways were grind shows on trailers and trucks, displaying world figures and entertainment stars. People would always pay a quarter to see Elvis Presley or John F. Kennedy — Jack Leipard's 1970 wax show used J.F.K. as a bally piece. Dead subjects were safe exhibits, but living celebrities could be a problem. Ward Hall says that when the tabloid press labeled pop star Michael Jackson a child molester, one wax exhibitor quickly turned Jackson into Diana Ross.

In the late 1960s, showman Jimmy Dixon partnered with Royal American Shows' train master Charlie Guttermouth to operate a wax show. The show was built into a semi-trailer, and at the old fairgrounds in Tampa in the early 1970s, it topped the back end. Dixon explains how he acquired his figures: "Some we bought and some we made. The Beatles figures came from a sculptor in California, but Batman and Frankenstein I made. I made them from plaster of Paris molds. The wax

New Highway 95 diverted Florida-bound traffic miles away from old routes. Highway tourist traps such as Boswell's Zoo outside Wilson, N.C., soon died. Harvey spent his last days behind a wooden stockade that surrounded his mobile home, a collection of small motel cottage units and show trailers. Inside one trailer was Harvey's planned final grind show. It contained the body of Marie O'Day, various pickled specimens, crime hardware, and wax figures of Siamese twins, a man with a horn growing out of his head, and John Lennon and Paul McCartney.

was poured in the molds to two or three inches thick and left to harden. I put the hair in the figures with a sewing needle. You cut the end of the loop that you put the thread through so it looks like a tiny fork. You put eight or ten strands of hair in that opening and press it into the wax head. I added eyelashes and glass eyes before taking it down to a local barber who cut the hair into the style of the character."

The 1969 press coverage of the Klondike Exhibition focused on "sex on the midway." Numerous articles protested there was too much of it. One writer quoted the grind tape on the Cargo of Death — "The naked truth, sensational, uncensored, more daring than sex" — while outside the House of Wax, the recorded spiel invited people to "See Cleopatra topless." "The sad part is it's all just a commercial come-on," one reporter concluded. "And even at rock-bottom midway prices, that isn't in the Better Business Bureau handbook. But any fair that comes up with a topless Cleo, even in facsimile, deserves marks for moving with the times."

Some of the last figures used in a fairground show under canvas were being sold in the 1990s by showman Harvey Lee Boswell. His 1994 list included 11 figures, including one of John Lennon "standing in a relaxed pose." Harvey had newspaper headlines of John's death to make good blow-ups from. "As always, after death of a famous person, the public wants to see them even more," Harvey reminded potential buyers. His freak models of giraffe-neck women, pinheads, and Ubangi women with Snap Wyatt banners sold quickly to collectors. Harvey boasted that they were all good figures with real hair and genuine wax — not resin rip-offs. The last time I saw Harvey, in spring 2000, John Lennon and the Chinese Man With a Horn Growing From the Back of His Head were still with him, propped up in a semi-trailer he had been framing for years as his last hurrah.

RIDE AN
Indian Scout
THE MOST POPULAR
MOTOCYCLE IN THE WORLD
WE USE INDIAN MOTOCYCLES
EXCLUSIVELY
BECAUSE THEY ARE DEPENDABLE
LEW

THRILLS, CHILLS, AND DOCTORS' BILLS

Motorcycle Maniacs on the Wall

Nothing on the midway stopped a crowd faster than the noise of motorcycles thundering around wooden drome walls. The show was noisy and the bally even noisier. On the bally, a rider rode a bike with its tires placed between metal rollers locked in a frame to the floor. To attract a bigger crowd, the talker shoved a hand-held siren against the side of the spinning front tire, producing a piercing wail.

Motordromes are unique show venues. The mark buys a ticket, crosses over the bally — usually a wagon or a semi-trailer — and climbs steep steps to the top of the drome wall. A walkway circles the wooden bowl, and on large dromes the back of the walkway is raised up a step so people standing behind you can also see. Down 18 feet, on the wooden floor, are three or four motorcycles and a go-cart or mini-car clustered around a center pole. The

Opposite: Thurston J. Apple's motordrome on Lou Dufour's short-lived railroad carnival in the early 1920s. Apple operated dromes and kiddie rides on carnivals for many seasons. He died at age 73 in Nashville, Tenn., in 1965.

Chapter 7

A Charles Miles photo of a trick rider inside the Cetlin and Wilson Shows motordrome during the 1950 Hagerstown, Md., fair. The painted line on the wall lets the rider know he's close to the safety cable at the top of the wall.

pole holds up the P.A. speakers and the overhead round canvas roof.

A heavy wooden door opens in one of the wall sections closest to the bally platform. Through this door the riders come off the bally and onto the drome floor. The door is closed, again becoming part of the circular wall that is 40 or 50 feet in diameter. The viewers' senses are first attacked when one of the riders starts his motorcycle. Another driver picks up a microphone and warns viewers to keep well back behind the safety cable that juts out a foot or so around the top of the wall. That's the only protection between the audience and the speeding motorcycle. Before he sets the microphone down, one of the riders guns the engine and roars up onto the main wall and the whole place shakes. The viewers' heads go from side to side as they try to follow the rider. They jump back as the motorcycle comes inches from them. Their eyes, ears, nose, and body are all assaulted at once.

A turn of the century bicycle ride carousel in Jean-Paul Favand's Paris fairground museum in the early 1990s. Each bike could carry three riders and their pedaling motion helped move the ride.

The motordrome's roots go back to nearly the mid-19th century. As early as 1864, Frederick Savage, an early farm implement and carousel builder at King's Lynn, England, manufactured what he called a Velocipede ride, a circular merry-go-round using bicycles instead of horses. Bike rides were found on European fairgrounds up into the 1920s. Bike racing as sport fuelled the bike craze, and in the spring of 1900 *Billboard* carried an ad listing for sale a "Novelty Bicycle Gallery" with round tent. For many years on European showgrounds, you could also find a show in which patrons tried their luck in riding bikes that where mechanically altered. More reserved people watched as others provided the hilarious entertainment.

Bicycle dealer George Hendee has been credited with developing the first practical motorcycle in America, in 1901. By World War I, motordromes were beginning to appear on midways. Before motorcycles, performers used bicycles to do a similar act on a wall made of wooden slats. The act became popular in circuses, on carnivals as

One of the early slant wall dromes. This one is quite large with a very short wood-slatted wall for spectator protection. Dick McFadden is the rider.

A further step towards the silo drome. The wall on this drome has a long slant section and then quite high vertical walls. Center steps and no roof covering indicate a very early drome. The 'Autodrome' name suggests they rode a car on the wall.

One of the early portable slant wall dromes on a carnival at Marion, S. Carolina, in 1913. Note the two riders on the bally with leather football-type helmets.

a free act, and on vaudeville stages. The act progressed from one rider to two, with crisscrosses and other tricks worked into the routine. To make the act more daring, the whole apparatus was hoisted up between vertical supports and then the floor was taken away. In circuses, the apparatus was often worked over the steel arena filled with lions.

One of the first to ride a bike on a fully perpendicular cycle whirl in the U.S. was a rider who called himself Cyclo. He performed his act on the Barnum and Bailey Circus the first year the show returned from Europe. A similar act was executed in 1904 by the two McNutts, Cane and Louisa, and their name certainly fit the frame of mind you had to be in to do it. One of the early showmen to present the cycle whirl as a paid show rather than a free act was Harry Cooper. In 1902, he built an elevated cycle whirl at his father's mill in Saginaw, Mich. The next year he spent 24 weeks on the Ferari Bros. Shows. Cooper's Bottomless Cycle Whirl was raised mechanically "50 feet" (no doubt an exaggeration) into the air while four bicycle riders raced around inside it.

The outdoor carnival business emerged from the incubator stage just before World War I. New portable rides were being invented and all kinds of show ideas tried out on the American public. One of the hottest was the motordrome. Several amusement centers had built motordrome tracks, and the chug-chug of the extended pipes on the bike's exhaust and the thud of the bike tires on the wooden oval tracks were instant crowd-pleasers. Various cities formed race leagues, and each team had home and away teams. The official size of most tracks measured four laps to the mile. The official bike was the eight-valve Indian motorcycle, from which the racers removed the mud guards and anything else not needed.

Brighton Beach became one of the best sites to see the sport. Races started late in the evening, when the cool ocean air was better for hot bike engines. By 10:30 p.m. on September 28, 1912, 10,000 people were packed around the "white saucer," watching the last race of the season. Five teams of two riders each roared around the track, periodically shooting up to the top of the inclined wall to overtake opponents. At midnight, the race saw its first accident. A tire on William Vandenburg's bike went flat while he was high on the wall and shot him out over the handlebars and rolling along the track for a considerable distance before tumbling to the bottom of the wall. He was picked up and rushed to the hospital tent, where he was treated for burns and cuts, and later returned to the race. By 6 a.m., after eight hours of racing over a distance of 539 miles, a winner was declared and the happy all-night crowd left the park and headed for breakfast.

O.K. Hager and his wife Olive's autodrome on Johnny J. Jones Shows in Youngstown, Ohio, 1927. In 1921, while on tour with Sheesley Shows, a blow-out on Olive's auto threw her into the protective cable at the top of the drome. She received 37 stitches but was back riding six days later.

The sport was outrageous. It ran all night, it was noisy and smelly, and it was pioneered by a bunch of roughnecks with colorful names who performed reckless feats of speed and daring. Distance and speed records were broken weekly. The media loved it.

Swartz and Turpin, owners of the Joy Amusement Co. and operators of the Swartz track at Coney Island, were the first to build and tour a portable drome, with the Herbert A. Kline Shows in 1912. Several other companies in Illinois and Michigan were soon producing their own dromes, each claiming to make the "only portable

The drome crew sets up the walls of a lion drome on the Cetlin and Wilson Shows in 1951. These walls are all in one piece. Some dromes had wall sections that were in two sections. The supports going from the ground braces to the wall are called "bumpers" as they take most of the pressure when the riders drive on the wall.

drome." Early dromes had no protection from the elements, but by 1915 circular canvas roofs were being used.

It took midway showmen only a year or so to figure out how to compress the large oval track into a smaller portable touring attraction. In spring 1913, David C. Whittaker toured his drome on the Rice and Dore Shows. Whittaker's daily gross statement for their July 4 date in North Platte, Neb., showed the drome topped the merry-go-round and Rice and Dore's famous Water Show, and more than tripled the grosses of any of the other 11 paid attractions. Whittaker's wife, Mabel, was a well-known diving and swimming expert, but she bought a divided skirt and took to driving a motorcycle on the wall. She may have been the first lady drome rider.

J. Frank Hatch, who engineered portable water shows for touring midways, worked out many of the physical aspects of portable motordromes. In 1914, the 15-season midway veteran set up a drome factory in Pittsburgh, Pa., and by March he had placed dromes on seven midways, including Patterson, Ferari, Great Empire, and Rutherford Shows, plus three autodromes in parks. His 50-foot-diameter drome, "the kind that gets the money," sold for $650. The 100-foot-diameter autodrome went for $2,000, and for those "too far away" Hatch sold blueprint plans.

Hatch kept patent attorneys busy registering all his designs for strengthening the upright portable walls. His new "Autodrome" or "Devil's Tub" was touted as the next midway sensation. Eight hundred spectators could stand around the 85- to 120-foot-diameter walls that were 24 feet high, angled at 12 degrees. Hatch thought the industry was very lucky to have no major accidents with the flimsy guardrails used on dromes — his new dromes, designed by geometrical engineers, featured inner and outer guardrails to protect both rider and public.

The Hatch Drome Co. placed 19 dromes at 269 fair dates in 1915. Their major competitor, American Motordrome Co. out of Norfolk, Va., had four dromes on shows and parks. By the 1920s, dromes were a fixture on every carnival, and Hatch was a successful film magnate.

Early dromes took days to set up and tear down, limiting their operation to only a couple of days at each stand. As one carny cracked in *Billboard*, "Your autodrome was up and running Thursday night, but what time did you start taking it down!" And there were other problems with the dromes: Flack's Great Northwestern Shows' *Billboard* ad looking for shows specified, "No Motordrome! Although dromes are money getters, the noise from them kills business for shows and concessions near them."

Despite the knocks, motordromes were the hottest midway show during the 1914 season. Everyone was jumping on the drome craze, including one booking agent who advertised that he needed a motordrome with a transparent front to play vaudeville.

The first dromes, "sugar dromes," had a small starting track and then all-sloped walls. In 1917, Harry Hogue turned out the

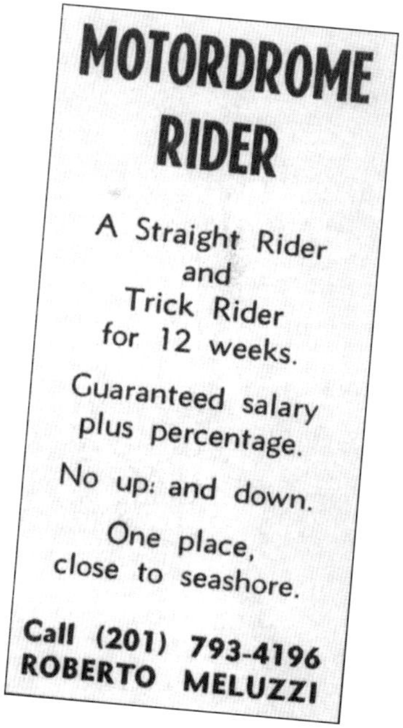

A young lion learning the lion chase act. By the late 1930s most of the big drome operators like Earl Purtle, Walter and Bill Kemp, and Joe Pelequin featured lions in the drome. One act involved lions sitting quietly on seats hung on the wall while the drome rider wove in and out between them, and another included lions being driven on the wall in cars.

first "silodromes," whose walls went straight up and down with a small slanted jump board to help the rider get on. The big dromes you saw in the 1940s and 1950s, like Walter Kemp's on Royal American Shows, were a "combination," using a starting track, slope or slant wall, and then a straight up-and-down wall. On early dromes, operators didn't own the motorcycles but simply advertised for riders with bikes, as most of the applicants came from the motorcycle racetracks. Within a few seasons, drome operators also supplied the bikes.

In 1915, Brison Wickwire, over on the Miller and Lachman Shows, was standing erect on the seat of his motorcycle while going full speed around the drome. More difficult tricks were soon being performed to lengthen out the show and excite the public, but they often resulted in accidents and injuries to the riders. Pioneer drome rider Otto Kecker, known as the Flying Dutchman, was killed inside the drome on Evans Greater Shows. In November, *Billboard* reported Pat and Johnny Dill, motordrome riders on Heinz and Bechmann Shows, were badly hurt trying out a new trick — a double criss-cross, only with the two riders going in opposite directions. They hit head-on.

By 1917, dromes were big business on carnivals. Johnny J. Jones' drome featured Margaret Gast, the only woman rider holding the 1,000-mile record and the only girl contestant to go into a six-day race in Madison Square Garden. Inside the drome she was noted for going 70 miles an hour and was one of many women riders who would claim the title "the Mile-a-Minute Girl" during their drome careers.

In a world where midgets got married on bally stages and fat women ran 100-yard dashes down the midway, it was only natural that the motordrome became the venue for unusual acts — and the chapel and reception hall for carnival marriages and christenings. In 1924, Harry Graff's motordrome on Miller Bros. Shows featured Herr Von Humer, from Germany, doing an act in which he rode the wall while balancing a horizontal bar with a girl on each end. During the Depression, to stimulate business, Del Couch's drome on the 1935 Dodson Shows held amateur nights every Friday to packed houses. The same season, Rudy Coombs, manager of the drome on United Shows of America, had special motorcycles made so midgets could drive them.

After two decades of risking death and crippling injuries while doing every stunt imaginable riding motorcycles on inclined walls, what could these daredevils add to the show to make it more dangerous? Speedy Babbs claims Carl Terrell was the first drome operator to use lions, on the Morris and Castle Shows in 1923. A 1926 *Billboard* reported that Egbert's Motordrome on the Bernardi Greater Shows was the scene of an innovative idea. As three riders attained their maximum speed in the bowl, two male lions were put into the motordrome. The lions tried to attack the riders, who kept a safe distance above the animals.

Earl Purtle spent over 40 years riding and operating dromes, including a lion drome. He had many spills and said each one had taught him something. Purtle told press agent William Lindsay Gresham that riding around his 34-foot-diameter drome was "like being flung around like a marble in a cup by a force greater than gravity." He wore a leather helmet, and never let anyone ride in his drome without one. Purtle also insisted on clean high-top boots so nothing could catch the handlebars or seat while the performer was moving into position in trick riding.

Lions riding in cars and chasing motorcycles seemed wild until you saw George Murray's act on the 1950 James E. Strates Shows motordrome in which he rode a lion around the drome. Giddy-up Leo!

Earl Purtle and his wife Ethel were lion-car riding pioneers. The lions were raised from cubs in their basement in Richmond, Va., and a whole succession of Kings and Queenies delighted motordrome crowds.

Purtle's career started in 1914 on the Parker Amusement Co.'s 50-foot-diameter drome. The frame of the drome was made from spruce and the floor was yellow pine. The show consisted of two riders racing around inside and doing the crisscross. Purtle told a reporter that you normally ride the drome counter-clockwise but in the old days you had to learn clockwise, too, for a trick where two riders crisscrossed from opposite directions. After a few seasons, drome operators dropped the stunt, as audiences never fully appreciated its danger. Purtle also claimed he was the first to use the safety cable. Up until then, riders often shot right out of the drome.

Purtle bought his first lion, Queenie, from a circus in 1927. One of the workers on the drome said he could train big cats,

so they put Queenie's small cage inside the drome. When they opened the door to her cage, she wouldn't come out. Purtle took the whip and gun from the worker, and his brother Dale got on his bike and rode it up on the wall. Queenie charged out of the cage and chased after the bike. Purtle kept her cage door closed until his brother had made a few rounds of the drome, then opened it and Queenie dashed back inside. This became the "Lion Chase" act, with Queenie chasing both the bike and an Austin car until one day in 1933 when Earl missed his timing and ran over her. From then on, Purtle altered the act so that Queenie rode in the car with him. In the 1960s, the Purtles sold their drome and settled down in Richmond, Va., to operate rides on a plaza and at the local fair.

The drome bike is built for neither speed nor comfort. The main goal is stability. Riders seldom go over 45 miles an hour — above that speed they risk "blackout" as high speeds increase the centrifugal force that draws blood from the brain. New riders become dizzy quickly, just riding the motorcycle in a circle on the drome floor. Once the new rider can go around the drome floor without getting dizzy, he graduates to the jump board or the 77-degree slope wall.

Once he masters that, he can try for the 90-degree main wall. A few weeks later, the new rider is told to gun the engine and go up on the straight wall for a single lap. A rider's first time on the high wall is like driving on a badly eroded dirt road. The hard bike tires jolt the body every time the bike goes over the abutments of the 18 or so wall sections, and the rider's vision is blurred. After weeks of two- or three-hour daily practices on the main wall, his vision clears to the point he can now clearly pick out objects on the drome floor and details of the wall. Many riders do not progress beyond this point, but those who graduate to trick riding can triple their pay. The average rider puts in about 50 miles a week riding the wall.

One of the biggest drome operators was the Kemp family. Walter B. Kemp, from Illinois, first rode in a drome on the L.J. Heth Shows at the age of 20, in 1919. The next season, he met his wife, Margie, on the same show when she got a job as a drome rider. From the early 1930s, the Kemps featured lions in their motordromes. After Walter was killed in a 1943 plane crash, his brother Bill and sister-in-

Marjorie Kemp and a male lion in their car on Kemp's combination drome. Note the small "jump board" from the floor to the slant wall and then the straight wall. Marjorie and Walter Kemp met on the L.J. Heth Shows in 1919 as drome riders. They drove together until Walter was killed in 1943 while working as an aviation instructor in Tampa, Florida.

The large combination motordrome on RAS as it finished out its last days on the road in the early 1980s. For years it lay rotting away inside wagons on the back lot of the show's winter quarters. In 1990, sections of the wall were donated to the carnival museum in Gibsonton, Fla., and the rest burned.

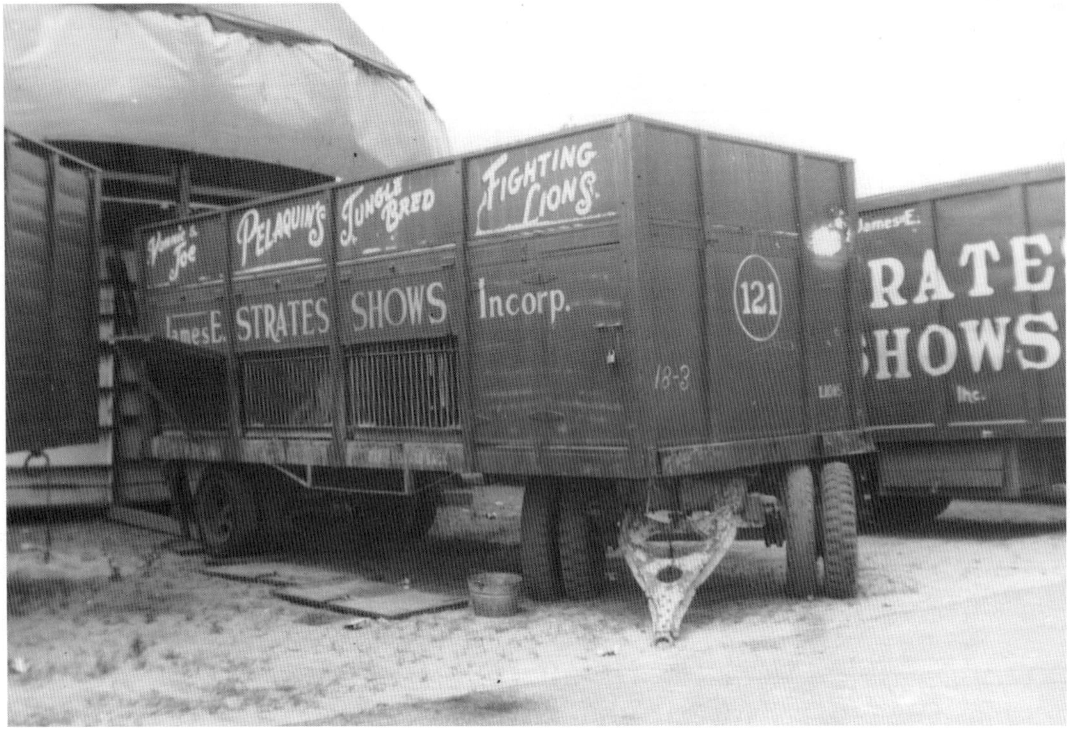

The wagon for Joe Pelequin's lions when he had the drome on Strates Shows in the early 1950s. When World of Mirth Shows folded in the early '60s, Strates bought the drome lions and the cage. He sent Joe with a tractor to pull it up to a spot on the east coast. When they arrived, show folks were shocked to see that the back door had fallen off in transit and the male lion happily laying there with his feet dangling out.

law Lolita continued running the drome on Royal American Shows.

Lefty Johnson, who now lives in Anchorage, Alaska, rode for the Kemps for years. In the early 1950s, he had been working on the Joie Chitwood Thrill Show as a "junkie" — a driver who did roll-overs in old cars bought cheap from wrecking yards. Lefty and another rider also jumped their motorcycles over a row of eight cars. "The show closed in Wichita, Kan.," relates Lefty, "and we were out of work. Someone said Bill Kemp needed motordrome riders. I stayed there ten seasons. I was making big money riding the drome — $150 a week. In the winter I was making only a dollar an hour at a town job.

"Elmo Ballard taught me to ride the wall," he continues. "It took about two months. It was easier for someone with no motorcycle experience to learn to ride the wall. A person with road experience wanted to fight what the motorcycle wanted to do as it was affected by the centrifugal forces. It felt odd, it looked odd, but you couldn't fight nature. You learned wrong if you went by what your eyes were telling you. You didn't ride straight on the wall but more on the side of the tire. You worked at it every day. They wanted you to go in there and drive the slant wall round and round to make some noise and get the attention of the crowd in front of the bally.

"I was riding away one day and Elmo told me, 'Go on up there.' Straight riding was just up, around, and down. I was riding two years before I was taught to trick ride. I rode with no hands, side saddle, both sides. I stood on the bike, and I also stood on one foot."

It took two or three hours for Lefty and the other riders to put up the drome, and two hours to take it down. On Royal, the drome loaded in several wagons. The big bally wagon carried the sills and steps and the front; another wagon carried the bikes, the top, and the racks for neon signs; the entire wall went into another wagon; the center ring went into the possum belly of the bally wagon — it took ten to 15 guys to move it.

Once the show was up, Lefty worked from 10 a.m. to 11 p.m. each day, giving two shows an hour. At the big fair dates, he started at 8 a.m. and didn't stop till midnight, riding a couple of dozen times in 16 hours. "When you were through," he says, "you went right to bed. No partying."

Was the work dangerous?

"I saw two people killed. One guy fell and the bike landed on top of him and the handlebars went through his stomach. One guy fell in Oklahoma City and hit his head on the floor. Just a small trickle of blood came out his ear. After that, Bill made us wear football helmets."

Another family with long careers as drome riders and owners were the Pelequins. Joe Pelequin was born in 1925; both his mother and father were riders. "Next thing I knew was the big round barrel and there I was," he recalls. "When I was going to grade school, my mother used to ride me in the drome on the handlebars. And when I was in high school, I met some people who had a lion act and I became a lion trainer.

"Then, in 1940, I went into the service, and when I came back in 1946, the Purtles took me under their wings. Earl and Ethel broke me into drome riding. Back in those days, I was just a drome rider. Then I became a trick rider. I became good at it. I married the Great La Vonnie, one of the greatest female trick riders there ever was.

"In 1948, I was riding for the Indian Motorcycle Co. The Indian was the finest bike made back in those days. I was racing motorcycles and I got my knees busted a couple of times. If you hit 100 miles an hour you broke a new speed record. Now they go 200 and something. Inside a 30-foot drome you only go 30 to 40 miles per hour — the speed you reach depends on

The Death Dodgers drome in the 1920s at Riverview Park, Chicago, was typical of the large park dromes built to drive autos on the wall.

Steve Camber's Canadian Daredevils out of Rexdale, Ontario, is one of the last dromes operating. It's a small drome that has largely been rebuilt out of aluminum, and loads on one semi-trailer. Here one of Steve's riders makes the "money run."

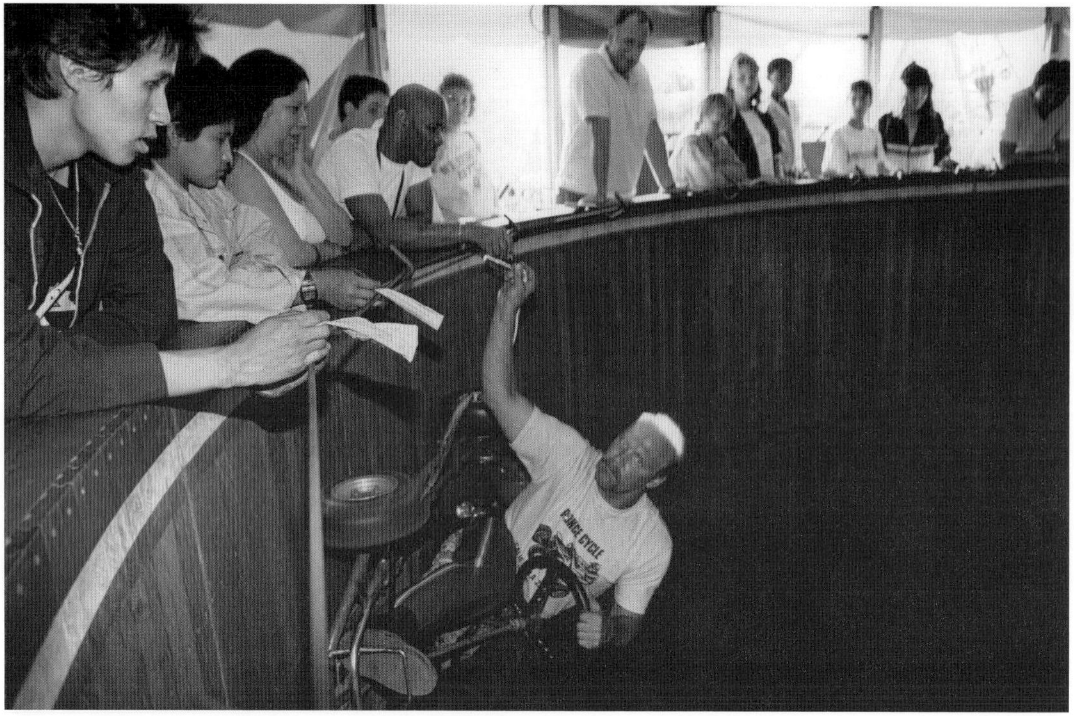

Steve Camber's aluminum drome at the Canadian National Exhibition in the mid 1990s.

the size of the drome. The largest drome I rode in was this big one built at White City Park in Chicago. We used to drive Austin cars on the wall there and that's what I used to drive the lion in."

Joe is the only person I had talked to that had actually been a chauffeur for a lion on a vertical wall. He explains how he got the lion into the car in the first place: "It was one hell of a job! You would take a piece of meat and throw it on the drome floor and he would lick that up. Then you throw another piece by the car — there was no door on the car. Then you throw a piece of meat on the dashboard, and he would jump in the car to get it. By that time you were sitting there in gear with two wheels backed up on the starting track. As soon as he leaped in, you took off! It was no job getting him up. He was too scared to jump out once you got going. We didn't chain him in there. Hell, no — he just sat there beside you. As soon as you got back on the flat surface of the floor, he was out of there. You better have that chute door open for him!"

Another character was Louis W. "Speedy" Babbs. In October 1929, he set a record for continuous drome riding in H.E. "Whitey" Hyan's Death Cheaters silodrome at Venice Pier, Calif. Later, he set a record for

Below: Robert and Mildred Restall, billed as Mildred and Bob Lee, toured Canada after WWII with Conklin Shows presenting their Globe of Death. In 1965 both Robert and his son died while excavating buried treasure on Oak Island, N.S.

looping the loop 2,500 consecutive times in a spherical "Globe of Death." Speedy was a character. In the 1950s, fair and carnival owners were especially liberal with passes to independent shows and rides. On one carnival, Speedy was fed up watching the show-owned girl shows and concessions make all the money while his drome was flooded with people bearing passes. He put up a sign: "Holders of passes, use third set of steps!" The locals with their passes would march around the silo drome looking futilely for the third set of steps. Those brave enough to ask Babbs where the steps were got this answer from him: "They're being installed Saturday night."

Late in his career, Babbs had his Globe act on Deggler Midway Shows from 1960 through 1966 and was also the show's pilot. After 56 broken bones, Speedy retired. He died at age 70 in 1976.

Motorcycle rider Bill Cadieux says that in the '70s he was doing four shows an hour: "Sometimes we did five or six if we were really cranking it. It took four or five minutes on the front to build the tip and turn it. Then you'd have about seven minutes of show, depending on the tip. If there was nothing on top, then it would be a quick show, but if we had a crowd it would go longer. We started with the 'dynamite ride,' a straight ride around the top of the barrel. The second act was the dips and dives of death — the driver goes around the top and suddenly shoots down to the bottom and comes back up. Then we did the fancy riding, where Jimmy Campbell rode side-saddle. The finale was the criss-cross race with two motorcycles on the wall dipping and diving in front of each other. Of course, if it was a big crowd we always did a 'money ride.' Jimmy Campbell

A team of stunt riders and their globe that operated on American midways in the 1970s, just before it became a big thrill act in circuses again. This one had even been on the Ed Sullivan Show!

would go up on his motorcycle and people would be holding money out over the rails and he would take it as he went by."

Besides the money ride and selling postcards, the most common "ding," just before the finale, was the "insurance pitch" — a necessity because of the crashes. "The money," says Cadieux, "carried the rider, paid the hospital, fixed the motorcycles."

Cadieux goes right into the pitch: "Ladies and gentlemen, I am sure you can see by now by watching the first three acts of the show that it would be next to impossible for any of our riders to obtain any kind of accident insurance. No insurance company will insure us because of the danger on the wall. So, we in turn have developed an insurance fund made up of two parts. One part: the riders contribute to the fund themselves. And the other part is you, the showgoing public. If you have enjoyed the show, if you would like to help and contribute to the riders' fund, simply take a donation out of your pocket; we don't care how small or how large. It can be from a penny to a $10 bill. Take it out now and drop it over the side of the wall and onto the floor. The riders will pick it up. Remember, the money is put in a fund, and all summer long the fund builds. It is there when a rider goes down to pay his hospital bills and fix his machine. Let's hear some coins jingling and let's see some paper floating. The riders thank you for your generosity."

During the 1980s, the "Globe of Death" act was revived in America by South American and Mexican artists, and it's still going in circuses and fairs. The Globes' timely reappearance was certainly helped by the absence of motordromes on many fairs and midways. For this act, motorcycle riders go round and round and upside-down inside a large, steel, latticed globe. High speeds and limited space make the act very dangerous.

The roots of this show go back to Thomas Eck, who in 1903 created an act in which he rode a bicycle inside a 16-foot-diameter globe built from steel strips and steel mesh. The globe was suspended at two points and revolved. The rider entered and went left to right while the globe turned right to left at 5 mph. This momentum allowed the rider to go along the sides and over the top. At the act's first season at Coney Island, Arthur Stone of Denver, Col., rode his bike around and above his lady assistant, who stood in the globe's center. The show lasted ten minutes.

Fred and Carl Greggs, billed as the Demon Twins in the early 1900s, worked various acts with cycle whirls, loop-the-loop apparatus, and a steel mesh globe. They were the first to go in opposite directions inside the cycle whirl and were the originators of many innovative leaping stunts while riding bikes.

Globe of Death shows were different from motordromes. They had to be set up inside a tent or an enclosure and behind a front like other carnival shows. In the 1930s, several were featured at amusement parks and were often advertised as "Suicide Globes" or "Cauldrons of Death."

Midway-goers' interest in the motordromes since World War II has risen and fallen depending on the popularity of motorcycle riding. The rise of biker gangs — and the films and books about them — kept dromes popular in the '60s. Today, interest in riding motorcycles is back, but there are few dromes left. Some of the small truck carnival dromes were sold in the '90s for less than the cost of the lumber in them. Most just rotted away in the back lots of show winter quarters, or in junkyards.

ney
MEAL
Lucky
CHEETER
Mile-A-Minit
MURPHY
2

WORKING FOR BANANAS

Racing Monkeys and Wrestling Chimps

The animal most seen on the carnival midway was the monkey. Most monkey shows worked in the open in a side-walled enclosure behind a large bannerline front. Others were framed platform-show style: the audience stood on a raised platform that ran the length of the bannerline and looked down into the performance arena, where the presenter put the monkeys, dogs, house cats, geese, ponies, and other small animals through various routines. Each carnival season saw a dozen or more monkey shows on the road. Providing an important performance show to any carnival's back end, they were steady moneymakers and not expensive to operate. Fairs loved them, as the monkeys always got their pictures in the local papers. Kids were instantly drawn to them. The games and other attractions on the midway all did well when a monkey show was on the lot — the monkeys made people laugh, and a happy crowd is a spending crowd.

Opposite: 'Mile-A-Minit Murphy' lives up to his name as he leads the pack coming into the last turn for the finish line. Watch out! Barney Oatmeal is catching up in lane three.

Chapter 8

The Carrells, Dotty, Leo, and son Tommy, had some of the biggest monkey and chimp shows on midways. They were a staple attraction on the Royal American Shows midway for years. Here they are on the bally of their show in 1952.

Leo Carrell and his big chimp Susie on the bally in 1952 on RAS.

Over the years, there have been many outstanding monkey show operators on midways. Reuben Gastang was a 1930s showman who had his monkey attractions on carnival midways and at world fairs. In 1937 he returned from Europe to be on Dodson's World Fair Shows with his Hollywood Chimp Show. Two of the chimps he was showing weighed over 200 pounds. The largest posed as an artist and drew life-like images of the other chimps on a blackboard. The chimps rode old-fashioned bicycles and took part in a cabaret skit, acting as restaurant-goers, waiters, and cooks. Gastang also played the CNE on the Conklin midway with a show framed like a hotel. Monkeys dressed as guests arriving for a night's stay were greeted by monkeys

Dorothy Lewis' monkey show on Wallace Bros. Shows at the 1946 Simcoe, Ont., fair. She operated this large platform-style show for years. The crowd stood and looked down into a side-walled performance arena.

Mae Noell was performing in repertory theater before she married Bob and went into the gorilla and chimp business. She is standing in front of their chimp farm in Tarpon Springs, Fla., where they looked after elderly chimps nobody wanted. She wrote *Gorilla Show,* one of the best books ever written on outdoor show business.

dressed as bellhops who carried their luggage away. One monkey at the reception desk kept banging on a service bell. The crowd loved it.

Don Carlos was another monkey showman of this era. After World War II, he had one of the top-grossing attractions on the back end of the James E. Strates Shows. Leo and Dotty Carrell were also successful monkey show operators who spent many profitable seasons on Royal American Shows and later, in the '50s, on the Strates midway. Their show, Hollywood Apes, featured chimps, monkeys, and mandrills. In the 1940s, a gentleman named Murphy operated the famous D. Rex Barnes Monkeyland, which spent ten straight seasons on the Gooding Amusements midway. The show consisted of 25 costumed performing monkeys and was considered one of the best grind shows of its time.

Sometimes the gems of the show world never show up on the big carnival midways, but thrive on the smaller shows playing firemen's festivals. Such was the case with Noell's Gorilla Show, the strongest back-end show in America from

Right: Bob Noell and Tommy in 1969 on the cover of *Science Digest.* When I first met him, we were only a few minutes into our conversation before he reached into his pocket and pulled out one of his fingers that the gorilla had ripped off a few years back.

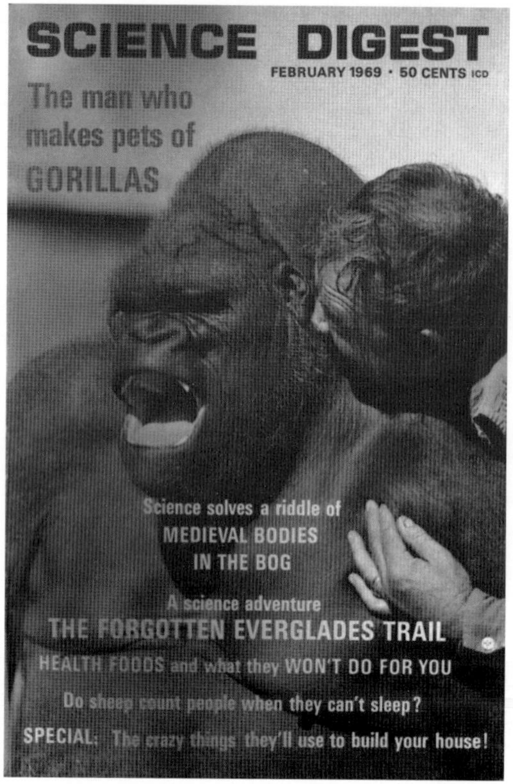

Bob Noell and a small chimp in front of Noell's Ark, one of the greatest back end shows of all time. Chimps billed as gorillas wrestled audience volunteers at each show, which were always packed. You can see all the rules and prize money written on the blackboards behind Noell.

the late '40s through the '60s. This show generated so much publicity everywhere it played that carnival owners often paid the Noells to be on their midway.

Bob Noell left home in Bedford, Va., at age 11 to work on a medicine show. This eventually led to the ownership of his own medicine show, which he and his wife, Mae, operated until 1938, before changing the show to a wildlife exhibit. They still gave a free show each night, but instead of pitching medicine they sold tickets to see a couple dozen animals that ranged from green rats to monkeys. They charged ten cents for children and twice that for adults.

The Noell's Ark on Wheels' main venues were small hamlets and crossroads where they could set up beside the general store rent-free. They bought their first chimp, Snookie, in the early '40s and changed their show title to Noell's Ark Gorilla Show. Their wrestling chimp act came about by accident and proved to be the best thing that could have happened to them. The other animals were sold off, and their exhibition truck grew from a small straight truck to a large Fruehauf semi-trailer.

From 1946 until they retired in 1971, the Noells' show was laid out in the same way, whether they were playing a midway back end or a vacant country field. The semi containing the chimps and a caged ring was parked perpendicular to the midway. The back of the semi faced the midway and the tailgate was lowered to make the bally stage. The back doors opened to serve as banners and 80 feet of white picket fence ran along the front. Canvas side walls started from the back of the truck and went completely around the semi in a big circle, leaving deep areas on both sides of the semi for the audience. The battle between chimp and man took place inside a wire mesh cage that took up half the trailer. Guardrails kept the public back three or four feet from the wrestling cage.

In 1960, Mae started issuing ape-fighter certificates to opponents who fought cleanly and obeyed the following rules:

1. Don't kick or hit the animal.
2. Don't pull on the animal's muzzle.
3. If your helmet comes off, put it back on!

Most challengers didn't care much about the $5 a second, maximum $20, offered to them if they could pin the chimp's shoulders to the floor. They wanted the certificate and a purple ribbon that read, "I am a member in good standing of the exclusive order of ape fighters by authority of Noell's Ark Gorilla Show." At one time, two gorillas, three orangutans, and five chimps were in the show. People would drive 100 miles from the last played town to see the show again. Over the years, the Noells played almost the same route up and down the eastern seaboard and developed not only a loyal fan base but also hundreds of relationships with owners of shows and stores where they were always welcome to stop and perform.

Bobby and Mae's son Bobby Noell didn't stay in the chimp business. He became a carnival game operator and a pioneer in "water games." He says the first chimp his parents got in 1939 was five years old: "The family was in New Orleans and wintering on the levee. We saw a show in a storefront in the city and this guy had a chimp there. Dad bought the chimp for $300. The chimp's name was Snookie, and me and another man went with Dad in a car to pick her up. On the way back, she was all over the car and us. Me and Snookie grew up together.

Most gorillas billed on midways were actually chimps. But these two weren't. Gargantua II and mate M'Toto were put on the Royal American Shows midway after Ringling Bros. Barnum and Bailey Circus closed mid-July under canvas in 1956.

"Our show at the time was a variety-type show. My father juggled and did vent and some small magic. My mother did cartoon artistry, a chalk talk act in which she drew pictures very fast. Snookie was added to the show. The first wrestling gorilla show we had, we kept the chimps in boxes in the front and brought them into the cage to lecture on them. Snookie put up a real fight being put into the smaller box in front of the truck. Dad moved her box into the big cage and set it in one corner. At one show, when we were struggling to put Snookie back inside her box, someone in the audience yelled out, 'Do you want me to come in there and help you put that animal in its box?' Dad said, 'Okay!' Well, it was very comical watching this towner try and put Snookie in her box, and the audience loved it. It looked like they were wrestling, and so from then on Dad would announce that at each show they would let a towner get in the big cage and wrestle with the gorilla. The show slowly evolved into a full wrestling show. When the chimp got tired, she would just go back inside her corner

box. Dad started offering towners $1 and then $2 if they could put Snookie on her back. If Snookie got tired, she would lay on her back, so Dad went further — the bet was to put Snookie on her back and sit on her chest. Nobody sat on Snookie's chest!

"When Snookie became tired, she also bit towners. Dad designed and made a muzzle, and from then on she safely wrestled with hundreds of people — including local sheriffs, Catholic priests, tough guys, blind people, and women. With blind people we would put a chair inside the cage and sit them on it. Snookie would play with their hair and take things out of their pockets."

Bobby explains what happened to more aggressive challengers: "If the would-be wrestler was a tough guy, Dad would put an old tire in the corner for the chimp to sit on. Dad then put a helmet and a white shirt — bought by the dozens at Goodwill for five cents — on the wrestler. The chimp knew that if an opponent had a helmet on it was a different match. Dad got between the towner and chimp and told the towner he had to put the chimp on her back and put her shoulders on the floor. Dad told the towner, 'No hitting, no punching, no kicking, and don't pull on the chimp's muzzle.' Then Dad looked the guy in the eyes and said, 'Are you ready?' and the match was on.

"Once Dad stepped into a corner of the cage and the guy advanced on the chimp — remember, the chimp is standing on this tire and can raise up to eight feet — Snookie would put one hand on the bar of the cage and swing out, and with the other hand grab the guy by his helmet and lift him two feet off the floor, then butt him in the chest and go back over and sit on the tire for a few seconds! Dad would jump back into the center of the cage and turn to the towner and say, 'Get him, Bill! Go get that monkey!' Most shows lasted only a few seconds, as most opponents gave up after their first encounter with a chimp, but occasionally the towner wanted another go at the monkey.

"On this second round, the chimp would get off the tire and come down on the ground and go quickly for the towner and grab his pant leg, the top of his underpants, or his belt, and go straight to the top of the cage. The opponent's pants would tear all the way around in a matter of seconds. Many didn't realize they were standing there in their shirt and underpants because it happened so fast. It was all over in less than ten seconds. Then Dad would tell the crowd to go back outside, this match was over."

The monkey speedway was the most exciting monkey show outside of Noell's Ark, successfully following motordromes onto midways during World War I. The

These monkeys sitting in their race cars on the bally of this 1920s monkey speedway are ready for the next heat inside the tent.

inventor of this monkey mayhem was Ohio native H.C. Hurlburt. During the winter of 1916, he operated his speedway in Detroit. He opened the season with K.G. Barkoot Shows in Toledo.

Hurlburt's original speedway was designed so that the enclosed track took 12 laps to make one mile. There were six cars for the monkeys to drive. Each was 3½ feet long and weighed 40 pounds. The races lasted 20 minutes and the winner was hard to predict. The crowds loved it and so did other showmen. The show not only made money but could also be upped and downed in under three hours.

The General Amusement Co. out of Detroit, with Barkoot as general manager, applied for a patent and started manufacturing the speedways. The Evans Company in Chicago, the premier carnival gaming-device builder, made a smaller version that worked as a game. If you put your money on the winning monkey, you won a basket of groceries. Operators claimed the original Detroit firm made the fastest cars — they could reach speeds of 35 to 40 mph. The monkey speedway could also work all winter as a novelty attraction in department stores.

About the same time the monkey speedway came along, A. Ehring out of Columbus, Ohio, had baboons driving motorcycles in a wooden-slatted drome eight feet high and 14 feet in diameter on the Keith theater circuit. He also had a unit ready for the 1916 fair season using gasoline engines. By the time the war ended, monkey dromes were a smaller version of the motordrome, built with slant walls and only a very small straight wall section. Cars used in the monkey drome were bigger than those used on the speedways. Harry Fee, the last of the monkey speedway showmen, told me the key was using gas engines and only putting a few drops of gas in them so the car went around about ten or 12 times before running out of fuel and coasting to the floor. The dromes were operated almost like a

Above: The big vinyl bannerline of Harry and Bee Fee's Monkey Speedway. It was the last big speedway to operate on midways.

Not long after humans began riding motorcycles inside wooden walls, entrepreneurs built a similar show for monkeys. Monkey dromes featured cars that were much bigger than monkey speedway cars, and the trick was to put just enough gas in the carburetor to get the car up on the wall, around a couple of laps, and back down. This is famed drome rider Bob Perry's show at the Houston Fat Stock Show in 1956.

Harry and Bee Fee line up the monkeys at the starting line. "Lucky Cheeter" looks pretty intense. Maybe he will be the winner this race? No doubt his name was inspired by auto daredevil Lucky Teeter.

grind show — they were small with limited viewing capacity, accommodating only a few dozen people at a time.

Harry didn't mess with monkeys when he was first in show business. In fact, he didn't start his outdoor career on carnivals, but on Billroy's Comedian tent show. In the mid-'40s, Harry and his wife, Bee, started touring their own animal shows. Working with monkeys in these shows led them into the monkey speedway business.

In these speedways, the racecars the monkeys rode in moved around the speedway juiced by electricity picked up from a brass rail between tracks the wheels traveled on. "The biggest problem back-end showman Glen Porter had was the pickup between the car and the track," explains Harry Fee. "The solution came from an old wino who used to hang out around Porter's place in Tampa. This wino had his nose stuck in there when Glen was discussing getting juice to the cars with another showman. The wino suggested windshield wipers! A wiper is placed underneath the car at the front and it would pick up the juice as the car went down the track. Glen did it and it worked. I built mine six or seven years later using the same idea."

However, the system didn't work quite that smoothly. "The motors burned out," Harry remembers. "I finally hit on the right motor — $9.95 power drills made in Greenfield, Mass. When I got them in the cars, I built a test track mounted on 4-by-8-foot plywood sheets and left one of the cars running all night. I got up the next morning and the car was still going around and around. The windshield wipers picked up the power and fed it onto the drill, which had a sprocket and a chain that hooked up to a sprocket on the front and back wheels, so the car was chain-driven like a bicycle." Next, Harry made a mold to build fiberglass bodies for the cars so they would last longer and not get dented like the metal cars. He even put colored dye in the fiberglass so he didn't have to worry about painting them.

The monkey speedway had a long bannerline, and the tent was open-fronted

This daredevil monkey just drove through a brick wall on Fee's Monkey Speedway track.

on the midway side like early pit shows. "The show was continuous," Harry explains. "You stretched the show out depending on how busy you were. Bee kept the show going and she would work harder when there were just a few people in there to hold them, so the people on the midway could see the tip in there along the track watching the races and be drawn in too.

"It usually featured three or four races, and then I had the brick wall. I had built a crash wall and we announced this monkey as the daredevil of the show. The car flew around the track with the monkey in it and — wham — right through the brick wall. I had a plywood gadget, so the wall opened every time and there was no catastrophe. The people liked that. Well, the only thing bad about it was the monkey got used to it. Imagine a car with a monkey driver heading toward a brick wall and the monkey is sitting there in the car with his hands folded in his lap!"

Harry got his share of flack from the do-gooders and animal activists. One lady got all excited because the monkeys were chained into the cars and Harry had to explain to her that there were 110 volts of electricity on the track, and if the monkey jumped out of the car while it was going he could be electrocuted. The monkeys were not chained in with a collar but wore little jumpsuits with chains sewn through the material. On the end of the chains were snaps that hooked into a ring beside the car seat like a regular auto seatbelt. "When you had those monkeys," says Harry, "it took two to tango. You eat, sleep, and shit monkeys. The guy who taught me to train monkeys told me, 'You belong to the monkeys; the monkeys don't belong to you,' and it was true. When Labor Day came, we headed south so they didn't get cold. When we made a jump and got into the next town, the monkeys were fed before we ate. I had one monkey that lived to be 38 years old. When we came in for good, I kept every monkey to the bloody end. The last one just died a year ago. They ate as well in my backyard as they did on the road."

Harry's favorite breed were ringtail monkeys. "They reason — they are not dumb animals. One day it was so hot in the tent that I went and got pieces of ice for the monkeys. One of them picked up a piece and dropped it because it was too cold. Tony, the guy I had for 38 years, got a piece of rag and picked his ice up with that!

"At the end, monkeys were getting scarce. When I started, you could buy four of those monkeys for $100. Same monkey today you can't touch for $2,000. I last had the show up at the Columbus, Ohio, fair when Ward Hall had the back end. I got a flat fee of $28,000 for the ten days. Two guys in business suits came in. I thought they were fuzz, but one was from the state agricultural department and the other from the federal government checking on the welfare of animals at the fair. At the same time, the grocer I did business with brings in the food and I start putting the bananas, apples, and oranges in the monkey cages. One of them says, 'Shit, man, we better move in here the way you treat those damn monkeys.'"

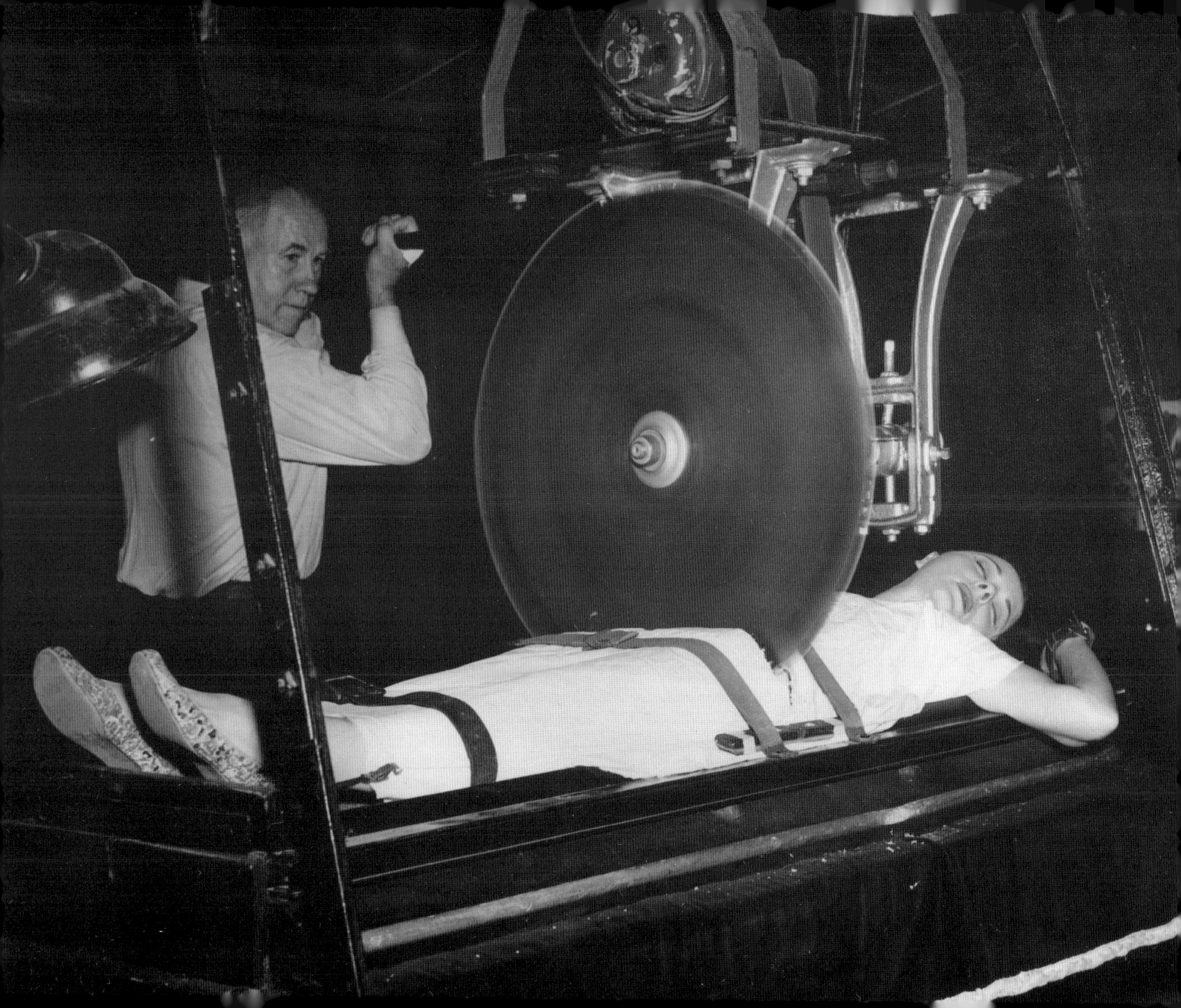

MORE THAN AN ILLUSION

Ghosts, Floating Ladies, and Gorilla Girls

Magic was the basis for many shows presented by early traveling showmen, and it still provides entertainment on America's midways. The headless girl, the girl with a snake's body, and the girl in the fishbowl are some of the last midway grind shows. Much of this midway deception is based on mirror tricks of the 19th century.

Opposite: Master illusionist Noel Lester guides the buzz-saw blade as it rips through his wife Phyllis' midriff on the Strates Shows in 1952.

A 19th-century Paris show called Phantasmagoria, first presented in London in 1801, used a magic lantern to create supernatural effects and horrify the audience. Etienne Gaspard Robert, a Belgian professor of physics, invented the magic lantern, which became both a home entertainment and a popular form of early show business. The Parisian show scared the audiences with images of fog and snakes and floating ghosts. Its illusions depended on a magic lantern with adjustable lenses mounted on a carriage track

Chapter 9

An illustration from *Mahatma* magic magazine at the turn of the 20th century showing how Pepper's Ghost Effect and the Cabaret du Néant works. This became the basis for girl-to-skeleton and girl-to-gorilla illusions.

behind a semi-transparent screen. The audience seated in front of the screen were frightened as ghosts came toward them and then quickly disappeared. The ghost scenes were created by placing an image of a ghost on a glass slide and blackening out the area surrounding the image, then casting the image on the screen.

The technique was advanced further in the theater setting, as described in Richard D. Altick's *Shows of London*: "In a small theater lighted by one hanging lamp, the lamp was drawn up fully into the shroud and the audience found themselves in total darkness. When the stage curtain opened in the dark, spectators saw a cave with skeletons and other frightening objects on its walls. A thin transparent screen, unknown to the audience, had been let down after the disappearance of the light and upon it flashes of light and ghosts appeared."

The thunder and lightning was followed by ghosts and skeletons with their eyes and mouths opening and closing. This illusion was created by means of double slides, which allowed a person's face to become a skull and clothed images to become skeletons. The show closed with figures advancing toward the audience and then sinking into the ground before them. Some spectators fled the theater in terror.

Several discoveries further advanced the presentation of the Phantasmagoria show. Henry Langdon Childe (1781–1874) strengthened the dissolving views by inventing a metal shutter that closed on one side but quickly opened on another so the audience saw just a brief interval of darkness during the change. Then Sir Goldsworthy Gurney invented limelight (oxyhydrogen), a gas made by applying a mixture of oxygen and hydrogen to a small ball of lime. The result produced a light that was equivalent to a dozen Argand lamps, letting showmen create sharper and brighter images from the slides. Shows featuring disrobing views soon became very popular on the European fairground. At St. Bartholomew Fair in 1833, De Berar's "Optikali Illusio," featuring appearing and disappearing ghosts, left its mark on the English language by coining the phrase "Now you see it — now you don't."

John Henry Pepper's visions have been amazing people since 1863, the year that he and Henry Dirks, a civil engineer, registered a patent for an apparatus for exhibiting dramatic and other performances involving the appearance and disappearance of a "ghost." Pepper was a professor of chemistry and honorary director of the British Royal Polytechnic Institute. The object of their invention was to put on the same stage a ghost and a real actor. The set-up in the theater required, in addition to the main stage, a second lower stage that was hidden from the viewers. The hidden stage was strongly lit by artificial light and could be rendered dark instantly while the main stage and the theater remained in normal light. A large glass screen is placed on the main stage and in front of the hidden one. The spectators do not see this glass screen but can see the actor onstage through it. When the ghost character lying on the hidden stage is illuminated, the ghost's image is projected onto the real stage, beside the actor. Darkening the hidden stage causes the ghost to disappear instantly.

Pepper's ghost illusion (which he called a "Strange Lecture") was first shown at a small theater at the Royal Polytechnic. The scene took place in the room of a student hard at work studying. He looks up and sees the apparition of a ghost. Frightened, he jumps up, seizes a sword, and stabs at the ghost, which disappears and then keeps coming back and vanishing. Pepper's assistant played the ghost, wearing a covering of black velvet while holding a skeleton with its lower half draped in white material. The assistant was seated on the floor so the skeleton appeared to be coming out of the floor.

Although the "ghost show" lasted only a few minutes, it attracted large paying crowds. The Polytechnic moved the show to a larger theater with a new performance based on Charles Dickens' "Haunted Man."

The method used to produce the ghost was soon leased out to London theaters and music-hall performers. By 1870, English

One of the best illusion showmen was Al Renton. He was encouraged by veteran sideshowman Slim Kelly to go into the illusion business. Here is his illusion 10-in-1 show on the Sheesley midway in the 1930s.

W.D. Ament's Ghost Show on the 1914 C.W. Parker and Con T. Kennedy Shows midway. In the London Ghost Show a man changed into a woman, glasses and bottles appeared instantly on a table, and a sword was thrust through people without harming them. Some of the favorite scripts used were: "Little Jim, the Collier's Child," "The Haunted Hotel," and "Over the Hills to the Poor House."

Sketch of the London Ghost Show.

inventors had patented 16 mirror tricks stimulated by Pepper's work.

In the August 1901 issue of *Mahatma* magazine, Henry R. Evans offers a good description of the type of show given in European theaters and fairground booths in this era. At the Cabaret du Néant in Montmartre, Paris, the proprietor presented a show where the patron entered a room that was draped in black and painted with emblems of mortality. Here the customers were seated at coffin-shaped tables and served drinks by men dressed as undertakers. After the drinks, customers were led through a passage into a crypt — at the end of which a coffin stood upright. A volunteer was placed in the coffin and wound in a sheet. Gradually he faded away and a grinning skeleton became visible in the casket. After a few chilling moments, the volunteer reappeared. Two men dressed as Capuchin monks then took up a collection in a skull and the spectators were led out.

The rapid growth of carnival companies and street fairs in the 1890s saw the "illusion show" take its place on the showgrounds next to the Oriental theater, the wild animal show, and the minstrel show. Professor E.E. Thorton's Palace of Illusions, out of South Bend, Ind., toured under a 25-by-40-foot tent. He presented Thauma, the

Living Mermaid, or Living Half-Girl, as well as the Beautiful Rosebud illusion. In Canada, a Brantford-based showman named Slantino toured Ontario fairs with his Temple of Illusions. Meanwhile, Prof. G. W. Van of Lockhaven, Pa., was using Galatea and the Living Mermaid in his tented fairground show.

Ghost shows were also a staple on the early-19th-century carnival midway. Scripted ghost shows were presented on theater and vaude circuits and even had their own posters, the surest sign that an entertainment was an accepted moneymaker with showmen. The father of the ghost show on the North American midway was fairground showman Capt. W.D. Ament. He introduced midway goers to the ghost show in 1902, along with illusions that featured the Flying Maid of the Sea, the Statue Turning to Life, and Poses Plastiques — showmen had to get those nude girls in there somehow! The next season, Ament's London Ghost Show was the top-grossing presentation on the 30-week tour of the Robinson Carnival Co. Other showmen hurried to frame ghost shows, but Ament warned, "Not one in 50 can run a ghost show after being shown how."

The illusion used in the ghost show was not difficult to pull off — the hard

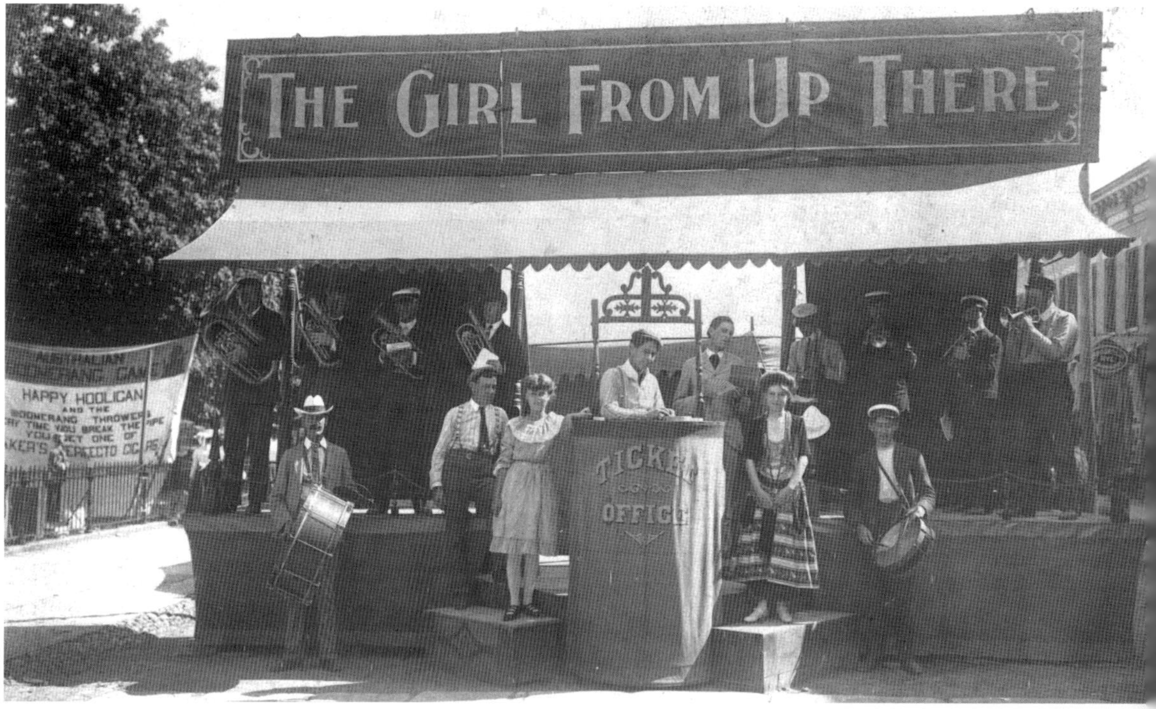

A suspension illusion show on a street carnival in Indiana in the early 1900s. The show band is on the bally along with the three or four performers in the show and a ticket seller. The man with the big drum standing on the ground is probably the talker. Note the boxes used to store gear being used as steps.

Roltair's illusion invention, "Pharaoh's Daughter," at the 1914 Mid-Winter Expo in San Francisco, Ca.

Heinemann's Olga Hess, the European headless girl, as presented behind a huge front on Dodson's World Fair Shows in the early 1930s.

part was getting that large plate of glass from town to town safely. Illusions like the Statue Turning to Life were often over in minutes, but the ghost presentation had more in common with dramatic theater, with scripted skits involving ghosts and other weird images. Ament's ghost show on the Robinson Carnival involved ten performers, including Whitey the Albino. There was also a piano player, a one-man band who played guitar and harmonica for the singer, and, of course, a pretty soubrette. The 20-minute routine involved a Dutch comedian as well as numerous appearances by apparitions as called for by the script.

Other illusions were soon popular on midways, but the ghost show hung on for years. Ament was still around in 1917, producing the ghost show on the Johnny J. Jones Shows.

Illusionist Henry Roltair was a genius at building elaborate illusion spectacles at world fairs and amusement parks, but few in the magic fraternity have paid the slightest attention to him. Born in London in 1853, he came to the U.S. as a teenager. Roltair's unsolved Rollo illusion saw him enter the stage riding a bike. As he traversed the stage back and forth, the bike rose higher and higher until he was 20 feet in the air. Roltair then reversed his zigzag trip back down to stage level. From his touring stage show, he branched out to creating complex illusion shows at expositions. His first was the Palace of Illusions at the 1891 Sydney Exposition. This was the era that saw growth in scenic theaters, and Roltair's presentations combined that form's techniques with mirror effects and illusions.

At the 1894 Mid-Winter Exposition held at San Francisco, he introduced Pharaoh's Daughter, a 30-minute sit-down spectacle based on the Biblical story of baby Moses. A male actor delivered a dignified narration while two attractive women performed, aided by strong lighting effects. The show was a big hit at Dreamland Park on Coney Island from 1904 through 1906, and was seen on many carnival midways for several seasons. Another Roltair illusion that found a permanent home on carnival midways as both a single-o show — a strong attraction that could stand on its own — and as part of sideshows was the Human Spider, also known as Spidora.

Roltair made a great impression on park and fairground showmen. He inspired Fred Thompson and Skip Dundy, the founders of Dreamland, to build their Trip to the Moon. This show, plus Roltair's Upside Down House, were the big shows at the Buffalo Pan-American Exposition in 1901. His Buffalo version was over 80 feet high. The house rested on its gables and spectators entered through a dormer window in the attic. Once inside, they found themselves walking on the ceiling with everything topsy-turvy, including views of the "live" fairgrounds from the windows.

Through the early 1900s, Roltair's major show, Creation, was worked by a large cast of performers, both human and animal. The show presented nearly every illusion known at that time to create the effect of life's formation and growth. It was the sensation of the 1904 St. Louis Expo and then moved to Dreamland, where it was a big attraction.

Roltair died in El Reno, Calif., in 1910 at age 57 while touring his illusion show. A year later his Creation show was destroyed in the famous Coney Island fire.

Among the most spectacular illusions were suspensions, acts in which performers appeared to hover over the heads of the audience members. One of the first suspension tricks in America was presented at the N.Y.C. Academy of Music in 1880 by magician/showman Baron Hartwig Seeman. His Electra illusion resembled a gun turret with the barrel projecting out between an opening in the curtains to suspend a flying subject over the audience. The barrel was of highly polished steel so as to reflect the curtains and hide its existence. In 1889 Will B. Woods presented a suspension called the Human Orchid, which F.E. Powell later toured as Edna. The early 1900s saw various crane or jib patterns for holding the flying person out over the audience. This was how the Lunette the Flying Lady illusion worked. Both Woods and later Nicholson turned out a belt that the flying subjects wore, enabling them to rotate once they were out over their audience. The belt worn by Lunette was made with roller bearings and was silent.

Noel Lester presenting the illusion known as the "Disembodied Princess" on the Strates Shows midway in 1951. The lady's head is actually a wax head and her body is hidden behind one of the doors.

Another suspension-show operator was Fred B. "Happy" Holmes, who presented the Girl From Up There on the 1903 Gaskill-Mundy show. His crew consisted of a head electrician with one

The "Spidora illusion" as presented in a sideshow during the 1950s. This was a midway illusion credited to Roltair. It's still presented today on midways.

assistant, a lecturer, a ticket seller, a soprano for the bally, and a piano player. His performers included picture dancer Millie Compion, illustrated songstress Grace Bolinger, Golda Spencer as the living statue, and Etta Louise Blake as the Girl From Up There. Etta didn't remain in the air long — in the teens and 1920s, she was one of the premier girl revue producers on midways.

John Henry Shields started his show-biz career in 1875 as a purchasing agent on the Barnum and Bailey Circus. He was later the ringmaster for Dan Rice Circus for five seasons. In 1884, he originated the "ten cent" circus and may have been one of the first circuses working for sponsors as he toured the south raising money to build Confederate war monuments. Shields managed the sideshow on several circuses before putting the first Lunette show on midways. He also made and sold slides for dance effects. His 1912 Lunette show on the Barkoot Carnival featured Lunette flying out over the heads of the audience and shaking hands with members of the crowd. In 1920 he retired to Tarpon Springs, Fla., after 55 years on the showgrounds. He died in 1938 at age 91.

Omar Sami, who would become one of the best carnival show talkers and Coney Island show operators in the 1920s, apprenticed with a Lunette show on midways. In 1909 he was on United Carnival Co. where he staged a production called The Beautiful Butterfly. A *Billboard* reporter wrote of it, "It holds audiences spellbound at every show. A lady dressed beautifully in white with a jewel-covered crown comes out before the audience and speaks to them and then flies above them."

Midway showmen proved that illusions were ideal midway presentations. The show's mystery was a natural draw, as were the lovely lady subjects, and the show could last from ten to 20 minutes, depending on the business. At the start of the 20th century, carnival companies were just developing. Illusions could be crated and easily shipped by baggage car and gillied to and from lots. Out of the 12 shows presented on the 1902 Robinson Carnival Co., one-third were illusion-based. They were Lunette, the Flying Lady; Galatea, the Statue Turning to Life; The Red Dome or The Girl From Up There; and SHE, a show based on H. Rider Haggard's novel *She*, in which the heroine suffers a horrible death by fire.

Illusion shows became popular on midways, and by World War I they were competing with the new 10-in-1s and holding their own. Zelma the Human Butterfly was big, along with the Spider Girl. While showmen seldom expose their tricks, in 1917 James A. "Fingers" Wallace wrote to *Billboard* to say he had been operating a Spider Girl illusion on midways for five seasons but this was the first season he had seen showmen exposing the trick for 25 cents. He wanted the practice stopped: "They have no regard for brother showmen who come in after them."

Builder and scenic artist F.B. Keller, the originator of the London Mystery operated out of Columbus, Ohio, advertised in the 1902 *Billboard*: "Hear Ye Carnival Shows. Some new startling scenic and illusionary effects for the coming season." He offered

Hall and Christ's Girl to Gorilla show in the 1970s. A key to the smooth operation of the show was choosing employees with enough brains to keep the gorilla behind bars when toddlers, cripples, and folks with babes in arms were in the audience!

WANTED ILLUSION SHOW LECTURER

Also Ticket Seller who can make second openings and small Man or Boy for Broom Suspension. Attractive proposition to experienced Carnival Illusion Show Lecturer or young Magician who can learn fast. Going into the big Fairs in two weeks. Can place working Man who drives semi. All must stay sober and help up and down. Top wages each week.

A. W. McASKILL

General Delivery, Boonville, Ind., this week; then Cedar Rapids, Iowa; with Des Moines, Lincoln, Hutchinson, Memphis and Dallas to follow.

Watch the girl as she slowly changes from Atasha to a gorilla. Pepper's Ghost never looked so good or so scary!

Phantasmagoria, Birth of Venus, Revolving Statuary, and Down Among the Sea Nymphs. Besides illusions, Keller designed and built elaborate fronts and sold more than 20 different scripts for ghost shows. The Sea Nymph's Show — like Fairies in the Well and other mirror illusions that Cincinatti builders Heck and Zarro offered showmen — was one of the early nude lady shows on carnivals. This platform-show presentation had higher-than-usual staging and steps so that customers peered down into a deep shaft or well and were glad they did! It was also one of the earliest fairground shows to be shut down by local authorities.

One of the leading shows on the early-20th-century midway was an extension of Pepper's Ghost, presented as The Statue Turning to Life, or Galatea. In 1903, Charles Weston of Lawrence, Mass., offered Galatea to showmen, stating in his *Billboard* ad: "GALATEA: is not a sideshow or a museum. It is a work of art that holds the people in dreamland as you place a stone statue on the machine and in three minutes have produced a living lady. We present her with a rose and then turn her back to stone. The

As the gorilla swings open his cage door the audience makes for the exit. No faking the look of terror on the lady's face in the bottom right-hand corner of the photo. She's probably the first out of the tent!

rose turns to stone one leaf at a time. In less than one second she is back to life and she hands the rose down to one of the audience.

"The next stage is DEATH. You see her eyes sink back in her head. She grows poor, pinched and haggard. Flesh leaves her mouth and she looks death-like. Then you see the flesh crawl off from her jaws and her eyes drop down inside of her empty skull. Her skeleton will then change to a bouquet of flowers.

"NOW FOR THE ADVERTISEMENT: Have some lady in the audience get on the machine and change her into stone and back again. Everybody in town will hear of it within 24 hours. The exhibition lasts 12 to 15 minutes and you send them out wishing for more. The machine will last a lifetime and costs no more than five cents a day to operate. A child can work it after it is set up. Ideal for man and wife operation. Can be set up in one hour. Runs on kerosene oil. The illusion is crated in three boxes that weigh a total of 350 pounds. No excess baggage. Galatea will pay for itself in four days in a storeroom at ten cents admission or two days in a park or in five hours at any good fair. Come right up to the factory and learn how to set it up and operate it. It will take you only two hours to learn. I will pay you $25 toward your car fare. Cost of show: $150."

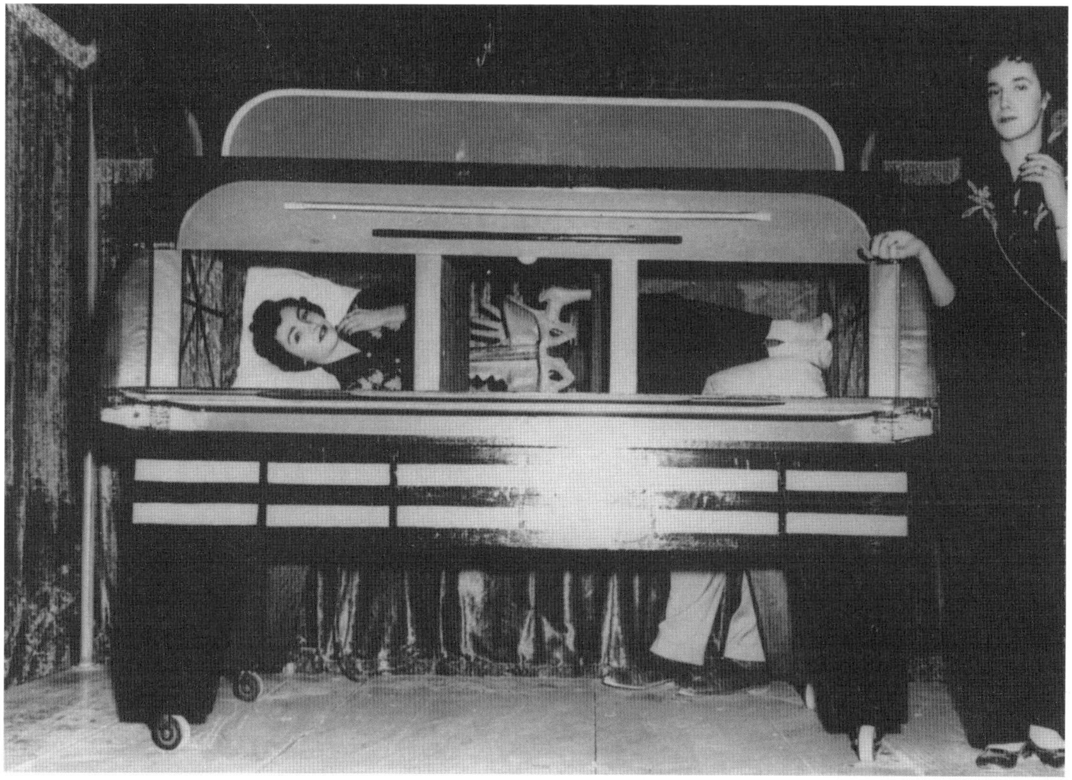

In the 1950s, Mae and A.W. McAskill's illusion show, "Helles Belles," was a big success on North American midways. Here they present the "No Middle Myrtle" illusion. McAskill would say: "Make a pretty show and they will always book you."

The show was presented under various names — one 1920s midway called it Anastasia, in which a mummy was brought back to life. The show was basic; the main thing needed was a black tent — usually 30-by-70 feet. The statue was generally made of papier-mâché and could be a full figure or just a bust.

Galatea was still going strong in the 1960s. Showman Karl Greenlaw says, "I saw this show on the Ross Manning Shows midway up in New England in the '60s. It was part illusion and part cooch — a statue turning into a lady. It was presented in a setup similar to how you would present a headless illusion. First you saw a statue,

The bally on Will Wright's Guillotine Show.

life-size and beautiful; as the lights dimmed, the statue slowly became a woman who stepped out of the box and did the coochiest cooch dance you could imagine. No smut, but a tent full of marks walked out with their hands in their pockets!"

In the '60s, the show was revived as the Girl to Gorilla Show to dazzle whole new generations of midway-goers. When Carl Sedlmayr, the owner of Royal American Shows, booked Hank Renn and George Duggan's Girl to Gorilla production onto his midway, he told a reporter that he started his carnival career as a talker for a Galatea show. He said the show began by changing a boy from the audience into a vase of flowers, which were given to the boy's startled parents or friends.

"See her change right before your eyes from a living girl to a live terrifying gorilla," the talker would tell his tip. The gorilla woman started out on the bally and inside the show in a steel cage as a bikini-clad beauty. The girl who changed into a gorilla on Royal American was Darleen

Left: This photo of the inside of Will Wright's Guillotine Show came from a rare postcard. The lady's hands appear to be still locked in the guillotine while her decapitated head is now across the stage resting on the blade of a sword. This was before "A" frames were popular and the tent center pole is right in the middle of the front of the stage.

Lions, billed as Atasha the Gorilla Girl. She claimed to do about 40 shows a day. Inside, she stood in the steel cage while an offstage announcer warned, "Those with weak hearts shouldn't stay in here," and then droned hypnotically, "Argo, Atasha, think gorilla, gorilla, gorilla, gorilla . . ."

GIRL WITH TWO HEADS ILLUSION: FRAMED in factory-built trailer, living quarters, with or without tractor. Priced to sell for cash. Anita Thompson, 1392 Worchester St., Aurora, Colo. 303; 366-2424.

Suddenly the beauty grew body hair, long arms, and big teeth, turning into a gorilla before the audience's eyes. The gorilla would approach the bars of the cage, fling the door open, and run toward the audience — or what was left of it. Most people bolted for the exit as soon as they saw the cage door open.

One thing about the Girl to Gorilla Show — you had to have the audience standing and the exit clear. When the final transformation takes place and the audience sees the gorilla in the cage, it's only a second or two until there is a loud ringing noise or a siren as the barred door of the cage flies open and the gorilla leaps into the audience. They may be skeptical, but when the gorilla charges, they run. That is why the main person on the show is not the girl or the gorilla, but the guy who yanks the curtain on the exit at the right time. You don't want the crowd running out through the side wall and falling on stakes or being cut by guy ropes. Duggan and Renn were experienced show talkers, and both made it clear in their opening that the show was "an illusion." But, once the gorilla escapes, people quickly forget what they heard outside from the talker. A wild stampede for the exit always occurs at the end of the eight- or ten-minute act. For showmen Renn and Duggan, that was good — a crowd running out on the midway only helped sell the show.

Sideshowman Bobby Reynolds says that what really hurt the Girl to Gorilla shows were the increased costs of public liability insurance after an accident in one of them. "The gorilla jumped out of the cage," he relates, "and this old guy turns around to flee the tent and runs smack into the first center pole. He's out cold. The guy in the gorilla suit bends over and tries to revive him. The guy comes to, sees the gorilla on him, pushes the gorilla off, gets up, and runs right into the second center pole and is killed!"

That was not the only headache to running this kind of show, according to

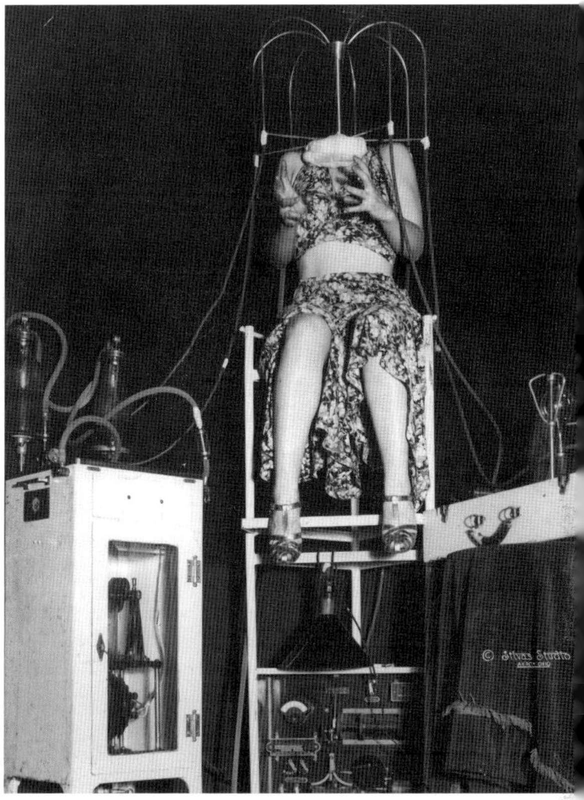

Egon "Dutch" Heinemann's headless girl illusion was the big attraction on Depression-era midways. It soon became a sideshow act, too, and after WWII a single-o grind show. The artwork on the show fronts keep getting updated but the illusion remains the same.

Zaro the Great's (Jimmy Dixon) magic show front in the 1970s. It had formerly been a girl show and was presented girl show-style on a stage with bench seating. The show was presented by Jimmy's large family (inset).

Bobby: "The gorilla suits were hard to keep from being liced up by the help," he says. "You had to clean them in gasoline and then hang them in the shade to dry, not the sun. At night was best. If you hung them in the sun, the gasoline ate the rubber in the face."

Every decade seems to be defined by a popular illusion. In the 1920s, it was the Sawing a Lady in Half act, which was big on the vaude circuit. In this well-known act, a woman is placed in a coffin-like box and sawed in half. The two halves of the box are pushed apart, and the woman — miraculously — wiggles her feet and waves her hands. Many showmen claimed to have created this spectacle. In 1921, in the pages of *Billboard*, Horace Goldin, playing on the Keith circuit, challenged P.T. Siebeit, who was on the Shubert circuit: "Let the wrong man destroy his illusion and never do it again."

Goldin was a veteran magician whose 47-minute, 35-person vaude show had shattered all records in 1913. Regardless of who invented it, the trick drew big crowds. Theaters had to hire extra police wherever Siebeit and Goldin were working. At the same time, Babe Ruth, "the Sultan of Swat" — who had never failed to draw crowds at the ballpark — wasn't drawing flies on his vaudeville tour, notwithstanding his $3,500 a week salary. In Canton, Ohio, when Goldin was playing the burlesque circuit at the Keith theater, a local butcher was selling "Pigs Cut in Half." And Prof. Francise Audrey, on the Lou Dufour Shows, offered a midway show of mind-reading plus an illusion in which a woman was cut in four. The climax of the show was the "Burning of She" cremation illusion.

In the 1930s, one of the best shows on the Conklin and Garrett midway was operated by Will Wright — an illusion titled Death on the Guillotine. One Winnipeg newspaper reported "youngsters' eyes almost popped out of their heads as they watched this alarming feat. The girl's head is neatly placed under the evil-looking machine. Down comes the blade and off comes her head into a box held by the assistant. He takes the head and places it on a chair several feet from the guillotine, where the hands are still seen. While apparently decapitated, the girl talks, winks, and answers questions freely."

Around the same time, the Headless Girl show began to appear on midways. It was reportedly brought here by "Doctor" Egon "Dutch" Heinemann from Hamburg, Germany. Heinemann exhibited a headless girl at the Blackpool, England, amusement park before coming to the U.S., where he landed his headless show on the Goodman Wonder Shows in 1937. It was a 10-cent grind show at the Golden Gate Exposition at San Francisco in 1939, and ran neck and neck with Cliff Wilson's bamboo-fronted monster snake show. Olga, the name Heinemann gave his headless lady, surfaced on dozen of midways in 1939, thanks largely to Edward Murphy of San Francisco who was selling plans for the illusion at $100 a set.

Tim Deremer's "Myrna the Mermaid" grind show is still working at fairs despite all the trouble to keep someone in the illusion. Tim never did say if he paid out the $1,000 reward when some dude complained there was nobody in there. The mermaid had stepped out for a break without telling him!

Harry Lewiston writes in his memoir *Freak Show Man* that he had bought the illusion for $700 from an illusionist named "Immelmann" after it didn't do well on midways. Lewiston says he hired a disbarred doctor in Chicago to rig it up with gaff tubes of liquids flowing in and out of the girl's neck. He obtained monitors, a control board, spark-makers, motors, and more from a medical supply house. One big tube ran into the center of the girl's neck, with six other tubes clustered around it. Lewiston claims to have made up the story of Olga, with which he framed his show. She was Olga Hess, he said, a Hamburg girl traveling on the Orient Express to Istanbul with her mother. The train had crashed and Olga was partially decapitated. A Dr. Landu, who was also on the train, just happened to be doing experiments involving keeping headless bodies alive. To save Olga's life, he had to

This bannerline painted by Ohio native Tim Franks for Tim Deremer's Palace of Illusions has been one of the nicest and flashiest bannerlines for the last decade on American midways.

FOR SALE FOR SALE

GORILLA SHOW

(Truck goes with it)
This is the show that grossed

$120,000 LAST YEAR

New Gorilla suit, new tent and banners-2 extra banners for she creature show can be changed in 20 minutes to another show: tapes, horn, milkes, amplifiers all go with it.

Can be seen at

GREATER JACKSONVILLE FAIR

CASH $10,000 CASH

CALL AFTER OCT. 28

GEORGE F. DUGAN

1712 W. Crawford, Tampa, Fla. 33604 (813) 933-2084 oc20

cut off her head. Lewiston was a constant promoter of his own greatness. Fiction or not, his story was a good one.

Many sideshowmen used Olga as a blow-off. When the tip was inside the show, the lecturer, dressed as a doctor or nurse, would select a volunteer from the audience to come up and feel Olga's pulse and her chest movement. The volunteers always stated she was indeed "alive." Lewiston says his set-up was so well-done that a coroner from one city showed up at the next place he exhibited to see if the body had decomposed. That didn't particularly bother Lewiston, but "people making the sign of the cross or kneeling in prayer before the headless girl tweaked my conscience." Olga was featured in sideshows and illusion shows for years.

In the 1960s, Olga was revived by grind showmen. The story was the same: for 50 cents, the public went into a trailer and stared at a headless lady, usually attired in a low-cut blouse or dress. The show generated publicity for the carnival, as a local reporter could be put in the illusion and write a story about her experience. One such story from a reporter who for a half-day was "Myra the topless lady" included quotes from the viewers. One male showgoer was overheard saying, "She's great from the head down," as if he had considered asking her out.

During the '60s and '70s, you might have seen shows presented by Jimmy Dixon at major fairs. Dixon had various grind shows out, plus a large sit-down magic revue. Other showmen I've talked with marveled at Jimmy's skills not only as a magician but as a pitchman. His father was a career military man and he had grown up in Germany, where he was fascinated by magicians on touring Armed Forces shows. When his dad invited some of the magicians back to their home, Jimmy got to see the magic tricks up close. From then on, he was hooked. He ended up joining the army himself, and when he got out, became a full-time magician. Club work dried up in 1960, and he went into the carnival back-end business.

Jimmy told me he played the Dallas Fair in the early 1960s with a grind show. Also in the back-end lineup was Archie and Mae McAskill's Helles Belles illusion show, which is where he got the idea to frame his own magic revue. Instead of placing the illusions on a platform, as in a 10-in-1, Dixon put his show on a stage like a theater magic show. His revue was framed almost like a large carnival girl revue. In fact, Jimmy's front was once a girl-show front, and inside the audience sat on girl-show-style seats. The show lasted 20 to 30 minutes, offering up dancers, variety acts, big stage illusions, and stage magic presented by Jimmy and his large family. When it was over, Jimmy would come out and make a special pitch to the audience. He told them that behind the stage were five additional attractions not advertised outside. Those wanting to see these illusions paid 50 cents or $1 more to pass by them. Among the visual illusions was No Middle Myrtle — you could see her head, lower torso, and legs, but her stomach area was just skeleton. Other illusions were Spidora and a head on a chair. None required long explanations, so the line moved quickly.

Another fairground magic show in the 1970s was Sebastian Adriani's Royal London Magic Circus. The show first opened in 1976 on Cumberland Valley Shows behind a 130-foot front, in a 40-by-80-foot tent. The show was presented 10-in-1 style and featured the usual acts. One girl doubled as the electric girl and the rubber girl. Dana Zornes escaped from a straitjacket while the audience counted to 30. Adriani, working under the name Zabrina, hypnotized a member of the audience who was then suspended horizontally between two chairs while Zabrina's assistant used a sledgehammer to smash a concrete block on the guy's stomach. The finale was a bullet-catch routine in which an audience member selected one of three colored bullets which was then put in a rifle. Zornes fired the rifle at Zabrina, who caught it and dropped it from his teeth into a glass flask, where the audience member identified it. Adriani had been a veteran sideshow worker on circuses and carnivals.

Boredom, and the fact that a person is often stuck for hours in one position inside an illusion, makes finding magic show help a real problem nowadays. Tim Deremer, out of Canton, Ohio, is one of the last operators of big illusion shows on midways. He has a mermaid show and a Girl to Gorilla show. He explains his strategies for eliminating the boredom of the illusion workers: "What I did with the mermaid and the gorilla show was switch the ape girl with the mermaid girl every two hours. That way, as the mermaid she can relax and get the air-conditioning while lying there. When she is the gorilla girl, she has time to stretch her legs, get a drink, go to the bathroom, and walk around a bit behind the tent between shows. So that worked out good."

For Deremer, the problems seem endless. "Every day, you wake up and wonder, 'Is everybody here? Do we have enough people to open?' Somebody quits and then you have to go out on the midway and find somebody to sit in the mermaid show. Once, when we couldn't find a girl, I had a kid who might have wished he was a girl, so we put a halter on him, stuffed it, put him in a wig, and put him in there. I was giving a break to the ticket seller and this black girl came out of the show and says to me, 'Mister . . . that's the ugliest mermaid I've ever seen!' I thought to myself, how many has she actually seen? Another one came back and said, 'Mister, that mermaid has bushy armpits.'

"Then I had a girl in an illusion projected in a bowl, and she was smoking in there. A guy came out and said, 'If that mermaid is underwater, how can she be smoking?' I had to go back and tell her, 'Don't be smoking in there. God, give me a break!'"

THE UNBORN
THE UNBORN
THE UNBORN

THE UNBORN

Will Their Souls Get to Heaven?

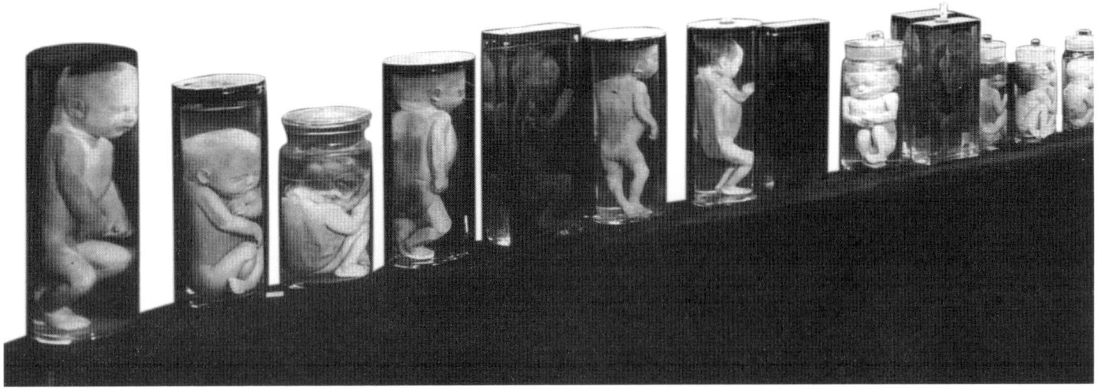

In the late 1960s, determined to buy a show, I visited my friend Harvey Boswell in Wilson, N.C. He said he had a semi that contained a Lord's Last Supper in Wax — it had formerly been a girl show owned by an ex-cop who worked it himself in drag. Harvey began preparing supper in a huge cast-iron frying pan. I needed to use the bathroom. "Do strange babies scare you?" he asked. "No," I replied and went in. I glanced at the bathtub. Something with a huge head was floating around in there. An oversized eye glared at me. I finished quickly, keeping my gaze on the upper wall. When I returned to the kitchen, Harvey was busy stirring potatoes, pork chops, and beans. He glanced over and nonchalantly said, "You got to soak 'em every so often. They get scummed up in those medical jars. Dust and whatnot gets in there."

Opposite: This two-word bannerline says it all in describing the pickled babies show that Montrealer Joe Kara had on Canadian midways in the 1950s. Joe is in the ducat box and ignoring the marks coming out of the tent.

Harvey Lee Boswell was a prominent back-end showman from the late '40s to the

Chapter 10

Harvey Boswell's freak-o-rama walk-through show on American midways in the 1970s featured stiffs, torture instruments, snakes, and pickled babies. Harvey was always proud of his candy striped bannerline uprights.

Marie O'Day's career has slipped a bit. At one time Hoot Black and Charlie Campbell exhibited her as a street exhibit in her "own palace car." Actually, it was a nicely painted semi-trailer with a sleeping area for the operator and Marie's exhibition room. Harvey Boswell in March 2000 had her propped up in a plywood case standing in his never finished grind show semi-trailer.

mid-'80s. He specialized in punks — babies in bottles. "My first year on the road," he says, "I framed a two-headed punk show in a 20-by-20 top and was going for 25 cents. I had various punk shows from then on. The only three-banner front I ever had was a punk show. It was titled Sons of Sex/Daughters of Sin. The door banner just read: 'EVE.'

"I framed a real nice baby show, Eternal Miracle, under a beautiful royal-blue top with a doctor's sign with a snake painted on it. I had a woman in a nurse's uniform work the ding table. The babies and specimens were lined up in rows and I featured the two-headed Siamese water-head girl, and a frog baby on turntables.

"At the Carmen, Man., fair a crew of miners bought tickets and went in the punk show. Allen Bedford was in the ticket box. They got mad, said it was a disgrace, and ended up busting a $250 medical jar. Bedford grabbed the top of the ticket box and nailed one guy and I hit another guy with a hammer. The punk in the broken medical jar quickly turned black in the air. I bought some bleach and got him back to his natural color, but the only thing I could buy to exhibit him in was an aquarium.

"Ever Since Eve" was a show that veteran show front builder and painter Jack Ray framed in the late 1940s. The front is made of wood panel sections hung on a pipe frame, and set up here at the London, Ontario, fair on Jimmy Sullivan's Wallace Bros. Shows midway.

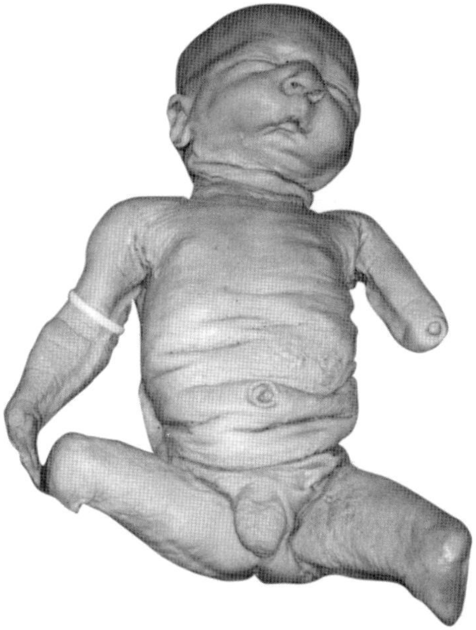

A rubber baby referred to by showmen as "bouncers" shows deformed arms and legs associated with Thalidomide drugs taken by women during pregnancy.

"Women reacted strongly to punk shows. They would cry. One said, 'How can their poor little souls go to heaven trapped in those jars?'

"On my big punk show, I had a blow-off with a two-door proscenium curtain separating it from the rest of the tent. The lettering read: 'Secrets of Sex.' Inside I had photos of odd sex techniques, piercings, and the worst-looking punks. Outside I had a sign on the ticket box that stated: 'You Must Be Over 16 . . . X-Rated.' That helped to sell it. We got 50 cents for the show and a quarter from the blow-off.

"I then developed my show more or less into a museum show that I called Palace of Wonders. It had banners painted 'Jungleland,' which was the shrunken heads and the snakes. 'Nature's Mistakes' covered the pickled and mounted freak animals. The 'Chamber of Horrors' was a small collection of torture devices. I had six pits. I featured the two-headed punk. I put the punks in the last pit closest to the exit. If the marks got mad, they were close to the exit doorway and this stopped them from going through the display mad, disturbing others, or wrecking the exhibits. Once I took the punks out, the business went way down!"

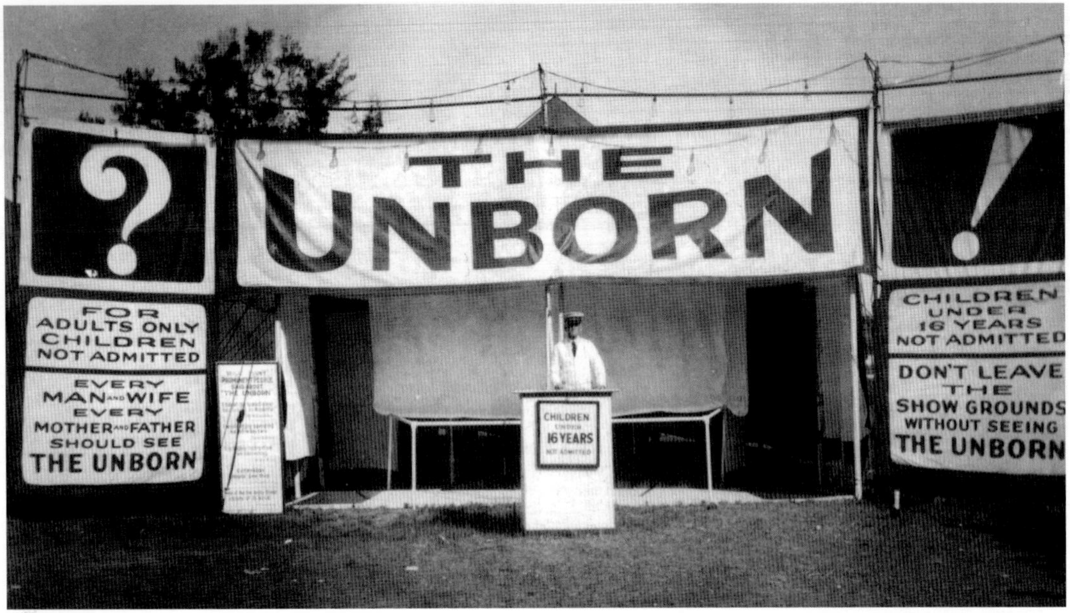

One of Lou Dufour's life shows on a midway in the 1930s. The under 16 age limit helped push the older crowd into the show.

Showmen referred to babies in formaldehyde-filled bottles as "pickled punks." Ads in the *Clipper* indicate a small but steady trade for those who supplied showmen with mummified, embalmed, or pickled real specimens. John Michael Schliesser, a New York naturalist and anatomical sculptor in waxworks, advertised himself in 1900 as the originator of the embryological exhibits in America.

Gretchen Worden of Philadelphia's Mütter Museum says the first exhibits in medical displays were "dried preparations." They were then coated with a preservative — usually arsenic, as alcohol was too expensive for preserving early specimens. John Dodge of the Dodge Company, one of the oldest firms in the country making embalming fluid, says that for fetuses, immersion in alcohol or formaldehyde was a better preservative than injection with fluids. Immersion covered the whole fetus and invaded every orifice.

Showmen, especially embryo and fetus exhibitors, worked hard to present their attractions as living wonders — "Born to Live" was a favorite slogan on ticket boxes and below bannerlines. Real specimens were highly prized by showmen, who seldom parted with them. Punks were sold and even rented through *Billboard* classifieds. In 1919, C. Colvin offered real two-headed and frog child babies for sale to showmen: "These cost more than paper stiffs, but you will not be ashamed to exhibit them. Send 25 cents for descriptions and prices. This small charge is to keep information from moms and children."

In 1921, Mrs. S. Godfrey of Eureka, Calif., even advertised her two-headed baby in the "At Liberty" section of the classifieds where performers, musicians, out-of-work carnies, and other show folks listed their skills and availability. Her ad read: "Two perfect heads on one body. Weighed 19 and three quarters pounds at birth, 10 inches across the shoulders. Preserved in five-gallon jar. For lease by a reliable show."

Some showmen felt uneasy hauling real dead humans around, and for them the solution was papier-mâché, wax, or rubber babies, also known as "bouncers." Bouncers mainly came from medical supply houses or were made by professional prop-makers. Before alcohol or formaldehyde were easily available as immersion fluids, showmen made do with freak babies made of paper and wax, exhibited in jars of water clouded with a few drops of tea or coffee.

One of the last big sellers of punks, both real and rubber, was showman Peter Hennen. His 1973 catalog listed a cyclops specimen: "One eye socket in center of forehead. Autopsied, re-sewed. $1,000." Another baby was listed as: "Waterhead Human Specimen, Negro, full term with long fingernails and hair. $1,500." He also offered for sale "Replicas of authentic freak babies. Human babies manufactured in tough vinyl from molds actually taken from genuine specimens. THESE MAY BE DISPLAYED IN WATER AND DEFY THE CLOSEST INSPECTION!" One such specimen was described thusly: "Six fingers, six toes, two noses. Each hand and each foot has six digits. Molded from a female infant which lived 11 days. $250."

Hennen's knack for this form of show-biz comes through in one paragraph in his catalog: "PRESERVED ATTRACTIONS COME 'ALIVE.' Use one of our turntables. Your tapes may then claim that your display is at liberty to say: 'As she slowly turns around,' etc. Strong tones that your jar is alive and living!"

For a brief time, live babies were also on display on midways. A 1902 *Billboard* story lists the Baby Incubator as one of the

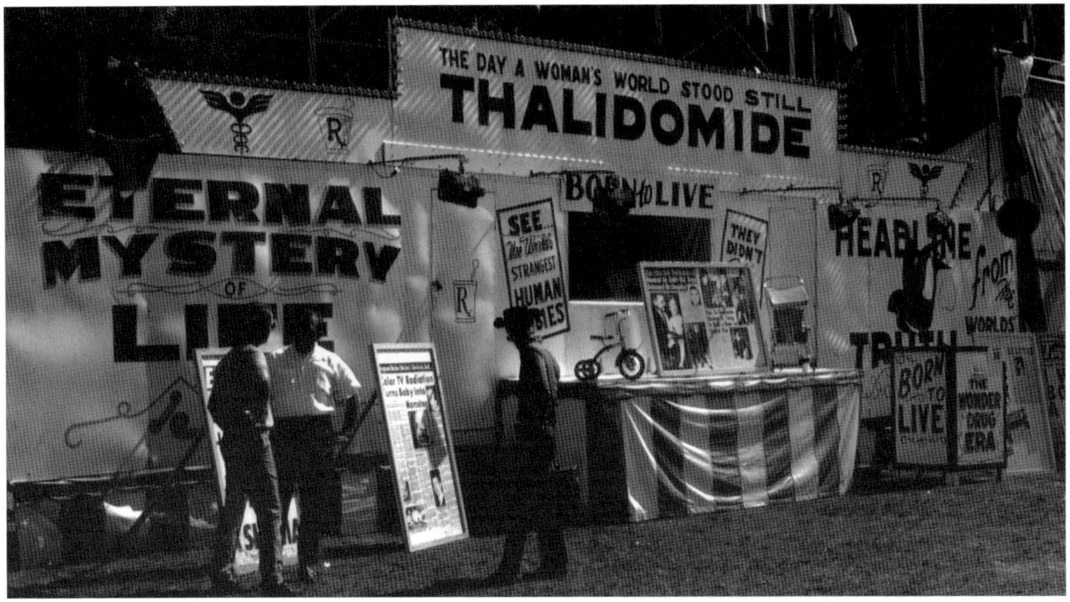

Peter Hennen's Thalidomide Baby Show in the 1970s. Hennen was a master at framing grind shows and spent hours putting together the right spiel and wordage for the show fronts. The numerous blow-ups, the tricycle, and the stroller are Hennen touches.

shows on the Dan R. Robinson carnival. Off the midway, it became a big attraction at Coney Island. Oliver Pilat and Jo Ranson wrote in their book *Sodom by the Sea*, "Only a man of rich personality and absolute integrity like Dr. Martin Arthur Couney could have made a continuous amusement attraction out of 'premmies' without drawing down on his head the wrath of the religious and medical authorities." The exhibit was unique in carnival lore because in 40 years they never had an imitator or

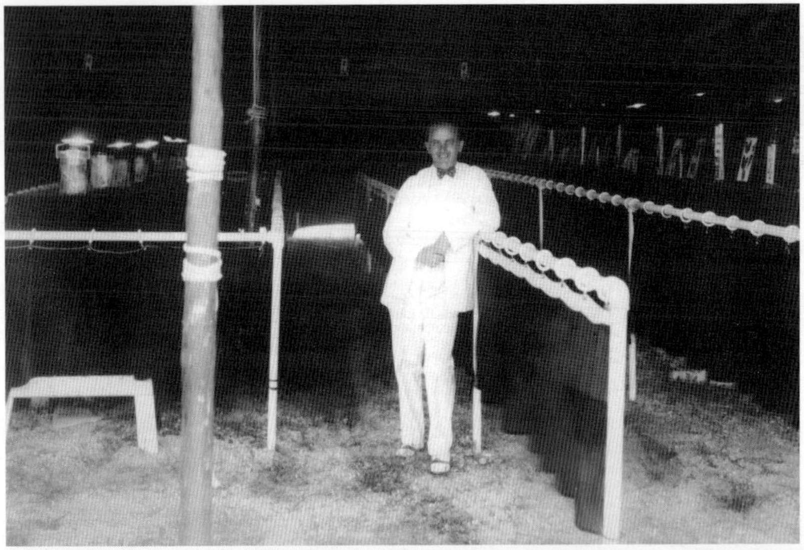

Lou Dufour standing inside his "Revelation" show on the 1928 Johnny J. Jones Shows midway. The Port Arthur (Ont.) *News-Chronicle* wrote: "It is doubtful, indeed, if a more vivid exposition of the formation of life was ever brought before the gaze of laymen."

A lecturer leads the tip through a Dufour and Rogers "Life" show made up of specimens bought from medical supply firms. At the end the tip were pitched sex booklets for 25 or 50 cents that were readily available free at any health clinic.

competitor. Couney had specialized in pediatrics at a Paris hospital in the 1890s. Back then, premature babies were left to die or placed under a blanket surrounded by hot bricks in a kitchen stove in a feeble attempt to provide the moisture necessary for life. He took his incubator to the 1896 Berlin Exposition in hope of embarrassing the French hospital authorities into giving him more funds. His exhibition became the butt of music-hall jokes and songs and one of the best-attended attractions at the fair. Frederic Thompson, the amusement park builder, suggested in 1903 that Couney place them in a permanent exhibition in Coney Island.

Babies were brought to the Coney Island incubators from all over the city and from cities that did not have adequate facilities for premature babies. The public were led into the incubator room and given a lecture and then moved on to the nursery. A staff of four or five wet nurses were kept on hand to feed the babies mother's milk. The smallest baby handled at Coney Island was

The beautiful plastic model of a woman that Lou Dufour used in his "Women" show. The birth of a baby film produced by Dave Friedman was rear-screen projected onto the dark area of the model's stomach area to the marks standing out front.

Dufour's last show was an elaborately framed affair. "Woman" debuted at the 1959 Tampa fair and toured on Royal American Shows with manager Mel Smith and lecturer Thomas Hart.

one and a half pounds. Couney's survival rate was 6,500 babies out of 8,000.

In the 1930s, showman Lou Dufour legitimized embryo and pickled-baby exhibits by putting them at several World Fairs here and overseas. In 1927 he was running an auction store on Dodson's World Fair Shows and, while at the Shreveport, La., fair, he watched crowds line up to see 20 specimens displayed in a tent by a local doctor named Jones. Dufour remembered back to 1920, when he had seen people at the Smithsonian stand amazed in front of displays of human embryos. He convinced Jones to sell him the display and renamed it UNBORN. The exhibit opened the next season on the Johnny J. Jones midway; soon he had dozens of the shows in parks and midways.

In 1933–34 Dufour teamed with Joe Rogers, another carnival hustler, to put two shows on the midway of the Century of Progress Fair in Chicago. One was the Life Museum and the other was a Live Two-Headed Baby. Felix Blei, the agent for the magician Carter the Great, had discovered a lady in Hong Kong who had given birth to a two-headed infant that lived. Contracts were signed, but the baby died a few weeks before the fair opened. Rogers and Dufour scrambled and managed to purchase a two-headed baby that had occupied a doctor's office for three years. For $1,500, they were back in business with their star attraction in a three-foot jar of formaldehyde. The artwork on the entrance was changed slightly from "LIVE Two-Headed Baby" to "REAL Two-Headed Baby."

Patrons entering the Life show were confronted by a refined lecturer dressed in a white hospital smock. He lectured on the contents of the medical jars, describing life from conception to birth. At the end of the displays, he pitched a booklet that dealt with sexual problems and pregnancy for half a dollar a pop. The same exhibit could be viewed at any natural or medical museum, and the pitch booklets contained information given out freely at clinics and hospitals.

Master exploitation filmmaker, author, and showman Dave Friedman laughs remembering Dufour's show: "I played the CNE a couple of years with Lou Dufour with

Hall and Christ's vinyl bannerline for their Children of Forgotten Fathers — World's Strangest Babies show. This was the show that was busted at the Grayslake, Ill., fair in the early 1970s.

the pickled punk shows, as I had this footage of the birth of a baby. You walked in and he had all these signs and explanations, and the mark would go up and down the aisles looking at the pickled punks and then come to a big clear area and we would gather the tip there where a tape announced: 'Now, look at the nude woman.' He had this woman standing there made out of plastic, a beautiful thing, and in her belly was a screen. We had a projector in back of the thing and I would start the movie. A voice said, 'You are going to see a natural birth. Now you see a Caesarean section, or birth by surgery.' Often a couple of marks would pass out when they saw that. Even in black and white. That first scalpel shot when the blood would start coming out, guys watching the film would drop like flies.

"Lou had that show framed beautifully. Soon as you got through with the pitch, you went in and rewound the film and got ready for the next tip. You had two books that you pitched, one for the men and one for the women. 'And I believe with all my heart,'" spiels Friedman, "'that a set of these books belongs on the living room desk or bedside table of every home in America. For if just one of these books can save a young girl from the shame of unwed motherhood or a young boy from the horrors of venereal disease — there is no telling how much they are worth. But we pass these books out to you people through the efforts of Women's Research Guild for the ridiculous price of $1 a copy, $2 a set. Take these books home and read them in the privacy of your own home. We have a chapter on conception. Any woman that can add two and two and read a calendar can keep and maintain herself and therefore know the time of the month that she is fertile.'"

Friedman pauses. "We probably got more poor girls pregnant with that phony crap, but it was the strongest joint ever set down."

By the 1970s, things were getting dicey on what you could and could not exhibit on midways. The punk business blew up in a small fair just above Chicago. Chris Christ and Ward Hall had their World's Strangest Babies show booked into the Lake County

Fair in Grayslake, Ill. Shortly after opening, Christ was arrested by detectives sent down by Coroner Robert Bobcox, who was acting on a complaint from someone whose daughter had seen the show.

Bobcox was quoted in the newspaper: "When we first saw the exhibits, we thought they were plastic or rubber. But assistant pathologist Dr. Vernon Zech examined them and found them to be human monstrosities. It was absolutely ghoulish." Christ was charged with transporting a dead body without accompanying permits, and 20 fetuses and embryos were confiscated along with signage and other parts of the show. Hall and Christ hired attorney Raymond M. Carlson to defend Christ and get their show back.

Bobcox was adamant that there was no way the babies were ever going to leave the morgue, except for a proper burial. "The only way anyone could obtain malformed fetuses and babies," he said, "would be to buy them from either a morgue in a large city, a second-rate abortionist, or medical schools. I will not let this practice go on." However, it soon became clear that these babies could be anywhere from one to 40 years old and virtually impossible to trace. Bobcox had a weak case, so he called police in Hillsborough County, Fla., to get Christ's

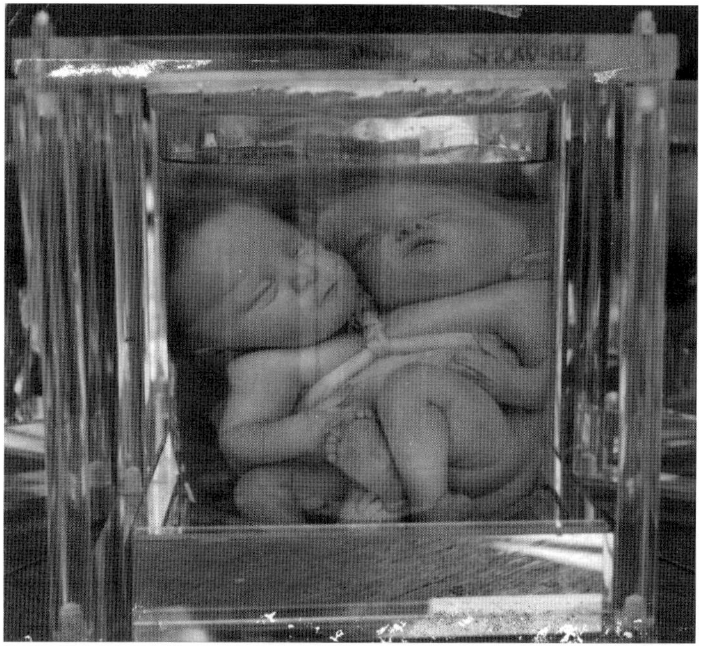

A current grind showman's double-body baby in a square medical jar. It is not presently on exhibition.

Below: Jack Constantine's baby show at the Hamburg, N.Y., fair in 1999. The three-banner front came from Hall and Christ. "As Seen On Hard Copy" on the ticket box front suggests a current realism to the show. The word "facsimiles" has replaced "born to live" and "real," but proves just as effective for luring in a new generation of marks.

Inside Jack Constantine's 1999 baby show. Jack was quite pleased with using bassinettes to prop up these bouncers but I think the final touch was the teddy bears.

Bobby Reynolds has used his two-headed baby as a blow-off in his sideshows and midway museums for several years. At one time the "boys" were shown behind a canvas partition with a doorway cut in it. More recently (2002) Bobby has placed them inside a Boler trailer and patrons wishing to see them look in the back window where the boys are displayed on a turntable. In 2001 he had the Boler trailer on the midway as a separate grind show.

records, which came up clean. But, at Hall and Christ's property in Gibsonton, police found 13 other human fetuses and embryos stored in jars inside metal containers. Some of the jars were wrapped in newspaper dating back to the '60s. A Hillsborough detective arrested Hall and he was charged with failure to register fetal death. In both cases the charges laid weren't consistent with the laws to which the court tried to apply them, so both men were acquitted. As part of Ward's deal with justice, he was instructed to give the babies a proper burial.

On November 17, 1977, Bobcox and ministers of the Protestant and Roman Catholic faiths, plus a Jewish rabbi, attended a graveside ceremony for 14 of the babies in Highland Park, Ill. The burial of the 14 plastic-foam caskets in a single grave was accompanied by a four-minute ceremony at which Rev. Richard Hunt commented: "We also bury the idea that human life should be a grotesque spectacle . . . that human life is cheap or to be exploited." The remaining six bodies had been given to medical schools. But the baby show continued on the fair route with the word "REPLICAS" lightly painted on the entrance banner.

Punk fever was rising in the carnival field. A lot of pickled punks were buried by showmen who feared interference from the law. Though it would be very hard for the law to make charges stick, if prosecuted, showmen could lose their attractions and spend thousands in legal fees. No one wanted to risk it — the showing of punks slowed down until there were only a few shows in the nation's backwaters.

In recent years, the biggest market for

punks both real and man-made has been collectors fascinated with the subject of death and sideshows. In the early '90s, Bobby Reynolds took a big chance and exhibited his real two-headed baby show at Coney Island. He was soon busted, but he won his court case. At the Hamburg, N.Y., fair in 1999, Jack Constantine had a three-banner baby show he had bought from Ward and Christ on the Strates midway. All the babies were bouncers, and were displayed propped up in individual bassinettes inside a single glass-faced box. "I had that punk show out on Strates because I needed three shows over there to make a go of it," Constantine says. I tell him I like the bouncers in the strollers idea and he laughs: "I got those at Wal-Mart. I had to figure a way for the customers not to fool with them and so I put them in the glass box and in those bassinettes."

The next season, Constantine didn't return to the Hamburg fair with his baby show, but Reynolds was back with his museum show. This time he was using his two-headed baby show on the midway; at 50 cents, it was doing steady business. "The boys," as Reynolds called them, rotated in a medical jar on a turntable. Each revolution brought new expressions to the marks' faces. People were fascinated. No one seemed disgusted. The spiel on the grind tape said it was a medical presentation — a warning to young mothers about dope and alcohol consumption during pregnancy. They seemed to buy it.

Reynolds was back to the Hamburg fair again in 2002. I went down a couple of days before the fair opened and brought him to see a mutual friend who had a large collection of shrunken heads. As we traveled along the freeway, I asked, "Bobby, are you bothered by owning and showing those babies?"

Reynolds responded without hesitation: "No. No. No. As matter of fact, at Christmastime I put the two kids under the Christmas tree and I have the train running around them and I get them toys. The kids love Christmas. They are the only kids who never ask for the keys to the car and who give you money. On top of the Christmas tree where the angel should be, I have a shrunken head. Those are my kids. I love them.

"I don't feel guilty about that. I'm doing a real service, telling kids not to take drugs during their pregnancy. Don't smoke, don't drink alcohol. I'm doing it in my own incorrect way. I'm not doing it for free, of course. You know, the kids that are

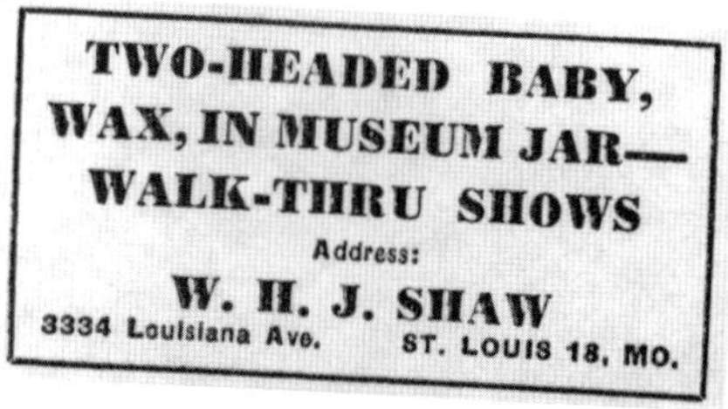
TWO-HEADED BABY, WAX, IN MUSEUM JAR— WALK-THRU SHOWS

Address:

W. H. J. SHAW

3334 Louisiana Ave. ST. LOUIS 18, MO.

around 13 years old ask more questions about drugs and babies. 'If I take drugs and I get a girl pregnant, will I have a freak baby like that?' they ask me. I tell them, 'Well, it's like a blender, son. You put an egg in, then you put some peas in, and some celery. Then you blend it all up. That's what happens when you get a girl pregnant. Your sperm; her eggs. So if you are taking drugs, you can screw up the baby.' I tell them that stuff. They like it."

Bobby looks at me and starts into the baby show spiel on the grind tape: "Mother Nature knows no rights, Mother Nature knows no wrongs when she brings these unfortunate children into the world. If you drink during your pregnancy, if you smoke cigarettes during your pregnancy, if you do drugs during your pregnancy, these things can happen to you. Don't do these things because your baby can't say no!"

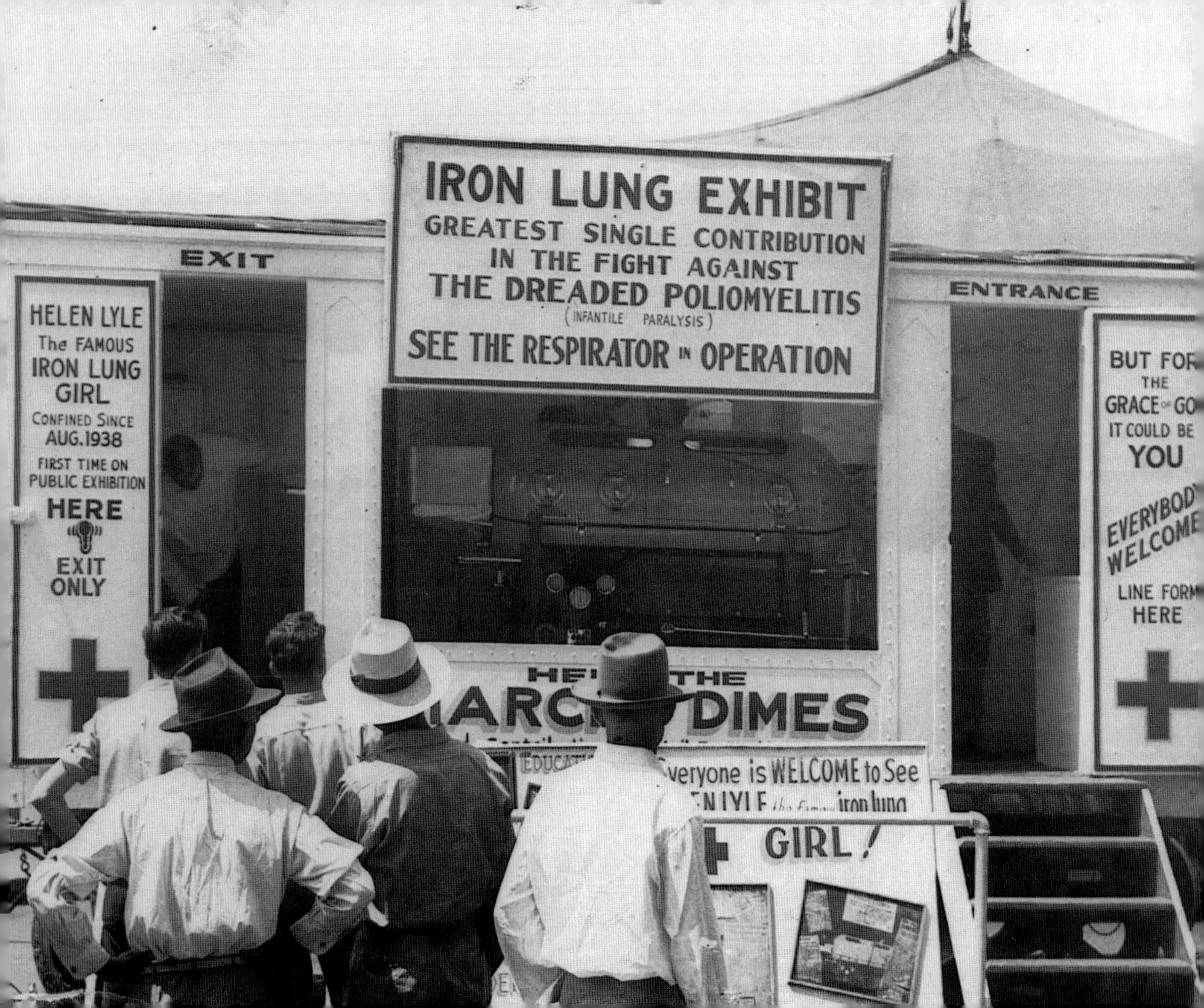
IRON LUNG EXHIBIT
GREATEST SINGLE CONTRIBUTION IN THE FIGHT AGAINST THE DREADED POLIOMYELITIS
(INFANTILE PARALYSIS)
SEE THE RESPIRATOR IN OPERATION
EXIT
ENTRANCE
HELEN LYLE
The FAMOUS
IRON LUNG
GIRL
CONFINED SINCE
AUG. 1938
FIRST TIME ON
PUBLIC EXHIBITION
HERE
EXIT
ONLY
THE
IT COULD BE
YOU
LINE
HERE
GIRL!

WALK IN, NO TICKETS

In the End, You've Got to Pay

In *Billboard* ads, showmen referred to the ding show as a "donation show" and sometimes a "needle show." These were shows that were advertised as being free, but when you reached the end of the exhibit, you were faced with a narrow exit and a large box with a sign suggesting you put something in it — preferably money. Incubators, unborn shows, war exhibits, miniature villages, iron lungs, and wildlife shows were some of the attractions that could be operated on a ding basis. Dings could be found on downtown city streets, and on circus and carnival lots, but mainly on carnivals. Crime exhibits were good ding attractions when worked downtown — especially if the showmen made a donation to the police.

Opposite: The Iron Lung show on the World of Mirth Shows midway in the late 1940s featured the occupant "Helen Lyle." Barbara Moody, wife of Al Moody (the show's trainmaster), worked as the "lung girl." Note the gentleman inside the exit doorway dressed in a medical smock who's in control of the ding box. Bill English recalled the spiel on the Greco brother's lung show, booked on Royal Crown Shows, as: "Come in and see beautiful 21-year-old Ella Webb. . . . She's awake now!"

Chapter 11

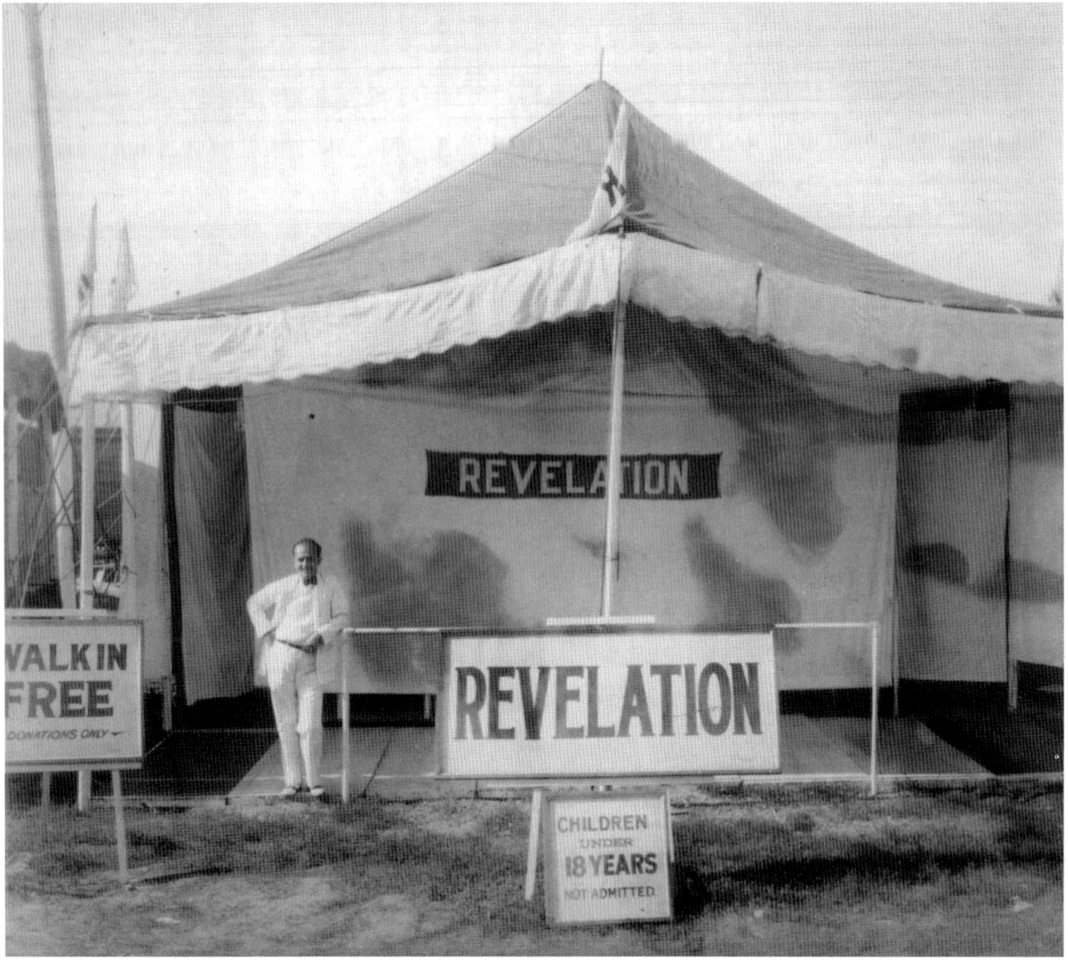

Lou Dufour's "Unborn show" called Revelation being worked as a ding show. Like medicine shows that gave free demonstrations to gather a tip to sell them phony medicines, Lou let the public in for free to pitch them sex and health booklets.

One of the things show people have in abundance is a good sense of humor. It is an essential asset to have if you are going to stay sane on a touring show. A prime example of this was Star De Belle, one of the best press agents in the outdoor amusement business. In the late '40s and early '50s Star contributed two weekly columns to *Billboard* that were hilarious tongue-in-cheek looks into the carnival and circus world. Here, from one of his columns, is the best description of a wildlife ding show you can find:

"Our Wildlife Show is operated entirely by animals. An ex-organ grinder monk works the mooch box. He's on the up and up and always gives the office a fair count. A trained goose leads the tip through. For protection purposes, should some stick wise up the mooch monk, we keep a parrot behind the piling table calling the donations, while another parrot does nothing but insult the patrons who drop nickels and dimes instead of quarters. The parrot has a big vocabulary and uses such phrases as 'Hey, jerk! Take that measly dime and buy the lady some bubble gum,' or 'Ack! Ack! A cheap John is showing his hillbilly gal friend a good time on a nickel!' I wish you could hear the parrot when someone doesn't give a donation. It's brutal."

And here are De Belle's comments on the iron-lung ding show: "We're using a retired chimp as beautiful Gladys Good, the girl in the iron lung. As the patient's body is hidden in the lung, a blonde wig and heavy makeup makes many a rustic's heart flutter for the poor unfortunate girl. The ape has had not less than 150 offers of matrimony from lonesome farmers that want to take her where she can regain her health in the open air."

During the World War II years and after, many dings were walk-through shows. The midway show Hitler and His Henchmen After Death — comprised of wax figures of Hitler, Eva Braun, Mussolini, and various war relics — was operated as a ding show on major midways in the mid-1950s. The panel and banner front had a sign over the entrance that read: "ENTRANCE — WALK IN." Another small sign on the ground read: "NO TICKETS SOLD." Like most small ding shows in a 30-by-50-foot top, it was laid out with exhibits on both sides. You walked toward the back of the tent and made a U-turn, walking back up toward the front, before leaving through a side exit, right past the ding box.

In the wintertime, the Kempf Bros. — famous for their miniature villages — exhibited their Model City and Bergmann's Famous Swiss Village in department stores and vacant shops. In some cases, they were paid outright by the department store or theater to set the show up; at others, they operated according to one of their brochures: "THIS EXHIBITION IS RUN ON THE PAY LEAVE PLAN. IF YOU ARE SATISFIED, PAY 10 CENTS ONLY." A very polite way of dinging the public.

After WWII many of the war shows found on midways worked on the ding principle. At the end of the visitor's trip through the carnage and gore of war was a carny wearing a veteran's uniform asking for a donation. Few turned him down.

Dingers on circuses were a whole different breed. They were part of the grift mob running the controlled games on the show. Games like three-card monte, the shell game, and razzle were usually worked in the sideshow. If the town was securely "patched," the dingers might work right out in the open on the lot. Usually they worked the parking lots and the streets approaching the circus grounds. Characters

Another "Lung show" built into a modern trailer. Several iron lung manufacturers provided showmen with the trailer and the lung.

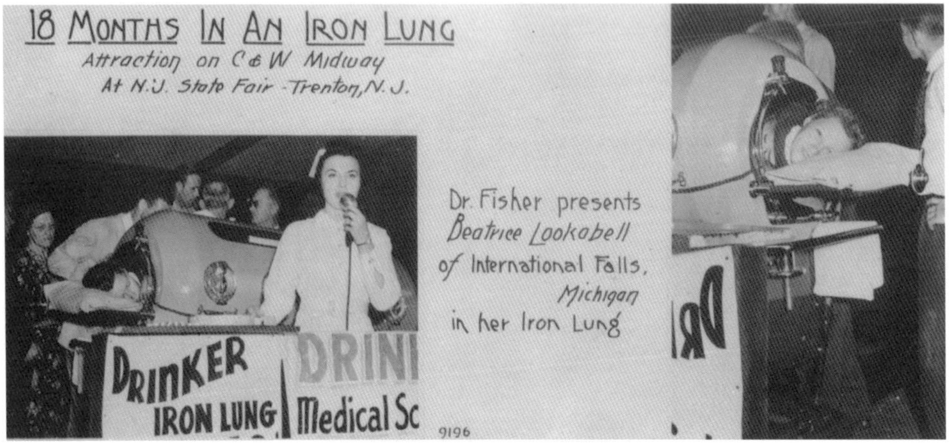

like Pistol Pete, a dinger on Dailey Bros. Circus, dressed in a veteran's military attire and simply pinned a small U.S. flag lapel pin on circus patrons as they approached the lot. If they didn't ante up a donation, he roughly removed the pin, often taking a piece of the lapel with it! Ding mobs are still out there working parades and gatherings.

One of the most effective dings from the 1930s through the 1950s was the iron-lung exhibit. Medical science came up with this machine that did the breathing for polio victims. But because new medical equipment was very expensive, fraternal groups and clubs held drives to raise money to purchase iron lungs for their hospitals. Several companies made the machines and were eager to get their product advertised — they had no qualms about putting them out as exhibitions run by showmen.

The key to the operation — or rather, the key to deflecting any heat — was the word "EXHIBIT," which appeared on all lung shows. It didn't stop the public from going and giving. If questioned, the operator could point to the word and say this was a

Money in the iron lung show business didn't all come from donations. Here is a pitch card sold to visitors to the iron lung show on the Cetlin and Wilson Shows midway.

demonstration to promote awareness of the disease and show how the iron lungs can help. The iron lung was one of the best ding shows; the eerie noise of the respirator alone drew people. And the best dings are those that leave viewers in a remorseful mood as they pass the ding box. What could be better than a pretty young lady trapped for the rest of her life in a groaning iron medical contraption to make you feel lucky enough to help out with some change? Staff dressed in medical garb and the spotless, gleaming exhibition area made the mark feel like he was in a hospital setting. Just don't hang around to see the unfortunate lady get up and leave when the show closed later that night.

A July 1947 *Billboard* ad placed by the Mullikin Co. offered four iron-lung trailer exhibits for $2,747 — $1,600 for a newly constructed trailer and $1,147 for the lung itself. A $747 discount was given if the operator retained the name "Mullikin Iron Lung" on the trailer.

GIRL WANTED

For Iron Lung, salary $50.00 week (including room). Permanent location. Young, attractive. Send photo. Experience not necessary. Join on wire. CHAS. W. STANLEY, 1472 Button Ave., Cincinnati 30, Ohio.

Wildlife shows almost always worked on the ding principle. This one on the Strates Shows midway in the 1950s has a unique red painted wooden bannerline with large cut-out signage with letters painted yellow and red. Somehow the workers put up the "Rare" sign in the wrong place.

Even before iron lungs were popular as stand-alone shows, there had been a case where one was used for a bally. At the 1938 San Francisco Exposition, the Incubator Baby Show lagged behind the other fair attractions until it was switched to a ballyhoo show using an iron lung and an almost nude girl to attract the curious. Lungs were also worked in amusement parks and as part of other shows. Sam Weriheimer's

ATTENTION!

Wild Life Show Operators

If you are interested in taking subscriptions for a sport magazine that really sends out the copies we have OUTDOORSMAN available at 25% turn in. Unless you already have account with us we require a $50 deposit.

MIKE WRIGHT
Trade Service Co.
139 N. Clark Street CHICAGO 2, ILL.

Floyd King had been an off and on circus owner since the start of the 20th century, but rarely made money with his own shows. He was successful with his wildlife show that appeared on his 1950s circuses' midway. In the wintertime, veteran agent Jake Rosenheim worked store fronts with it.

A wildlife show next to the motordrome on the 1957 Strates midway at the Hagerstown, Md., fair has suspended its ding operation in favor of "Ten cents to everyone" — no doubt what they were averaging when patrons were dinged.

FOR SALE—BARGAIN

WILD LIFE SHOW EQUIPMENT

1 G.M.C Truck, special bed
1 Anchor Tent, 30x60, complete 8½' side walls
13 Cages, 23"x42"x26"
13 Cages, 28"x52"x30"
3 Cages, 16"x24"x12"
26 pair Jacks for same
1 Knockdown Display Cage, 4'x8'x5', with top
1 Donation Table, elec. wire, lights
1 Eureka Tent, 25'x40', complete, ready to set up with cages

Write, don't phone.

W. D. LEAVENGOOD
401 East Francis Ave., Pittsburgh 27, Pa.
P.S.: Walter Stoffel, get in touch with me.

Pleasureland sideshow at Coney Island in 1951 also included an iron lung run by Tom Norner, with Ella Webb as the lung girl. But the main iron-lung exhibitors were the Greco Brothers. These Miami showmen had a half-dozen units out on various midways with a national charity tie-in. As late as 1958, "Squawk" Riley had his lung set up for the combined carnival and Christiani Bros. Circus date in Philadelphia, but by the 1960s, they were gone from the midways.

Another show that worked on the ding principle was the wildlife show, which consisted of a display of wild animals in cages. Most of these were smaller animals who could cope with small cages, and many were animals you would find in the woods or near lakes, like a fox, otter, or skunk. Some — anteaters, coatimundis, and monkeys — were small jungle creatures. The wildlife

One of the nicest framed wildlife shows booked onto the Cetlin and Wilson Shows midway in 1951. It was presented under a beautiful gable end tent with a big cage holding Himalayan Bears right up at the entrance. This show featured a big chimp advertised as a gorilla.

The Lord's Last Supper in wax was an ideal ding attraction. This one presently is working hard as an annex attraction to James Taylor and Dick Horne's Dime Museum in Baltimore, Md.

WANTED FOR CASH

IRON LUNG

WILD LIFE

Shows with or without trucks. Address

BOX D-303, Care The Billboard, Cincinnati 1, Ohio

show was often framed and painted to look like a display the Park Rangers, Lands and Forest, or Fish and Wildlife departments might exhibit at a local fair. Some shows did carry one or two big animals as a drawing card. For several seasons, the wildlife show on World of Mirth featured a cage holding two lions. Some showmen exhibited bears in their wildlife shows, and one even advertised a gorilla.

This kind of ding show had its drawbacks, though. Patty Conklin, one of the leading showmen in the carnival business from the 1920s to the 1960s, always said he would never own anything that eats. Once you own an attraction that eats, you

The ding lung show owned by Cavalcade of Amusements set up at this fair. It had earlier been the doctor's office on the show. When the lung craze died on shows these wagons reverted back to other uses. The lung wagon on WOM Shows became a Mickey Mouse Circus.

have to keep working all the time to feed it. This certainly applied to the wildlife business and was one reason you could find wildlife operators in the wintertime showing downtown in a vacant store.

Showman Don Prevost's mother and father had been in the wildlife business since the late 1920s, and after they died, he carried on their shows. At one time, Don had five wildlife units out on various

"Unborn" show on 1951 Cetlin and Wilson Shows. Creating show fronts in royal blue with white trimming was a clever way of displaying ding "unborn" shows on 1950s midways. Inside, the exhibits were finely labeled, backed with rich drapery, and properly lighted, and pickled babies inside medical jars rotated on turn tables.

midways. He says the secret to operating a wildlife show on the midway was the "WALK IN . . . WALK IN" signs. Once you got the people in there, all the signage pointed one way and you had backfire men that moved the people forward and didn't let them come back out the entrance.

"On the midway," he remembers, "I had a 100-foot spread with two big knock-down cages at each end of the top. Something big in each cage on the end of the bannerline. I had a 40-by-80-foot top. I had wallabies in one of the big cages. Inside we had raccoons, skunks, kickapoos, coatimundis. You walked [people] around in there — down one side around to the next side rows of cages. All the signs read 'ONE WAY.' The backfire men stood in the corners to keep them from turning around.

"The real trick to running the wildlife was you had to flash the thing, make it look inviting and appealing to people walking down the midway. On the ding, you had to flash the ding table with money — ones and fives. Sometimes a family would give you a fin, which was a lot of money in those days. You had to ask everybody! We tried to make it look like those exhibits the conservation officials put out at fairs. We had green-painted cages and all the staff wore green pants and white shirts."

Don was adamant about staying off the carnival midway if he could. "If you were on the carnival midway, they would often set you at the end of the joint lineup with the walk-through," he says. Did they put some of the most exotic animals nearer the ding box? "No," says Don. "We just spread them out. A bird, an animal, a reptile — just so you keep the people moving through. I put the chimp in the back where they couldn't see him but they could hear him. You let the people walk through; you don't hurry them.

"In the 1970s, the animal activists started coming in and asking how big the cages were, how much water does that animal drink? They were never satisfied, raising the requirements another step once you met their last ones. No matter what you did, it was never good enough. "So, in 1974 I gave up the wildlife business and went into concessions."

Ding-show operator Frank Hansen showed a "Lord's Last Supper" exhibit. "I have not used it in years," he says. "I have all the heads and hands in storage. They look like the original. In fact, as far as Christ is concerned, people cry when they go through it. Little kids would say, 'Why don't they say something, Mummy?' We exhibited it at shopping centers, too. Everything was on dollies, just wheel them in. It was a ding show, but it worked real good. You walked through gates at one end — one-way gates — and they couldn't get back out. If people forgot to leave a little something for their appreciation on exiting, I wouldn't press the lever to make the turnstile work. People would look at me and I would say, 'Maybe you forgot something?'"

SOUL ON SAWDUST

Black Nightclubs at Your Doorstep

In the mid-1960s, I was a teenager working on the Gene Cody and Kipling Bros. Circus as it limped along in Western Canada. When the show closed for ten days to give the agent time to set more towns, fire-eater/sideshow manager Carlos Leal took me into the Regina Exhibition to see Royal American Shows. Carlos was an aging sideshow and carnival veteran — a flaming gay Mexican who looked like Little Richard on a bad hair day. He knew everyone on Royal and we were given a free run of the midway. We saw all the shows, but the one that impressed me the most was Leon Claxton's Harlem in Havana.

Back in high school, I bought up the town's supply of black shoe polish and talked a group of friends into doing Harlem in Havana for the Christmas concert. We recreated the show, complete with a big set, an eight-piece

Opposite: Dancers in Leon Claxton's 1965 Harlemites chorus line in which the big number had them adorned with baskets of fruit on their heads. Memphis sax player extraordinaire Bill Harvey led the band. He was B.B. King's first band leader.

Chapter 12

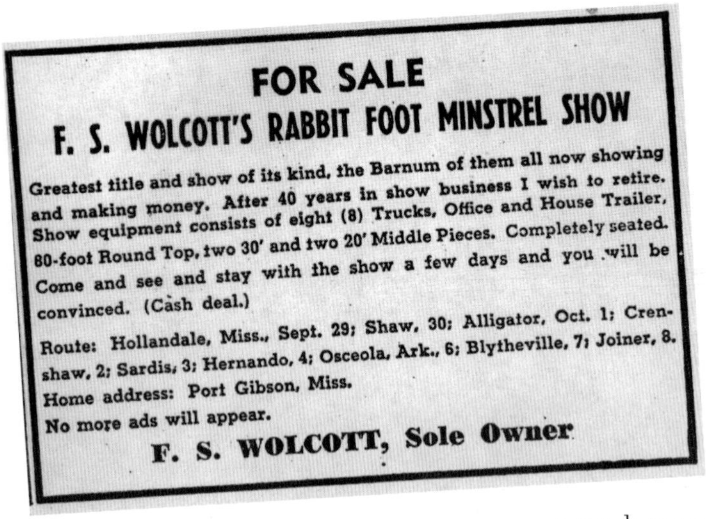

FOR SALE

F. S. WOLCOTT'S RABBIT FOOT MINSTREL SHOW

Greatest title and show of its kind, the Barnum of them all now showing and making money. After 40 years in show business I wish to retire. Show equipment consists of eight (8) Trucks, Office and House Trailer, 80-foot Round Top, two 30' and two 20' Middle Pieces. Completely seated. Come and see and stay with the show a few days and you will be convinced. (Cash deal.)

Route: Hollandale, Miss., Sept. 29; Shaw, 30; Alligator, Oct. 1; Crenshaw, 2; Sardis, 3; Hernando, 4; Osceola, Ark., 6; Blytheville, 7; Joiner, 8.

Home address: Port Gibson, Miss.

No more ads will appear.

F. S. WOLCOTT, Sole Owner

Besides black revue shows on midways, the minstrel show had also developed into stand-alone black shows touring under canvas and playing one-day stands like circuses. The oldest of these was Rabbit Foot Minstrels, which started in Tampa, Fla., in 1900 by black entertainer Pat Chappelle. The title derived from a popular song of the era. Here the show sits on a southern lot in 1953 awaiting a packed night crowd.

R&B band, and a chorus line of seven girl dancers balancing wicker baskets of plastic fruit on their heads. Everyone, including the teachers, liked it so much it was dragged out several more times during the year. When it came to listing "Probable Occupation" under my name in the yearbook, I was bold enough to put "Jig-Show Producer."

Referred to over the years as "Ethiopian minstrelsy," "coon shows," and other coarse names, the minstrel show was nonetheless an American original. Much of the talent and many of the early routines came from the touring American circus, where some performers blackened their faces and sang songs in Negro dialect. In the late 1820s, a white performer named Thomas D. Rice put together the song-and-dance format that became the minstrel show. A decade later, Barnum made a tidy profit promoting jig-dancing contests between a black New York City dock worker named John Diamond and anyone who would challenge him. Such contests and prize fights were the big spectacles of the day. And for a time, many American opera singers and theater actors came from the minstrel stage.

When black performers got involved in the minstrel entertainments in the 1840s, black show business began in earnest. By the 1860s, black entertainers were the hottest acts in the show world. In language common for the day, the *Clipper* called it "Niggerism," reporting on November 3, 1860: "Barnum's Museum was doing immense business because of one sole figure: What Is It! The little nigger does the business. The Siamese Twins ain't much. Years ago they took down anything in the show line before the Nigger Trade loomed up. Why? Because their faces aren't the right shade. Let them black up like the minstrels. Look at the Albino Children. See how they are run after. They are of African breed with some white color to their skins."

The popularity of minstrel shows lasted through the 1870s. White variety acts were "blackening up" with burnt cork so they could get work. At the peak of the minstrel business, there were both white and black companies — both "blacked up." The 1910 *Billboard* list of blacks in show business included 1,279 actors, 100 showmen, 521 stage hands, 84 theater ushers, 0 theatrical agents, 50 fortune tellers and hypnotists, 100 park attachés, 46 ticket sellers, 93 owners and

This was Leon Claxton's Hep-Cats 1944 front on Royal American Shows, around the time that Charles Kidder built a girl show for World of Mirth Shows with an overhead balcony. This style of front never caught on for girl shows but almost all the big rail carnivals adopted it on their black revues. The balcony got the big bands away from the center of the bally stage, yet allowed them to remain on the front and play while the tip was being turned and entering the show over the bally.

managers, 5,604 musicians. The total was 8,866, but the unofficial estimate — including smaller clubs, circuses and carnivals — almost doubled to 15,000 show people.

But black entertainers were barely represented at the 1893 Chicago World's Fair. An exception was the woman who made pancakes while portraying Aunt Jemima, a Negro character created in 1889 by an employee of a flour company who'd seen a minstrel show. Fair officials at the 1894 New Orleans Cotton States and Industrial Exposition tried to do better — they included a "Colored Department" —

Irvin C. Miller made a name for himself producing black tab shows that featured chorus lines of light-skinned girls. His troupes were featured in movies and for several seasons on the James E. Strates Shows, seen here with colored neon lights, which were popular decorations for all carnival show fronts in the 1940s.

Charlie Taylor's rock n' roll show on World's Finest Shows in Canada in 1960.

and when the fair was held the next year in Atlanta, it celebrated the joining of the South's new culture of segregation with the North's growing industrial and consumer culture. All the exhibits were open to whites and blacks, but the fair itself was segregated — blacks had to view performances from separate seating and could only get refreshments in the black exhibition building. The organizers tried to boost black attendance by promoting a special "Negro Day."

The Midway Heights area of the Atlanta fair had a show titled Old Plantation, owned by whites and run by a former minstrel man. Featuring songs and dances by blacks of the old South, it received a lot of publicity when it was the only midway show President Grover Cleveland visited in 1895. The Old Plantation show, although mixed in with anthropological exhibits and exotic villages on the pike, was the show that became a permanent fixture on touring carnival midways for the next seven decades.

The black shows on early carnivals were all called plantation shows. Unlike the minstrel show, whose main performers were black men, the carnival show featured black musicians, dancers of both sexes, and black chorus lines from the start. The "plant" show, with white-lipped black comics on the bally, looked like a minstrel show, but inside they were right up to date. You heard the latest music, saw the latest dances, and laughed at current black jokes. Boogie-woogie, jazz, Dixieland, and rock'n'roll music kept black revues at the forefront of midway entertainment. Except for shows in the South and at lots near neighborhoods with large black populations, the black revue shows' audiences were largely white.

Midway black-show performers in 1904 were doing the new buck-and-wing dance called the Wedding Cake, as shown for the first time that winter at the Chicago Horse Show. The 1915 Washburn Mighty Midway Shows carried a plant show called The South Befoo' Da Wah. World War I shows advertised a dance called "the Black Bottom." By the 1920s, when the remaining minstrel shows were those featuring only black performers, the term "plantation show" was replaced with "minstrel show," a designation used by carnies into the 1970s.

Show titles progressed from the early crude names to Darktown Strutters, Cotton Blossoms, Georgia Minstrels, Darktown Follies, and Jazzland Minstrels. Shows were named after dances, cities known for black music, and even colors of skin — hence Black and Tan, Chocolate Strutters, and Brown Skin Models. Well-known locations for hot black music like Harlem, New Orleans, and Memphis were found in producers' titles. The most notable were Dave and Lucky Wiles' Gay New Orleans shows on World of Mirth in the 1950s and '60s, and Leon Claxton's Harlem in Havana on Royal American. Claxton used his title from 1953 until the Cuban missile crisis, when he changed it to Harlem in Revue.

From the '20s through the '70s, carnies also referred to black revues as "jig" shows. The 1938 newspaper ads for Hennies Bros. Shows played on the reputation of the Ziegfeld Follies by calling their black revue the Jigfield Follies.

The word *jig* once referred to a form of dance, but it eventually became a slang term for black people in and outside of show business. Alex Albright, who has researched black entertainers working in minstrel and black tent shows, says he interviewed a chap that had been in black producer Irvin C. Miller's troupe, and when Albright referred to the artist as working in "blackface," the man said he found the term offensive. And while he was fine being known as a "jig performer," black organizations like the NAACP objected. One black performer who kept a diary referred to the color of audiences as "Jig" or "Ofay."

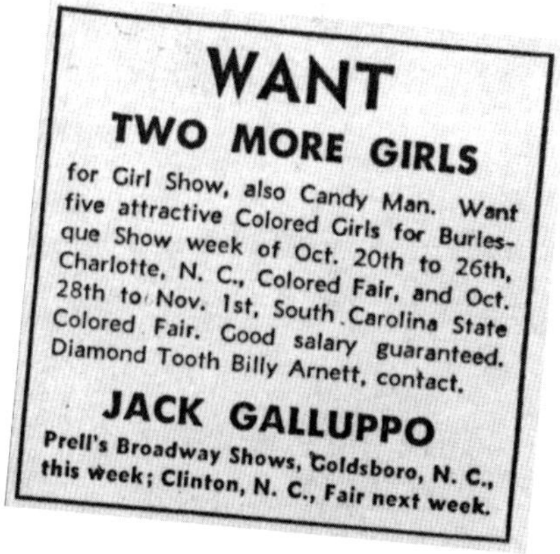
WANT
TWO MORE GIRLS
for Girl Show, also Candy Man. Want five attractive Colored Girls for Burlesque Show week of Oct. 20th to 26th, Charlotte, N. C., Colored Fair, and Oct. 28th to Nov. 1st, South Carolina State Colored Fair. Good salary guaranteed. Diamond Tooth Billy Arnett, contact.
JACK GALLUPPO
Prell's Broadway Shows, Goldsboro, N. C., this week; Clinton, N. C., Fair next week.

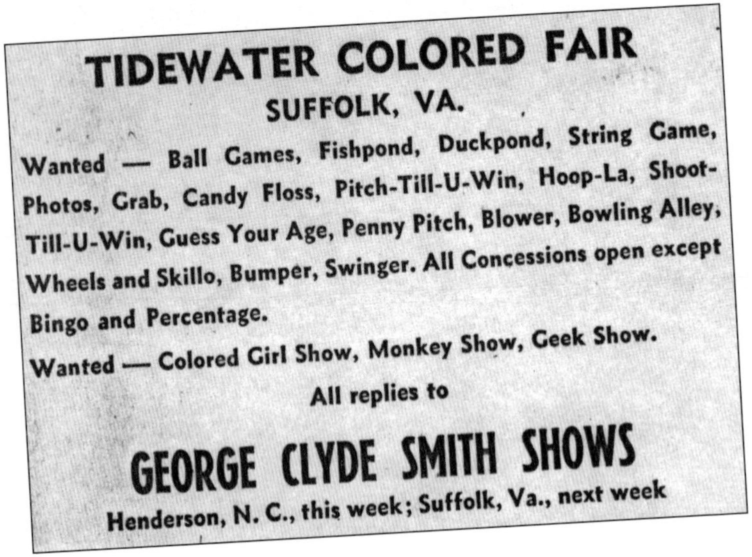
TIDEWATER COLORED FAIR
SUFFOLK, VA.
Wanted — Ball Games, Fishpond, Duckpond, String Game, Photos, Grab, Candy Floss, Pitch-Till-U-Win, Hoop-La, Shoot-Till-U-Win, Guess Your Age, Penny Pitch, Blower, Bowling Alley, Wheels and Skillo, Bumper, Swinger. All Concessions open except Bingo and Percentage.
Wanted — Colored Girl Show, Monkey Show, Geek Show.
All replies to
GEORGE CLYDE SMITH SHOWS
Henderson, N. C., this week; Suffolk, Va., next week

Lucky Orr, one of the last producers of black revues and girl shows on carnivals, says she found the term "jig show" offensive, while Verna Mae Smith, a long-time dancer on Leon Claxton's Black Revue on Royal American, says simply, "'Jig show' — was what the carnival people always said."

Blacks remained segregated on the show train and in the cookhouse of most of the larger circuses. Circus, carnival, and theatrical people were marginal at best in the eyes of town people — circus owners didn't need the color issue causing additional troubles. On rail carnivals, blacks usually slept in segregated coaches, but ate and went where they wanted on the lot.

Southern segregation greatly affected carnivals at fair time. Some of the biggest Southern fairs excluded blacks except on "Black Day," which they sometimes tried to dress up by calling it "Negro Achievement Day." On these days, fair boards expected the white girl show to be closed, but most girl show operators kept working by hiring all black musicians, performers, and dancers.

There were also exclusively black fairs in the South. A 1921 issue of *Billboard* reported 46 such fairs: "The colored fair proved to be the salvation of several carnival companies during the summer and fall." Often the black fairs took place the week after the regular fair, and many of the independent shows, concessions, and midway companies played both. In addition to the major carnivals that played these fairs were a handful of independent black carnies with shows, rides, and concessions playing black fairs exclusively.

In August 1964, *Amusement Business* reported that, as the fair season approached, many showmen were nervous about the new Civil Rights Act of 1964. At their conventions, fairs failed to deal with the issue, and a situation remained where there were fairs restricted to white-only patronage, fairs that had a special day for blacks, fairs that had been integrated for years without trouble, and fairs that were slowly lowering racial barriers. By 1963, some fairs were boycotted by black groups. Fire departments that hosed blacks during segregation demonstrations and marches saw blacks boycott their carnivals and fundraisers.

Alvin Cube, the talker for Lucky Orr's black revue on Gooding Amusements, told me about the problems they had during the integration of the 1960s: "One of the nights of the Nashville fair, we had a bomb threat. Someone phoned the fair board office and said they had placed a bomb inside the New Orleans show tent. We quickly cleared everybody out of the tent and told them if they came back tomorrow night and said they had been at the show that was canceled we would let them in free. Of course, the next night there were 1,000 instead of the 400 or 500 that said they were at the canceled show."

Verna Mae Smith remembers that "before segregation, Royal went into the Tupelo, Miss., fair one season. The fair had the original Confederate flag up on the front gate and

On World of Mirth the crew from Lucky Orr and Dave Wiles' Gay New Orleans Show "jungle up" in one of the wagons. That's an outdoor show term for everyone throwing in some money, someone going to the grocery store, and everyone helping to make a meal.

Charlie Taylor's Club Ebony bally at the Toronto C.N.E. draws in the crowds. Besides the Kit Kats, the show featured Tommy Hodges, a one-leg dancer, seen here on crutches on the bally. Taylor produced many black revues on Canadian midways.

Sedlmayr Sr. asked them to remove it, as it was an insult to us. They didn't, and the show didn't go back in there. The year of all the race riots when we played Jacksonville, Fla., we had to have police protection from the show train to the lot."

The Tampa fair was held in February while both the white and black revue shows on Royal American were preparing their new productions, so Tampa patrons always saw the previous year's show. Claxton would call the acts in for this ten-day run, then many would take jobs in the cigar factories or in clubs in St. Petersburg until rehearsals for the next season started a couple of months later. In April, Claxton would rent a bus and the show would play its way up to Royal's opening in St. Louis, visiting clubs in Jacksonville, Atlanta, and Memphis.

"On this one trip," recalls Verna Mae Smith, "we pulled into this bus depot in a Florida city to eat. There was a little cubby-hole restaurant in there run by this lady with about eight kids and none of them had shoes on. We had to go and sit in the back and she wouldn't come back and wait on us. Claxton was on the bus waiting for us, and he had a short temper. He finally came in to see what was taking so long. We told him she wouldn't serve us and he put a cussing on them people. Then he walked up to her and peeled off two $100 bills from his bank roll and said to her: 'Buy your babies some shoes!' Then he told us to get back on the bus."

Over the years, there have been some excellent black revue operators. Irvin C. Miller had made a name for himself as a producer of black tab shows — a form of

Singer Faye Adams, featured in this poster, had the first big rock'n'roll hit titled "Shake a Hand." Lucky and Dave Wiles featured her in their carnival show for one season.

condensed musical comedy — and his troupes had been in early black movies. One of his earliest productions was a 1921 tab troupe he called Chocolate Brown. Mainly a theater show producer, he put a unit of his famous Brown Skin Models on the James E. Strates Shows for several seasons starting in 1948. Verna Mae Smith, who danced in his shows and Claxton's, says, "Irvin C. Miller believed in very light-skinned girls. I am not what you say 'black,' but I was the darkest girl in his line. I wouldn't have got the job if I couldn't have danced good. On Leon's show, if he had a lot of light-skinned girls, then the dark-skinned girl would be the soubrette and in the middle of the line, or if there were more dark-skinned girls in the chorus, then he would make the light-skinned girl the soubrette. The soubrette would be the lead dancer."

Canadians were familiar with black revues produced by veteran Charlie Taylor and his wife, Vivian. Their daughter Audrey Jane was a feature dancer on their shows. Taylor had produced shows for Conklin at the C.N.E. in Toronto, but his best-known revues were a fixture for many seasons on Jimmy Sullivan's World's Finest Shows playing the western Canadian B circuit and all the big Quebec and Ontario fairs. In 1961, Taylor had four units out, featuring what Taylor called "the finest in sepia entertainment." Taylor put on one of his last big revues in 1965 for Quebec carnival owner Jules Racine. Charlie ended up as a doorman in Las Vegas.

When segregation ended in the 1960s, Southern fairs dropped their special days for black attendance. By that time, the big black revue shows were fading from the midways — and the white girl show was not far behind them. Some white girl show operators started featuring both white and black strippers in their shows — carnies called them "salt and pepper shows."

I found Lucky Orr in North Carolina. She spread a half-dozen photo albums out on her coffee table and told me how she got into the black revue business. "I met Dave Wiles in the early '40s when he came through Tarrsboro, N.C., with Winstead's Mighty Minstrels," she begins. "The 'jitterbug' was hot. In town we had a character named Hot Pappa Sharpe who was a good dancer, and he took me to this show. Dave was married at the time. He was originally from Jackson, Miss., but was living in Detroit. His first carnival experience was working for Irvin C. Miller's Brown Skin Models on the James E. Strates Shows. Dave separated from his wife and in 1948 managed the black revue produced by S.H. Dudley on Frank Bergen's World of Mirth Shows. That's when we got together. The help all liked me and called me 'Mom.' I loaned them money for car payments and made sure they sent money home to their families."

By 1959, Dave Wiles' Gay New Orleans show had opened its tenth season on World

Above: Lucky Orr, with exotic Lovi Lovi to her left, talks to her show girls before showtime.

Talker Al Cube holds the tip on Lucky and Curtis Orr's Gay New Orleans revue on the Gooding Million Dollar Midway Shows. Lucky was the last big producer of both black revues and girl shows on American carnival midways.

of Mirth at New Brunswick, N.J. The show, which had been playing clubs and theaters, featured recording artist Maybelle Hunter and a band under the direction of Joe Bradley. The show also had a six-girl chorus line, the exotic Sajja, drag performer Princess Ernestine, and comics Lucky Berry and Bob Davis.

Besides Maybelle Hunter, Lucky Orr and Dave had some big names on their shows. One year they featured Faye Adams, who had a big hit with the song "Shake a Hand."

"We featured her name heavy on the show and bally, and people would say, 'If Faye Adams is not in there, we are going to come out and beat your ass,'" recalls Lucky with a laugh. "Well, she was in there."

In 1960, Dave and Lucky left World of Mirth and went over to Gooding Amusements' main unit. They ran the black revue there and later the girl revue. Wiles died in 1964, and two years later, Lucky married New York newspaperman Curtis Orr. He went on the road with her each summer and helped on the revue. Curtis died in 1993.

Alvin Cube says, "Nashville was one of the big spots when Lucky was with Gooding. One Monday, we had a $7,000 night, which was big — really big for me, as I was getting 10 percent as the talker. Columbus, Ga., was another big spot for

One of Lucky's revues featuring 300-pound rhythm and blues shouter Agnes from Jacksonville, Fla. In the wintertime Lucky toured nightclubs and played burlesque theaters with her shows. Each spring a new show was put together in her backyard in New Jersey.

the rock'n'roll show. All day long it looked like a tar pit out there in front of the show. The black people just kept filling up one show after another without us ballying. We just kept selling tickets and giving shows."

I asked Lucky why she was so successful with her revues. "We always carried young musicians and played what was hot on the charts," she says. "We gave a 40-minute show and we didn't cut it. If you gave too short a show you got complaints, and I didn't like complaints! The chorus girls opened the show, then the comics came out, then my feature stripper, followed by the chorus line. And we always had a strong novelty or acrobatic dance number in the show. One year, we had the Jubilaires out of St. Louis. For many seasons, my feature stripper was Lovie Thomas, who worked as Lovi Lovi.

"I had people offering me year-round work in clubs and theaters. One season I put a show on Broadway for Sherman Dudley and was offered work in Europe. I had played burlesque houses with my revue in New York City for Leroy Griffith, but I could make more money on Gooding Amusements."

By the 1950s even black revue shows had to have an exotic star. Sijah was featured one season on Lucky's carnival revue.

In retirement, she misses the road and the action back in New York — Lucky is a city gal. To keep her hand in things, she hosts card games several nights a week. A small building behind her home still holds all her show costumes, just in case she gets a chance to go back on the road.

The Midnight Ramble Show was a special red, hot, and blue show put on the last show of the last night the black revue was in town. Seasoned midway-goers knew what to expect on Leon Claxton's Harlem in Havana.

"Oh yeah! It was different from the regular show," says choreographer and feature dancer Shirley Bates. "The costumes were more abbreviated with see-through mesh, and the comic routines were more risqué. They sold tickets to it all week and it would be jammed inside the tent. When I was over there in the 1940s, there were no strippers in the show. That wasn't allowed."

By the time Verna Mae Smith, known on the show as Burnside, joined the show in the late '40s, things had changed. Says Smith, "We had two shows with complete new wardrobe and routines for each one. The regular one was for anybody, where

The Kit Kats, a veteran acrobatic dance duo, are seen here performing in one of Claxton's productions.

children could come in. No one under a certain age could get into the ramble. Leon paid off to do the ramble and it didn't work in every city on the route. It worked up in Canada and was especially big in Winnipeg. It also worked in Tampa, Memphis, and St. Louis. The ticket price went up because there was nudity. The end of the show was a stripper — that was me." On a show like Claxton's Harlem in Havana, which played the same towns every season, the Midnight Ramble left the faithful counting the months until the show returned.

But besides the brief flashes of female flesh, audiences flocked to the shows to see first-class black singers, dancers, and musicians. Major black performers — including comic duo Butter Beans and Susie, comedians Al "Fats" Jackson and Sugar Dap Willy, and rock legend Little Richard — appeared on black carnival revues over the course of their careers. Claxton's Harlem in Havana shows of the 1950s featured a one-legged dancer named Clayton "Pigleg" Bates. In his mid-40s and weighing 182 pounds, Bates had one leg and a peg and did intricate dance routines and tap-dancing. "I don't want to dance only as good as a person with two legs," he told a newspaper reporter, "I want to dance better."

Bates grew up in a Southern cotton-farming village. At 12, during World War I, he started working in a cotton gin. One day the lights went out, and he fell into an auger, losing his left leg and two fingers. A good athlete before the accident, Bates went back to school on crutches and was determined to dance, swim, and play sports again. By his teens, he was appearing at theaters, carnivals, and minstrel shows with his dance act. In 1928 he starred in a Broadway musical with Bill "Bojangles" Robinson. He toured in Europe for several years, then returned to the U.S and bought a 65-acre resort in the Catskills.

While performers like Bates captivated audiences, the real star of any carnival show was the talker out front who got those audiences inside the tent. My favorite talker was a gentleman named Milty Levine, a pen pitchman out of Coney Island who turned the tip on Tony Mason's 1960s Coppertone Revue for many seasons. Near the end of the evening, Milty didn't waste words. He would cut the soul band off in mid-tune, turn to the tip, and say in his raspy Brooklyn-accented voice, "Enough of that shit — let's bring out the broads!"

Banner painter Johnny Meah, who was also once a jig show talker, relates a story

Gwen and Leon Claxton on the stage of their revue on RAS in the 1940s. All advertising said "Leon Claxton presents," but Gwen, a former show girl, helped produce the show and worked very hard to raise a family of three kids on the road.

The "lip" worn by black comedians came out of the minstrel era, but remained with many of them into the 1950s. Two such old timers are seen here doing their routine on Claxton's show.

Big band and chorus line production numbers made up the bulk of Claxton's shows. Talented black recording groups, lady blues singers, exotic striptease stars, and the best tap and acrobatic dancers that could be found were also included in the mix.

about his experiences on the bally: "I was taught a jig show opening by one of the best talkers of jig shows. In his opening, he would step down the steps from the bally into the tip. He would point back at the entertainers and say, 'These people are negroes. They are black and they are the best performers in the world.' Joe Sciortino had his jig show at the Michigan State Fair and that's where I first talked on a jig show. I went down on the steps of the bally and looked into the tip of mostly black faces. Pointing back at our performers, I repeated the old-time talker's words: 'These people behind me are negroes.

They are black. . . .' Before I could get the last part out, this big black guy looks up from the tip and yells at me, 'No shit!'"

Leon Claxton was one of the top producers of sit-down revues under canvas on carnivals. He was born in Memphis, where his father was a drummer. When Leon was very young, the family moved to Chicago. He grew up around music but didn't go past tenth grade in school. As a teenager he was a workman on the Ringling Brothers Barnum and Bailey Circus. Someone there taught him to be a contortionist. Verna Mae Smith describes Claxton's act: "He was his own emcee. He would do his steps and flips, and each time he came out to introduce a number in the show, he had on a complete change of wardrobe from head to toe. His wife, Gwen, would have the next set of wardrobe waiting for him in the dressing room."

The first mention in *Billboard* of Claxton's acrobatic dance act is for the Get Happy show on the 1928 Nat Reiss Carnival. In 1929, he was the stage manager for the minstrel show on the Melville-Reiss Shows, and in 1933 he was engaged by Duke Mills to produce the Show Boat revue at the Chicago Century of Progress Fair. Carl Sedlmayr saw the show and told Leon he would be pleased to have him produce the black revue on Royal American Shows the next season. He and Mills split up, and Claxton became the stage manager for Sedlmayr's black revue mid-season. Next year, as producer, Claxton developed his show into the premier black revue on carnival midways. The show remained with Royal for over three decades.

Claxton was first married to a showgirl named Ruby, one of whose friends was a dancer out of Kansas City named Gwendolyn Bates. Gwendolyn came on the show with her older sister Delores, and later with her younger sister Shirley. Things didn't work out for Ruby and Leon, and in 1939 Leon married Gwendolyn in Saskatoon while Royal was playing the fair there. She became a key part of Leon's show.

A 1957 *Color* article on the couple described Gwen's day. She started early in the morning on the show train, getting their three kids fed and dressed before doing the grocery shopping for the meals to feed their 40-member troupe on the lot. Back on the show train, she got lunch for the family and then worked in her office on the lot until show time. She handled the payroll and professional deductions, taxes,

Al "Fats" Jackson working on Claxton's stage the year before he died. Besides his comic routines, Al rolled his eyes à la Eddie Cantor and did a song and dance take off of Al Jolson.

As Claxton's show moved along with hot roll'n'roll and Caribbean music into the 1960s, the Harlemites' costumes grew sexier as well. Band leaders Jinx Simon, Bill Harvey, and Henry Raymond recruited the best musicians out of Memphis, Chicago, and St. Louis to keep the band jumpin'.

and social security, as well as advancing employees money and auditing the concessions revenue from the previous day's candy pitch, program sales, and drink sales. Then she'd check out the show receipts before putting on her makeup and wardrobe for the opening number. Between shows, she fed her kids supper. Her day ended around 2 a.m. when she prepared a snack for herself and Leon on the show train.

Color said she got her biggest laugh from Leon's remarks, like: "Honey, next year you won't have to work!" In Tampa during the winter, Gwen kept busy working for black charities and helping to get the new show produced and costumed. When she did find some time to herself, she went fishing.

Gwen's sister Shirley was a modest person. A top dancer and entertainer, she appeared in an opening act for Sammy Davis Jr.'s show in Las Vegas. Shirley has fond memories of working on Claxton's show: "They would take a month or so to rehearse the new show in Tampa. For a while I did the choreography and then Leon hired different ones to do it. He had three different choreographers. When I was there, the choreographer was from Detroit. Then I learned how to do it. He also had a Cuban guy who was very good. He had the know-how and the overall picture of how it would look. Gwen and I would do the steps. You had mostly the same chorus girls coming back with maybe only two or three new girls each season."

Asked about the music, Shirley says, "Basically the dancers would get the type of music they wanted for the dance numbers and the musicians would arrange it and write up the score. They stayed up on current dances and music. That was Claxton's thing. The show was designed to show off the acts like in a nightclub.

"He had comics," she adds, "but as the years went by, he cut down on them. He used to have a couple of guys who worked in blackface, but he cut that too. Then he just had a single comedian and no comedy teams."

Claxton and other black producers of his era ran a tight ship based on the fine system. You had to look sharp and always be on time. He fined his employees for wardrobe violations and for breaking any rules he set down. Claxton wasn't the only operator who got tough. Peter Garey, who had talked on the front of Dave Wiles' revue on World of Mirth, says that on payday "some of the entertainers didn't have much in their pay envelope because Dave had fined them 50 cents here and a quarter there." To keep employees from leaving before the season closed, many operators held back two weeks' pay and didn't pony up extra money earned around shows until employees finished the season. For blacks, the practice was even harder to tolerate, as they had fewer places to go if they quit.

But Verna Mae Smith speaks with admiration about Claxton's reputation as a stern employer: "He would have a meeting about once a month if things got a little rough. He had 50 people over there and we were living and eating together and we were all young. He had rules. How your wardrobe looked. How you looked when you walked down the street. He was very strict on those things, and it took all of that to make it such a terrific show. To all the boys and girls that had been good all season, he handed out diamond rings and watches."

Verna Mae had toured with Irvin C. Miller's Brown Skin Models and had seen Rabbit Foot and other black tent shows by the time she came over to Claxton's show as a teenager. "When I went there," she remembers, "I didn't expect it to be as good as it was! I enjoyed every bit of it. You didn't go downtown at night and get drunk around Claxton. You better be well-dressed when you got off that show train. That's the way Claxton wanted you to be. He taught me a lot of things my mama didn't tell me about. A lot of the girls, it was their first time away from home. He taught us about pimps and everything. Some girls didn't listen and the pimps stole them off the show and ruined their lives. But I listened."

In the end, Leon grew tired of the deteriorating help situation on shows. Lamenting that he couldn't find chorus girls and talented performers, he told newspaper reporter Gene Telpner in the 1960s, "Talent? You can't even hire anyone to take out the garbage because nobody wants to work anymore. Years ago, kids used to run away from home to go with the carnival. Now I guess they just go to love-ins and become hippies." Claxton died in 1967 at age 64. The revue closed before the season ended.

Leon Claxton was proud of being black, and along the route he was active in putting on special benefits for black hospitals, orphanages, and handicapped children. He left an impact on those who worked with him and especially those who were entertained by him.

EMPF'S MODEL
THE WORK OF A YOUTH
5 YEARS TO BUILD
FAMOUS INVENTION
ON EXHIBITION
A PERFECT
AN INTERESTING STUDY IN ART SCIENCE
TICKET OFFICE

A SMALL, SMALL WORLD

Mechanical and Miniature Shows

Miniatures have always held a kind of fascination. Today people fill their leisure time with miniatures-related hobbies that can range from building model train layouts to putting up elaborate doll houses with electric lights and running water. Families still gather in European cities to watch clocks that parade out a miniature army on the hour. People collect miniature houses from various countries and elaborate Christmas scenes that can be augmented each year with another limited-edition piece.

Miniature shows run by clockwork have been on display in England since the late 1600s. In 1709, German artist Jacobus Morian invented and introduced to Londoners a moving or mechanical picture show — a frame enclosed a painted backdrop in front of which cut-out shapes of animals

Opposite: Kempf's Model City as it was first presented at street fairs and celebrations in the early 1900s. Note the snap-together banners that could be used anywhere and the bannerline of nailed-up lumber to support them. A fellow playing the guitar provides the noise to attract the tip.

Chapter 13

Bergmann's Swiss Alpine Village was built between 1850 and 1867 in Switzerland. Barnum acquired it in 1872 and exhibited it in his museum. The last owner was Jacob J. Summerfield who displayed it at the 1884 Mechanics Exposition in San Francisco, Calif. He was from Lansing, Mich., and that's where the Kempfs found it in 1916. It had been badly damaged by the Grand River flood in 1907.

and people were moved by hidden clockworks. The figures performed repeated motions in one place, or traveled across the frame opening.

The same year fair, booth showman William Pinkethman was presenting a show with over 100 one-foot-high figures. From 1717 to 1724 he toured a show he called "a musical picture" — a mechanical scene in a cabinet. Competition at the same game came from clockmakers Christopher Pinchbeck and his son. Besides making clocks, they made barrel organs and presented mechanical shows at various London fairs. By 1742, Pinchbeck's son had combined the little mechanical scenes with organ music — in a show he called the Panopticon. Soon such mechanical showmen were presenting battles and sieges at fairs and other venues.

In 1741, Henry Temple built the Microcosm, or the World in Miniature, which had 1,200 wheels and pinions to move the displays. He toured England, Europe, and English America with it for over 40 years. In 1776, Henri-Louis Jaquet-Droz, a member of a famous Swiss clockworks family, presented in London a "spectacle mécanique" in which miniature figures enacted various scenes. Droz also displayed three large automaton figures. In 1789, a show presented at St. Bartholomew Fair consisted of puppets, conjuring tricks, and a miniature opera, ending with the exhibition of a musical clock in which 900 figures were shown working at various trades. The automaton was a big success in Europe, and is still seen today on the European fairgrounds in both its original form and its modern equivalent. The new versions include three- story-high monsters and figures that gyrate, gesture, and talk to the crowd, beckoning customers into dark rides and fun houses.

The village and the busy city were the main themes of many of the early miniature shows on carnivals. In 1885, H.G.

Cooke, a pioneer miniature showman out of Warsaw, Ill., toured a model called the Great Electric City of Jerusalem, which he touted as being one of the "finest automatic or electric wonders" of the world. Cooke had recently spent ten weeks at the Great Chicago Museum and five weeks at Broadway and Trevor's Museum in St. Louis. He was still going on carnivals in the early 1900s with his City of Jerusalem behind a carved gold front.

Other early model exhibits depicted coal mines. Popular in Europe, these showed a cross-section of mining operations including all the underground tunnels, somewhat like an ant farm. One model in Germany was even accompanied by thumbs of former miners in jars — in desperation, some men had cut off their thumbs so they would be unable to hold a pick or shovel, making them unemployable underground.

Miners have created miniature mine scenes, just as sailors have built ship models. The miner's folk art consisted of small mines and grottos built from metals and crystals found underground. Disabled miners often constructed the exhibits used by showmen; the miniature mine was built into a box with doors on one side and straps on the back for carrying on the showman's back. Early photos of these models show them exhibited out in the open, where the exhibitor either collected a fee before he started his mine demonstration or passed the hat around afterward.

One earlier supplier of model shows to showmen was Chas Hood, working in Cambridge, Mass. While early mechanical shows were hand-cranked, in 1900, Hood offered one that depicted a Battle Between the Boers and the English that could be converted to motor power if the showman so desired. In 1904, he had four ready to go — including mechanical shows depicting scenes of the Baltimore Fire and the Russian-Japanese War — for $125.

During and after World War I, the midway saw many models of the war on display. A model called Europa, consisting of miniature battle scenes and art reproductions of the war, trouped on the Great Patterson Shows from 1915 through 1917. It was run by a man who sold the tickets and did the talking while his wife did the lecturing.

Bruce and Irving's model showing a streetscape that included the Opera House with five different vaudeville acts rotating on the theater stage in miniature. Streetcars ran on electrified tracks and all the building interiors were lit up.

I saw this small Alpine Village at the Toronto CNE when I was a teenager. It was built into an old-time European show wagon. You entered one door, walked around three sides of the display, and exited out the other door. It was owned by Hy and Willi Stein and in the 1950s was on the Strates midway for several seasons.

The other hot miniature show of the era was the Panama Canal Show, which covered about five acres at the Panama Pacific International Exposition held in San Francisco in 1915. A moving platform transported visitors slowly around the canal, which was sunk down about 20 feet so everyone had a bird's-eye view of it. Telephones hooked up to phonographs provided the lecture for the 20-minute show.

Carl La Dare was an early builder and exhibitor of Panama Canal shows on midways. His were compact shows, but the lecture took the visitor through the entire Canal Zone with scenery and working locks. This was a time when travel was not affordable for the average person, so such shows made an impact on the public, allowing them to "travel" for just a dime or so. In the 1920s, La Dare built a huge miniature-ship exhibit for the C.A. Wortham shows that had to be hauled by four 20-foot wagons. The front was made up of a series of lighthouses with revolving beacons. Inside, ships and subs provided the show in a 100-by-40-foot tank.

The biggest name in the model show business in the early part of the 20th century was that of the Kempf family, who came from the village of Lich in Germany's Black Forest region. Jacob Kempf arrived in

America in 1850 when he was 21 years old and settled in the German community of Sherbogan, Wisc. Jacob and his wife had 11 kids. One son, John, a bootmaker by trade, ended up in Imlay City and the Capac, Mich., area, where he married a local schoolteacher. They had four children: Fred, Bruce, Irving, and Hazel.

While Fred was in high school, he started building a miniature city. Within a few years, his father loaned him enough money to rent a tent and exhibit it at the fair in Imlay City. Everything in Fred's small city moved. The elevator in one of the model buildings worked, and even the theater curtain in the opera house raised to show six animated acts. At 10 cents admission, it was a big hit, and made Fred a lot of money. He took it to the state fair in Detroit and from there he started booking it on carnivals.

Fred's brothers Bruce and Irving joined him on the tours. They spent the summers with a carnival company, while during the winters they exhibited the model city in large department stores like Hudson's in Detroit and Marshall-Fields in Chicago. Stores paid the Kempfs a flat fee to bring the model city in, and they usually set it up in their auditorium or in a vacant upstairs room. Customers who

Above: Fred Kempf building his mini city in 1902 behind the family house in Capac, Mich.

The first busy city that Fred Kempf built with the mountain at one end to hide the motors, gears, and pulleys that automated the whole set-up. A small amusement park is located halfway along, behind the church.

purchased something from the store were given a free ticket to see the village. This was a popular promotion. The village toured in the U.S., Canada, England, and Holland, and in other European countries.

In November 1915, while touring with the Con. T. Kennedy Shows, both Fred and his wife Blanche were killed in a train wreck. The report of the accident in *Billboard* said the Kennedy Shows had completed a profitable week in Atlanta and were en route to Columbus, Ga., around 1:40 p.m. when a passenger train hit the show train head-on about eight miles from its destination. The collision occurred on a sharp curve where both trains were doing about 30 miles an hour. The engineers leaped from their trains before the collision and were only slightly shaken up.

Nine flat cars from the show piled up on top of one another and the hot coals thrown from the locomotives quickly set show fronts and canvas on fire. The debris was piled up 30 feet high and 100 feet in radius. Kempf's truck had been on the first flat car after the engine on the show train, and Fred and Blanche wound up at the bottom of the debris. Before the crash, Fred had managed to throw their daughter Hazel Helen clear and she survived. Five other showmen and one woman were

This is Fred Kempf's truck loaded on a carnival show train flat car. Fred, his wife, and their daughter Hazel lived in the first small portion of the truck. The truck was parked perpendicular to the midway and the two sides and end opened up so patrons could see the miniature city on three sides.

Hazel Helen Kempf standing beside her parents' headstone in the Imlay City cemetery. They were killed in the 1915 Con. T. Kennedy Shows train wreck that demolished their exhibition truck. The railroad later paid out $30,000 to the Kempf family.

killed in the accident, and three dozen people were injured. Manager Walter Stanley led a crew of show people who pushed the rest of the show train back down the track away from the fire.

The first Kempf Model Village was completely destroyed, and it took Bruce and Irving three or four years to build another. In the meantime, they were eager to get back touring, and for several years followed leads on P.T. Barnum's Swiss Village. In 1916, they located it in Lansing, Mich., and acquired the Swiss Village for mere shipping fees. Hazel Helen recalled it was in pieces and her uncles brought it into the house in boxes and baskets. While they built their new village, they worked on the Swiss Village and added electricity to it.

This Swiss Village of Barnum fame was 14 feet long, nine feet eight inches tall, and seven feet four inches deep. It had 43 moving figures and depicted life in an Alpine village, from the beer-garden drinkers to the shoemaker. It had been carved from spruce wood by a Swiss watchmaker named Joseph Bergmann who started it in 1850 and finished in 1867. The village was first displayed publicly at the Paris Exposition and then toured in Europe. It was on display at the Crystal Palace Exposition in London in 1871, the year

Above: By 1916, Fred's brothers Bruce and Irving had built an even bigger model city and toured on carnivals with a nice show organ on the front. Note the searchlight for the nighttime bally inside the wagon that holds the organ.

The new Kempf Model City that Bruce and Irving built from 1916 to 1921. The village was built so that one half of the traveling case hinged down and the other portion pushed up and was supported by rods. Inside the tent a railing kept patrons from touching the model.

Bruce Kempf met his wife Dorothy on the midway where she was a feature rider on Will Jones' motordrome. After they were married she worked as a "Human Mannequin." Here she is doing her act in front of the model village at Meridian, Miss., in 1923 billed as Dollie Dot. In the wintertime she did her act in large department store windows.

Bergmann died. An agent for Barnum bought it for $30,000 and shipped it to America, where Barnum displayed it in his New York museum and then toured it. In 1876, it grossed $100,000 at the Philadelphia Centennial Exposition. After 1883, it was sold and resold many times.

In 1921, the Kempfs were touring both the restored Alpine Village and their new Model City. The Model City was built to one-eighth scale and could be stretched out for 40 feet. It had over 17,000 working parts including cars and trucks moving on the streets, bridges lifting to allow ships into the harbor, and trains pulling into the station. The Kempfs opened on Dodson's World Fair Shows, then went over to C.A. Wortham. They played the CNE in Toronto and at Christmastime were in the Sanger Bros. department store in Dallas, Tex. In 1924, they acquired a 56-key German Gebruder organ that they carried on a 14-foot wagon. For a short time they had this $9,500 organ with 14 working figures as part of their inside show. In 1925, they rebuilt the organ to play Wurlitzer band organ rolls, using it on the front of their show to attract patrons. The show now had a five-banner front and was under a 28-by-24-foot khaki tent.

The Kempfs toured with various midways, including Morris and Castle, Wortham, Johnny J. Jones, Rubin and Cherry, and Conklin. Tiring of the road, they focused on playing amusement parks. The Kempfs quit touring their show in the early 1940s, and their Model Village was stored away in the shed behind the family barn where it was first built. Bruce Kempf died in 1964 at the age of 78. Irving died two years later at 77, and shortly after that the model village was sold.

When niece Hazel Helen found the village again, it had been in storage for 20 years. She bought it for $60,000 and it is now on display at the Capac Historical Society Museum. In the fall of 2000, the museum put up a new building to properly display this historic piece of Americana.

One subject that was often modeled in miniature was the circus. An 1892 *Clipper* carried an ad in which a sideshowman, juggler, and jewelry worker offered for sale a miniature circus he had toured. It was three by six feet and described as "Lifelike with everything moving and suitable for museum or sideshow." And in the 1920s, half-man Johnny Eck and his brother made a beautiful model of a carnival that they set up while they were on the road in whatever sideshow they were working in.

The building of model circuses grew into a hobby in the 1940s, aided by several articles in craftsmen's magazines. But, as an attraction it was not big on the fairgrounds. Why look at something that has been shrunk when you can see the real thing only feet away? Still, the odd one was out there. In the mid-1950s, Harry K. Smythe of Angola, Ind., toured his half-inch scale model Ring Bros. Circus inside a school bus, boasting that it had 5,000 moving parts. In 1959, Harley Barber had his miniature circus on King Reid Shows in a 40-foot semi-trailer. This model, along with Bill Hall's complete miniature of the World of Mirth Shows, were two of the last miniature reproductions of circuses and carnivals seen on the midway.

In the 1950s, there were several prominent miniature showmen. One was Dick Dillon from Youngstown, Ohio. Dick had acquired a miniature village made in Denmark that consisted of 251 animated characters, 30,000 working parts, and 50 European scenes. He told people that the builder took eight years to carve it with a pocket knife. The show was on three large semi-trailers that were parking U-shape

Dick Dillon on the left shows film and radio star Bob Burns part of his miniature village display, which he had on the World of Mirth carnival in 1948.

with a tent over them, with a front made of wood carvings. In the winter, the show played southern shopping centers and northern sportsmen's shows.

Another showman of this era often found on midways was Earl B. Walsh with his Matchstick City, a model built from six million matches and 3,080 tubes of glue. It was 18 feet long and four feet high. In 1958, Walsh had two semi-trailer shows out. One trailer featured a Great Cathedral model that was 20 feet long and made of matchsticks, while the other held a 40-foot animated display of the Ten Commandments, also made of matchsticks. In 1959, the units played 36 fairs in 14 states. Walsh worked year-round at fairs, schools, and shopping centers.

In the 1970s, I saw a hand-carved show operated by the Port Colborne Lions Club at the Welland Fair in Ontario. The show originally belonged to French-Canadian woodcarver and showman Archélas Poulin (1891–1969). While he was working on a log drive, a load of logs had fallen on his

Thousands of matchsticks and gallons of white glue went into building this display, Earl B. Walsh's Great Cathedrals of the World, exhibited on the Cetlin and Wilson Shows midway at the 1958 Reading, Pa., fair.

This is a Kobel photo of Harry K. Smythe's Ring Bros. Circus carved in 1/2 inch to the foot scale. Smythe, from Angola, Indiana, had it on exhibition for many years in the 1950s; besides fairs, he claimed he could make $100 a day playing drive-in theaters and shopping malls.

The Canadian province of Quebec is famous for its wood carvers. Moise Potvin was born in Farnham, Quebec, in 1876 and was known for being a fine violin maker. His other passion was creating miniature scenes of life. He died in 1948 but then Ralph Delrae of Atlantic City Boardwalk Delrae Fudge fame exhibited Potvin's carvings for many years afterwards on a ding basis.

back and injured him. Poulin started carving the Stations of the Cross while he was in bed recovering from the accident, which left him crippled. He began exhibiting his work to raise money to live on, but in Boston, the carvings were stolen from his exhibition trailer. He returned to Canada and carved a new exhibit he called the Life of Man, and later, a huge dancehall scene, which became the last model you saw as you left his trailer. Poulin toured his exhibit from coast to coast and lived in it while on the road. The last time I saw the trailer, it was parked behind a barn outside of Hamilton, Ont., its doors open to the elements.

This is Archélas Poulin's exhibition truck as I last saw it parked behind a barn south of Hamilton, Ontario, in the early 1980s. He played fairs and city streets with his exhibit all over North America, often on the ding basis.

Model ships of all kinds have appeared on circuses and midways over the years. The Barnum and Bailey Circus in 1903 featured a miniature copy of the White Fleet. The display, exhibited free in the menagerie tent, contained models of every type of American warship, from submarines to enormous battleships. The 1903 courier — a promotional flyer — for the show described them as "Magnificent, Majestic, Modern Marine Machines and Monsters of Marvelous Might. Huge Leviathans that Belch Fire and Flame, Smoke and Shot. Now seen for the first time on land!"

In 1917, several submarine shows were on midways and appearing in *Billboard* for-sale ads. One was operated by Carl Reinhold of Revere, Mass. His submarine was displayed in a portable glass tank; it submerged and rose at the will of the lecturer. Another sub show presented by wireless expert John Baughman of Dorset, Ohio, had the boat maneuvering, sinking, firing cannons, blowing a whistle, and ringing bells. Operated by wireless, it was eight feet long and weighed 130 pounds. Baughman also had a show he called The Destruction of Germany, which boasted various wireless effects, including blowing up a warship and firing a cannon. In 1915, Tangley Mfg. Co. of Muscatine, Iowa, known for making calliopes, also produced a mechanical model show based on The Sinking of Lusitania.

Midway-goers gawked at various marine-themed shows, including deep-sea diving exhibits, dead whales, and live sharks, but they would never have witnessed anything like the ship show built by Conklin Shows in 1978.

The story starts with Sergei Sawchyn, one of North America's great show-business impresarios. His career has spanned from managing the Winnipeg Ballet to bringing the only performing panda bear out of China to North American circus audiences. "I was just reading an article in the *Weekend Magazine* one day about this guy who had built a model of the *Bismarck*," Sergei recalls. "The builder had put 10,000 hours of skill and work into it plus $4,000 of his money. I tracked down the builder, Paul Gresser, north of Toronto. The boat was in his garage and by this time he was a beaten-down man over it. He was a cabinet maker and had German navy exposure." Sergei thought this would make a great midway attraction, and approached Conklin with the idea.

"Jim Conklin paid all the bills," says Sergei. "Jim paid $57,000 for it. I paid nothing, other than all my energy, labor, and paying everyone in my office who was helping to put it all together." Jim Conklin's involvement with a show of any kind was unusual, for his father, Patty Conklin, was one of the first major carnies to abandon

Marine exhibits were a popular midway show in the first decades of the 20th century. The model ships used in the show are seen here on one side of C.W. Parker's carnivals.

the back end. But 1978 was an experimental year for Conklin Shows — they had been awarded the prestigious Western Class "A" fairs and were out to show that their midway was not only different management-wise, but looked like what the carnival of the 1980s should be. The game trailers were built to look like a Western town. A whole antique carnival was created and hauled along with the regular show on the route. "The whole thing came about with Jim Conklin wondering if shows couldn't be brought back to the midway again," Sergei says, "But in a different format and maybe of a better caliber than those he had been seeing."

Jim gave the go-ahead for Sergei's idea for a show based on Gresser's model of the *Bismarck* and work began. Sergei remembers being directed to a military club in downtown Toronto where someone gave him a blue leatherbound report filed in 1941 on the sinking of the *Bismarck*. It was marked "Classified Material — Property of her

The massive 80-feet-wide and 20-feet-high Conklin Shows Bismarck model battleship show was at the Toronto Canadian National Exhibition in August 1978. Sometimes shows are too good for the midway and people avoid them. This was the fate of the Bismarck show.

Paul Gresser's wonderful scale model of the Bismarck that was winched off the semi that carried the show front. Patrons walked around it on raised stairways and exited at the top of the show front down high stairs onto the midway.

Majesty's Navy." Sergei next contacted a navy museum in Massachusetts, who loaned the Conklin Shows some anti-aircraft guns and a 15-foot torpedo, which they would lay out in front of the show. Sergei then had local artist Jim Haines do some sketches for the layout of the front and an outline of what the show should look like.

The show was built on two 45-foot semi-trailers at Tony Lerno's shop in Princeton, Ont. One trailer had the front and held the boat, while the other housed all the signage, walkways, and additional exhibit material, along with a staff living area. The front opened up to 80 feet long and 20 feet high. Along the top were big metal can letters that spelled "BISMARCK."

The two trailers were parked parallel to each other with a space left in the middle. The boat was winched out on rollers from the front trailer and put in the central space. The main exhibit area was four feet off the ground. The viewer walked up steps to floor level in the front trailer and along walkways, seeing a complete reproduction of the boat's history on the wall. A detailed tape gave viewers the history of the boat — and of the model as well. The museum was double-decked, and the viewer exited from the top floor. Pat Power lectured on the exhibit, starting her spiel with: "The Bismarck appears exclusively for the Conklin Group of Associated Amusement Companies." Conklin leased it for the tour from Paul Gresser, who traveled with the show and lived in the crew quarters. Gresser had rebuilt the model for the road, adding a new deck and metal pieces on the guns. The model was almost 40 feet long. Dick Marvin painted the front, and the exhibit area was covered with a blue canvas top.

Problems developed early. The exhibit was late being framed and missed the opening of the show's western route starting at the Red River Exhibition in Winnipeg. If construction was slow, though, the publicity campaign wasn't. A special window card was printed and distributed. An elaborate program titled *Souvenir of the Fair — Bismarck* was printed for sale inside the show. Another sale item was a special 45 rpm record with Johnny Horton's hit "Sink the Bismarck" on one side and Conklin's large German band organ playing "The Gladiator's March" on the other. In case those items didn't get the extra coin inside the show, Jim Conklin installed a half-dozen nautical-themed arcade machines on the top deck that patrons had to pass when leaving.

The last detail worked out was the sound on the front. "Jim Conklin met this weird sound-effects artist somewhere in the States," recalls Sergei. "He put the sound together for it and did all the engineering. I wrote the script and produced it with a local Toronto actor doing the voiceover. It was done in stereo, and so as you walked past the front on the midway, these explosions from ship guns would follow you right along, traveling on the show-front speakers!"

But Sergei felt let down once the show went on tour: "Management seemed eager to have something different from the traditional midway offering, but in the end they just wanted another fun house or dark ride attraction that was all Day-Glo colors, flashing neon, and garish airbrush artwork. I assumed it would be located prominently on the midway, but instead it was never in the midway lineup. On the western circuit it languished on the independent midways, and at the CNE it was placed off the midway up near the Princes' Gates, where you normally found government displays and

local radio station mobile units. By the time the Bismarck reached the CNE, the aircraft guns had been 'red-lighted' — eliminated. It never made money and was taken off the road after Toronto."

Later, in fall 1978, Sergei got a phone call after midnight from someone at Conklin's winter quarters in Brantford, Ont. The caller's message was brief: "The *Bismarck*'s on fire!" The show had been soaked in gas and destroyed by an arsonist. The only thing salvaged was a few of the block letters that had spelled out "BISMARCK." Perhaps as a tribute to suckers everywhere, Conklin later used them to rename a Wild Mouse ride the "MARK-V."

THE MURDER OF
JESSE JAMES
GEO. W. ROLLINS PRESENTS SCOUT YOUNGER'S (BISON BILL)
ORIGINAL
LAW AND OUTLAW
A $65,000 ART PRODUCTION
THE OLD PRISC
AT FORT SMITH, AR

DOES CRIME PAY?

Gangster Death Cars and Electric Chairs

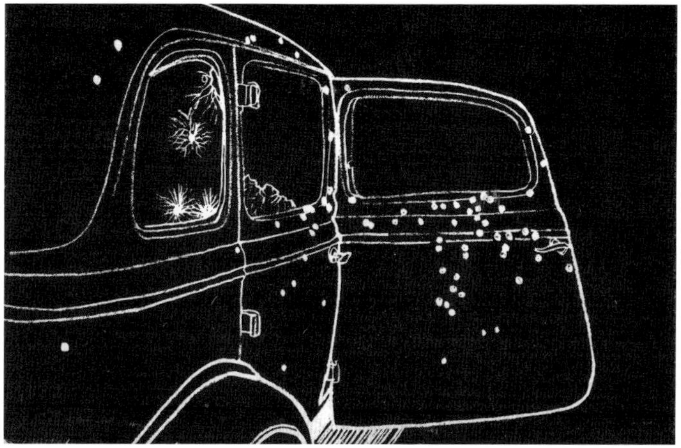

Early peep-show views featured battles, war carnage, and grisly crime scenes. The December 22, 1888, *Clipper* reported a direct link between American show business and crime exploitation. Vaude manager Fred Wilson surprised the amusement world with his patented electric act intended to portray an execution onstage. The act was to exactly emulate the first apparatus passed by one of the states to be put into operation in 1889. Showmen got the controversy they needed when Thomas Edison got involved in trying to decide which current, AC or DC, was best for frying human flesh. Continuing debates over capital punishment have made the electric chair a permanent prop in both crime shows and sideshows.

Americans were fascinated by tales of bandit shoot-outs, stagecoach robberies, and

Opposite: Geo. Rollins was an early wild animal showman on midways, but in the 1920s he turned to the Crime Does Not Pay show craze. Scout Younger was displaying these shows on midways and also building them for other showmen.

Chapter 14

A typical crime show on the midway. This one features a century of "public enemies in wax." Jesse James, Cole Younger, Bruno Hauptmann, and others who ran afoul of the law drew customers to these shows.

Indian massacres. In the 1880s, no bandits were more publicized than Jesse and Frank James and their cousins Cole and Jim Younger. The Bonheur Brothers were early showmen who cashed in on the James gang's notoriety. From 1880 on, the Bonheurs' lantern show portrayed Western life. The brothers carried cameras to get their own pictures and toured extensively in Missouri, often meeting and photographing the James gang. As the gang's infamy increased, the Bonheurs added their photos to the show, and after Jesse James was assassinated, the photos became even more valuable to their exhibit — they were said to be the reason the Bonheurs did over $10,000 in just Ohio and Indiana one season.

In 1903, Frank James and Cole Younger fronted the Cole Younger and Frank James Wild West Show, formerly Buckskin Bill's Wild West Show. Sen. Stephen Benton Elkins of West Virginia, one of the backers, had put up $20,000 to get Younger out of prison. Their friendship went back to the Civil War, where Younger had saved his life. Frank's performances included rescuing the stagecoach from Indian attack, and James claimed that at no time in the performance would the public witness unlawful acts. One stipulation in Cole's early release was that he was to not take part in any public exhibitions, so he limited himself to being the show's treasurer. The only tales of the outlaw's exploits were in Cole's book, sold on the show.

Many preachers and newspaper editors were outraged about the ex-bandits traveling and capitalizing on their crimes. Over 100 people had been killed by the James and Younger gangs, and there were lots of victims' relatives wanting revenge. Younger and James were said to be very suspicious of people, and paranoid that someone would shoot them. Both had frequent nightmares, and Frank often paced the floor in his train car at night wailing, "My God! Have pity on an old man." The show carried heavy grift, and disputes between the show managers closed it that fall.

When Frank wasn't an outlaw, he was a ham. He had acted in a dramatic show in

The lecturer leads the tip through a crime show with the wax criminals laid out in rows on one side of the tent, while the crime figures standing on the other side are held up by the reader boards explaining the life of the prone wax figures.

1901 and after his circus experiences ended, he went back to the stage in a 1904 play titled *The Fatal Star*. In 1908, Cole opened a Wild West show with Frank on board, but it too lasted only one season. For four years, Cole and partner Lew Nichols ran the Cole Younger and Nichols Theater Amusement Co. out of Lee's Summit, Mo. Cole died there March 21, 1916, at age 72.

The February 22, 1915, *Billboard* carried a story by Tom L. Wilson about the recent passing of Frank James. Wilson recalled being on the Dan B. Robinson Carnival Co. in 1911 at the fair in Miles, Ohio: "On the midway, we had as a feature on the show a show called *The James Brothers in Missouri*. It was a talking picture show. Word got to the carnival office that Frank James himself was the official starter of the horse races and that he was coming onto the midway as well. The Robinsons were afraid Frank might object, since the show depicted the James Brothers in a negative way because of their crime sprees. They wondered if Frank, angered by the show, might shoot up the place.

"At 4 o'clock," wrote Wilson, "Frank

The crime show lecturer helped to make the show of wax figures longer and more interesting for the tip and was also there to guard his charges. Hats, canes, fake guns, and rings were constantly being stolen off the dummies. Obviously the midway crowd hadn't paid much attention to the showman's banners stating "Crime Doesn't Pay"!

Ruth Snyder in the electric chair as modeled in wax and sold by B.W. Christophel from his St. Louis studio.

showed up at the ticket box of the show. He was short in stature, then middle-aged and graying, quiet and unassuming. He went in and sat down and watched the movie. When he came out, he asked permission of the talker to say a few words to the crowd that had gathered. He said: 'My friends, inside this top is a representation of myself, my brother Jesse, the Youngers, and our former gang of bad men, depicted true to life and nature. The pictures, the scenes are correct, and while looking at them I found food for thought and saddened reminiscences. I advise you all to go in and see them.' He turned and thanked the announcer and then quietly walked back to the judges' stand at the race track."

These early bandits also inspired midway showmen to put on crime shows they called Law and Outlaw shows. Showmen liked them because the wax or papier-mâché figures were light and easily boxed up for travel. The show could be worked on carnivals and in storefronts year-round. Best of all, the actors and actresses didn't eat or draw a salary. St. Louis wax sculptor W.H.J. Shaw, who specialized in making and selling wax outlaw shows from the 1890s on, called Jesse James the King of American Bandits. In 1903 *Billboard* ads, he offered showmen the latest wax figures, "the Union Bank Robbers," and offered a list of other bandits ready to ship. For a public curious about electrocutions, his 1915 *Billboard* ads offered crime showmen the life-size wax figure of murderous cop Charles Becker, with electric chair, death cap, battery, and wires for $50. For $20 more, you got the banner.

WANT SPONSOR FOR CRIME SHOW

Wife of one-time No. 1 bad man. Have played stage and carnival. Loads of newspaper clippings and magazine stories.

BOX D-385

BILLBOARD, CINCINNATI 22, OHIO

B.W. Christophel, also based in St. Louis, Mo., offered showmen wax figures starting in the mid-1920s. In 1935, he offered showmen several Public Enemy Wax Figure shows. The characters on his roster included John Dillinger, Pretty Boy Floyd, Baby Face Nelson, and Bonnie Parker. Showman R.E. Norman wrote Christophel in 1932, asking if he could make him a seated wax figure in an electric chair to mount on the front of his crime display truck. Christophel wrote, "I can provide a figure of Ruth Snyder, but she would have to be all made of papier-mâché as the wax would melt in the sun. I can make delivery in about 10 days after receiving order as the papier-mâché must be properly dried and seasoned. Would appreciate you placing order soon as possible to avoid the spring rush as many of the carnivals have their wax shows repaired and furnished shortly after they open."

For the cash-strapped showman, Chas. T. Buell out of Newark, Ohio, was offering walk-through peep shows in 1929 for as little as $125. His Under World, Great Chicago Gang War, and Prohibition King Killing shows came with 20 viewing boxes, 52 enlarged views on panels, plus the lecture. During the 1930s, Buell turned out a constant line of gangster shows with titles such as Gangland: Its Crimes and Punishments. This show was quite elaborate for a Buell peep show. It came with an electric chair and a big five-banner front, plus a dozen Verascopes and six of Buell's latest invention, the Buellscope. For the bargain price of $285, Buell threw in 36 glass frames containing over 100 crime photos.

Future carnival owner John Francis' Life in Sing Sing show on the 1915 C.A. Wortham Shows was called a new idea in pit shows. The old convict ship *Success* was doing big business the same season visiting Atlantic coastal cities from Boston to Norfolk. In San Francisco, it averaged about 9,000 people a day at 50 cents a head. A December 1917 *Billboard* ad described it as "the only one of the Ocean Hells built in the 1790s and made of Burmese teak wood. Aboard her are shown the airless dungeons and cells, whipping post, iron-tipped cat-o-nine-tails, branding irons, punishment balls, coffin bath, manacles, and other fiendish inventions of man's brutality to fellow man."

In the 1920s, Scout Younger was considered the top Law and Outlaw showman. The March 1925 *Billboard* reported he was at the Chicago wax studio of Gustus Schmidt and Sons, supervising the building of his wax shows. He also ordered a wax figure of himself. Younger had contracts to place wax shows on George L. Dobyns, John M. Sheesley, and Nat Reiss carnivals, plus storefront shows in Detroit, Denver, and Long Beach.

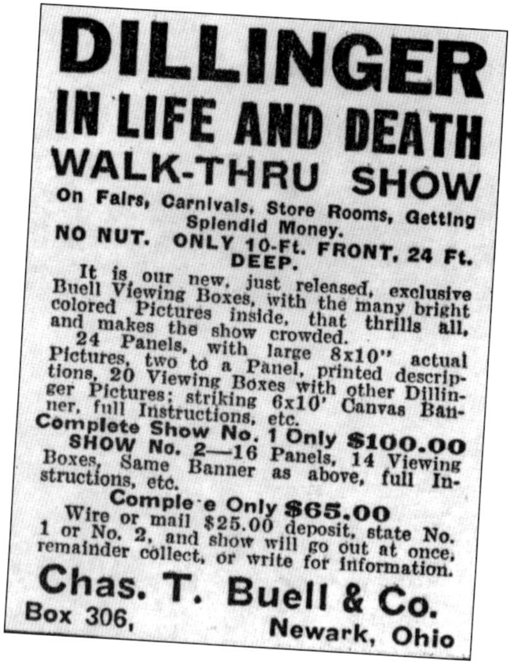

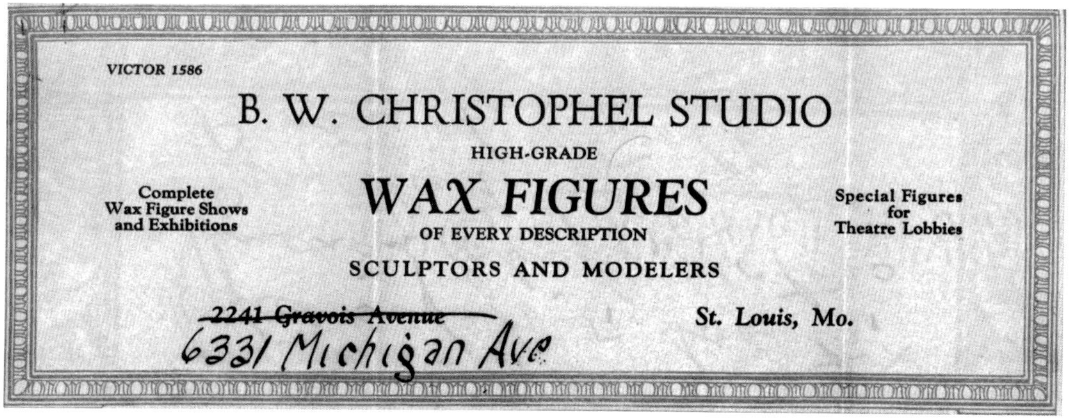

A crime show banner depicting the killing of John Dillinger that was auctioned off at one of Jim Conklin's carnival auctions in the 1980s, when Conklin Shows vacated their old winter quarters in downtown Brantford, Ontario.

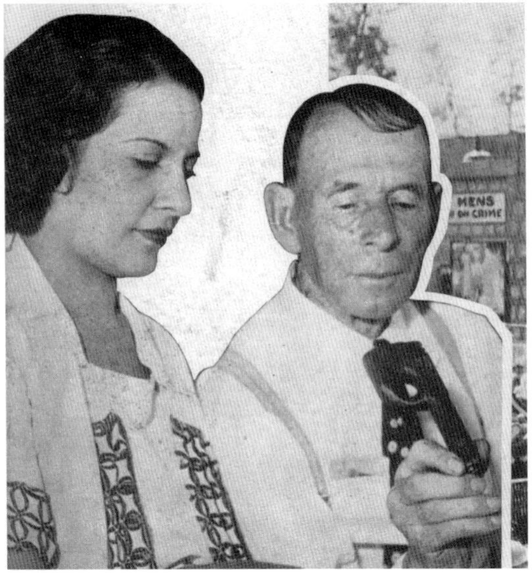

John Dillinger's father shows Evelyn Frechette the wood gun his son used to bluff his way out of the Crown Point, Ind., jail when the two were featured on Johnny J. Jones Shows' 1936 International Crime Exhibit.

The storefront shows contained 44 wax figures of famous outlaws, and the carnival shows each had 24 to 30 figures. The shows toured under the banner of "Scout Younger Bison Bill." Outlaws sculptured in wax included Wild Bill Hickock, Cole Younger, Scout Younger, Bob Younger, John Younger, Jim Younger, Detective Pinkerton, Bud Ledbetter, Belle Starr, Bill Dalton, Bob Dalton, Grat Dalton, Cherokee Bill, Red Kelly, Bill Doolin, and Sam Barr. In 1929, Younger retired, selling his Wax Attractions to Dodson World's Fair Shows. He died in 1938 in Tulsa, Okla., at age 64.

In the 1930s, crime showmen added escape artists and ex-criminals or their relatives to their shows. Outlaw J. Dillon joined the Does Crime Pay? show on the Western States Shows. In 1934, Mrs. John Castle, whose husband was part owner of United Shows of America, hired both Clyde Barrow and Bonnie Parker's mothers for her Crime Does Not Pay shows. In 1935, escape artist John Caterino joined the show, and soon J.W. Dillinger, the father of John Dillinger, was on board, too. He appeared in the crime show dressed in his son's clothes and holding the original wooden gun used by his son to escape from the Crown Point, Ind., jail.

Scout Younger, before retiring, had talked John Dillinger's girlfriend Evelyn Frechette into working on his show after her unconditional release from the Michigan State Prison. She was described as a handsome brunette and an interesting

Above: Lou Dufour and his partner Joe Rogers made crime shows larger and more elaborate for World Fair midways like they did their "Life" shows. This one is set up at the 1935 California Pacific Exposition at San Diego. Lou had written the police chief in Tucson, Arizona, and obtained the loan of personal effects of John Dillinger and Harry Pierpont for the show.

People looking at the execution scene on the front of Dufour and Rogers' Crime Show at the Belgium World's Fair in 1935.

For $100 a week Floyd Woosley was executed 20 times a day inside Dufour and Rogers' Crime Show at the 1935 Belgium World's Fair.

A Crime showman's truck painted to ballyhoo his exhibit. A five-banner front with one banner lettered "Facts Not Fiction" brought customers into the tent where the show itself was on film.

conversationalist who had learned that crime doesn't pay. Frechette drew big crowds in each town where Younger's Arizona Dust Bowl crime show played with the Dodson World's Fair.

Sexploitation movie operator C.R. Dent and his wife ran crime shows on carnivals during the summer. After touring on the 1936 Johnny J. Jones Shows, they had Frechette, several wax gangsters, and a gangster movie playing towns in Kentucky, West Virginia, and Ohio. The Dents told *Billboard* Frechette was a real trouper — she had been showing for four months without a day off. She was saving to buy a carnival ride.

Next season, Dent had his International Crime Show with Beckmann and Gerety Shows, and Frechette was the big attraction. Press releases described Evelyn as a black-eyed beauty with Indian bloodlines. The lecturer introduced her by saying, "She didn't talk out of the side of her mouth or tote two guns. All she ever did, really, was love a rascal." Frechette and Dillinger's dad were the exceptions to the warning that "crime doesn't pay." Both continued to work on carnival crime shows and lecture tours into the 1950s.

Lifelong showman Lou Dufour and his partner Joe Rogers presented elaborate crime shows on World's Fair midway zones. They had large crime shows at the Belgian Fair, the America's Exposition at San Diego in 1935, and the Cleveland Great Lakes Exhibition in 1937. The San Diego show, titled Crime Never Pays, contained hundreds of artifacts and photos, plus Dillinger's crime car, a section on scientific crime detection, a special piece on the St. Valentine's Day Massacre, plus a live re-enactment of Floyd Woosley's last steps to the death chair. Dufour himself played the part of the warden.

Dufour also had Doc Lamarr's dope show as a blow-off. Departing customers were greeted with a huge sign over the souvenir stand that read: "The officers and exhibitors of this International Crime Prevention exhibit appreciate your visit and hope that it has been beneficial to you." It was signed "Lewis E. Lawes, Warden, Sing Sing Prison." A sign over the souvenir shop urged, "Take home a souvenir made by a convict in prison."

Phillips H. Lord, producer of the radio show *Gang Busters*, produced Dufour and Rogers' 1939 New York World's Fair crime exhibit. The show was tied in with CBS radio, and featured items once belonging to John Dillinger, Harry Pierpont, Baby Face Nelson, Pretty Boy Floyd, and Legs Diamond. The live part of the show was handled by Juanita Hansen, the heroine of many silent movies. A reformed drug addict, she waged a militant fight with her anti-drug presentation.

Amusement Business carnival correspondent Irwin Kirby wrote about outlaw showman Doc Danville, who wintered his show in a carnival quarters in 1929–30 at San Bernardino, Calif. Times were hard in that period, and some of the carnival help broke into Doc's show and took the hats, clothes, and boots off his wax outlaws. When he went to open the show that spring, he found all his dummies nude. Doc quickly garnered outfits from the local Sally Ann.

Occasionally, wax crime figures surprised more than just the public. When a scene for the television series *The Six Million Dollar Man* was shot inside the Laugh in the Dark ride at Long Beach's Nu-Pike Amusement area, one of the funhouse figures fell off its hook. When the crew went to hang it back up, they saw what looked like a human bone protruding from the arm. A coroner examined the dummy and found it to be a real body. Exploitation showman Dave Friedman later identified the remains as gangster Elmer J. McCurdy.

"Elmer was part of an outlaw gang and

The John Dillinger crime car exhibit on the James E. Strates Shows in the 1950s.

he was shot and killed by a posse of deputy sheriffs after trying to rob a bank near Pawhuska, Okla.," recalls Dave. "The body was embalmed locally with arsenic and it turned leathery. Back then, a couple of sharp showmen from the Patterson Shows said they were relatives and claimed Elmer. He has been on tour for years. My old friend and former policeman Louis Sonney was on carnivals in the 1930s, and he had loaned a carny $500 and taken Elmer as security. The carny never returned and later Sonney exhibited him in his own carnival shows, retiring him after World War II. By

Crime shows were still appearing on midways into the early 1980s. This one appeared on Royal American Shows in the 1970s.

then, Sonney had founded a film business in Los Angeles and Elmer was laid up on a shelf in the office."

In 1968, Sonney's son Dan sold the body to the Hollywood Wax Museum. Later, the amusement park operators bought Elmer from the museum, along with a bunch of wax figures. Says Friedman, "They always assumed Elmer was made of wax. The coroner opened Elmer's chest and not only found a copper-jacketed bullet in the abdominal cavity but a tag printed 'Property of Louis Sonney.' My friend Duane Esper had Elmer out on tour for a time with his dope film and told audiences the body was that of a dope fiend."

"Dummies and signs fail to show real death row" was the newspaper headline after an Edmonton reporter's trip through a 1970s midway crime show. Her article explained: "The show was charging 35 cents admission and the loudspeaker spiel dared you to come inside the trailer and see death row as it really is. Inside on your right are iron bars, and inside the cell are figures of a priest and a convict. Posted on the wall in back of the cell is a sign that reads: 'Co-operate with your local law enforcement officer.' Another sign asks: 'Would you spend your life in this cell?' Following

Crime showman Tom Hughes' Al Capone car show at the Phoenix, Ariz., fair in 1960. One of the signs states that this display is "Combating Juvenile Delinquency." The show is framed on a semi-trailer truck and charges 10 cents.

along inside the trailer you come to a figure kneeling beside a guillotine with the dummy's head already off. In a case you see a 1929 Thompson machine gun with a tag saying it was the same type as that used by Bonnie and Clyde. Another case has a selection of weapons made by convicts. In another glass case is a figure of a convict in the electric chair with a doctor taking his blood pressure. A sign says it takes 60,000 volts of electricity to execute a person." The entire trip through the show took the reporter four minutes. When you compare this show to Dufour's massive crime show, it is lucky for the operator that poor showmanship is not a crime.

By the late 1930s, showmen were adding crime cars to their walk-through shows. The crime show on Hennies Bros. in 1941 had a bullet-ridden gangster car parked behind the bally platform. Although the guy on the bally wore prison garb and leg irons, the show inside was on film. Continuous news clips and stock footage depicted the execution of Richard Hauptmann, the killing of Clyde Barrow and Bonnie Parker, and the shooting down of John Dillinger. An exposé of sex maniacs of the underworld was the blow-off feature.

For years, crime cars could be lucrative draws for a savvy showman. But establishing their authenticity and tracking their owners was another story, as the tale of Al Capone's "original" car attests. Harry E. La Breque, secretary of the New Jersey State Fair, owned attractions at East Coast amusement parks. In 1933 he bought Al Capone's 1931 Lincoln, built by "Bronx Beer Baron" Dutch Schultz. He sent it to England for a tour of fairs and amusement zones. In 1956 it was placed in storage there and a story circulated that it had been removed from exhibition at the suggestion of the U.S. State Department, who wanted to play down gangsterism in America. Two years passed before Tony Stuart bought the vehicle and returned it to the States. In 1959, Frank Platten of Sacramento, Calif., offered showmen for $1,500 Dutch Schultz's armored 1931 Lincoln on a new trailer with lettered panels that opened to make a 40-foot front.

Meanwhile, the Mighty Sheesley Shows exhibited an Al Capone car in 1936, and Carl Sedlmayr Jr. fronted a Capone car on

the 1938 Royal American midway. Visitors to the Minnesota State Fair in 1975 stared not only at Al Capone's ride, but met the driver, 76-year-old Morris "Red" Rudensky. Red, Capone's chief safecracker and driver, had spent most of his life in jail. He had even shared a cell with Capone in an Atlanta prison. In 1963, Paul Elkins, owner of the Gay 90s Village in Sikeston, Mo., had bought Capone's 1931 Cadillac from a millionaire living in Arizona. Elkins had found Rudensky working at a 3M plant in St. Paul. Red attested to the authenticity of car, claiming that only 43 Cadillacs with this particular body shape had been made, and Capone had paid another $50,000 to have it customized. It had holes in the window for machine guns and weighed 10,000 pounds.

But who owned the real original was still a mystery. In 1984, Wally Yee Shows in Hawaii offered a 1934, 16-cylinder armored Cadillac also billed as Al Capone's car. Yee's ad read: "My sale price is $50,000, or highest offer! Some have asked me to prove it is the real car. If I could prove it, I would be asking $150,000!"

Tom Hughes moved from owning rides to operating grind shows when he bought a crime car for $900 in 1948 and toured it as a Dillinger car. This 1931 eight-cylinder

Back-end showman Hank Renn poses with the "real" machine gun Clyde Barrow was using when he and his girlfriend Bonnie Parker were gunned down by Louisiana lawmen in the bullet-ridden car. The Bonnie and Clyde death car appeared on the 1971 Royal American Shows midway in a lease agreement with owner Ted Toddy.

Lincoln with 33,000 original miles was completely armored, including the roof, and was custom-built with one-inch bullet-proof glass windows and a secret machine-gun compartment. The windows had holes from which to fire guns. In 1957, Hughes had both his Siamese-twin show and Dillinger's gangster car on tour with Art B. Thomas Shows. In 1961, he advertised the Dillinger car for sale in *Amusement Business* for $1,000.

Charles W. Stanley was called a crime expert and continuously framed new "blood operas" for the carnival midway and amusement park. He was said to be the original owner of the "real" Bonnie and Clyde car, which he had on his 1939 crime show on the Hennies Bros. midway. Stanley used the death car outside for bally purposes; inside, a film showed the actual ambush. The 1948 season found Stanley operating his show at Coney Island before joining Cavalcade of Amusements at Sedalia, Mo. His latest show featured educational films that dealt with sex, crime, and juvenile delinquency. He added a Dillinger crime car and toured with Gooding Amusements and Hennies Bros. Shows.

In 1951, Stanley toured the Mosser Family Massacre through theaters, spent a short time at Coney Island in Cincinnati, and then joined the Cetlin and Wilson Shows for the season. *Billboard* carried his 1952 ad offering the "Bonnie Parker and Clyde Barrow world-famous bullet-riddled DEATH CAR" for sale. The same season he retired from the road to manage the Coney Island amusement park in Cincinnati. He was still exhibiting the car there in 1960.

In 1949 sideshowman Charlie Hodges exhibited a Bonnie and Clyde car along with his large 10-in-1 show. In 1968, long-time promoter Frank Siro also had a Bonnie and Clyde car on midways. In 1969 he toured it at Texas fairs with a Valley of the Apes show, an all-crime show, a marine

The 1971 Bonnie and Clyde death car show, framed on a wagon in Royal American Shows' winter quarters, was quite elaborate with this beautiful fold out front. The viewing of the car included a brief film of the ambush.

exhibit, a Frozen Creature show, an outer space attraction, and a Fish Girl show.

In the 1960s the "original" death car seemed to have been acquired by showman Ted Toddy. In October 1969, *Amusement Business* reported: "Ted Toddy has won his suit for an injunction over the use of the Bonnie and Clyde name. Johnny and Marilyn Portemont, owners of Johnny's United Shows, will have to find another title for theirs!" Showmen were warned to avoid using the title, especially around Toddy's home in Atlanta.

In 1971, Toddy leased his car to Royal American Shows, who promised to build a $50,000 trailer and front for it. The car and a short clip of the ambush film of Bonnie and Clyde from May 23, 1934, were shown that season. Royal's bookkeeper Guy Gardiner leased the car, and had it on the midway in 1972. An article in the February 1973 *Amusement Business* said the trailer and exhibition equipment would be sold off after the Tampa fair and the car returned to Toddy.

In the fall, *Amusement Business* reported: "Operators of Bonnie and Clyde cars may find themselves clear of legal entanglements this year with the sale of Toddy's original to a Nevada casino. Peter A. Simon of Oasis Casino, Jean, Nev., paid $175,000 for it. The amount paid rubbed out the previous record paid for an antique automobile. The record of $153,000 was previously held by the Hitler car auctioned off a few years earlier by Dean Kruse of Auburn, Ind." The reprieve was short. Toddy wrote *Amusement Business* the next week saying its story "definitely encourages fakery, dishonesty, and crookedness, and plainly says that anyone can now put out and show a fake car. The new owner will vigorously protect his rights, more so than I have."

A bullet-holed postcard from Whiskey Pete's Casino and Hotel in Primm, Nev., boasts that both the Bonnie and Clyde and the Capone-Dutch Schultz cars are in their present collection.

Still, crime shows did have their lighter side. Dufour told a story in his *Amusement Business* column about rival Joe Glacy lecturing on Al Capone's car. As Glacy was explaining how futile it was to lead a life of crime, a mark broke in with, "Don't give me that booshwah; I'm driving around in a second-hand broken-down $500 Ford and Al Capone has a $6,000 Pierce Arrow. You're telling me crime doesn't pay?"

This crime show at a Canadian fair claims to be exhibiting the $19.95 gun that killed John F. Kennedy.

LARGEST SNAKE IN THE WORLD. LENGTH 27 ft. WEIGHT 300 LBS
10 CENTS

GEEK 101 FOR DUMMIES

One Trip Too Many

My experiences with snakes have never been good. They scare me shitless. When my only partnership in the circus business ended, my share of the splintered boards, warped tent poles, rotting canvas, and aging trucks also included two Burmese pythons. One had fallen out of the snake-pit show while we drove through downtown Edmonton early one morning. A young policeman ran over it before we could back the truck up and collect it. Taking no chances, he reversed and rolled over it a second time. Incredibly, the snake survived — with four deep grooves bearing a tire-tread design that contrasted greatly with the rest of his markings. He made it to the end of the season and expired shortly after he became 100 percent mine.

Opposite: A platform-style snake show at an early fair. Such lumber fit-ups were preferred by showmen traveling on gilly shows or in freight baggage cars.

The other, bigger python resided in our basement most of the winter, until I returned one day to find the glass top of his box open

Chapter 15

When showmen saw that snakes alone were not pulling in the crowds they combined the snake, a pretty girl, and an illusion to present Serpentina. This one is built on a wagon with fold down sides and ends to make the show platform and hold the pit.

a couple of inches and no snake inside. My wife heard me scream as I passed her on the cellar steps and slammed the door. Regaining my composure, I opened the door an inch, and yelled down that the snake was out. We searched all over but never found him until the spring thaw, hanging headfirst from a crack in our stone foundation.

That spring, I built a new snake-pit show and a snake box that should have rivaled the greatest illusion ever built. It looked more like a blade box with four doors on each side of it. The top came to a point, with two hinged glass flaps. Wherever Mr. Snake was, I was going to be able to get in a position where I was behind him!

Ever since the incident with the apple in the Garden of Eden, poor working snakes have been trying to overcome their bad reputations. Snakes were among the earliest creatures put on exhibition by showmen, since they could be carried in a small box and were a frightening curiosity. Early snake performances involved snake charming or the performer's fearless handling of poisonous species like the cobra.

Some of the earliest advertisers in the *Billboard* and *Clipper* were people who sold snakes to showmen. In July 1873, F. Mondy and Co. in New York City took out ads offering anaconda snakes — "largest in U.S." — for $100. On Broadway, the D. Burns Dog Store was also offering anacondas, perfectly healthy and shedding, ten to 12 feet long, for $35 each. An 1886 ad for Chas. Reiche and Co., animal importers on Park Row, read: "Will sell or let to any responsible party the snake that escaped and was captured in City Hall Park Oct. 9, the largest snake in America on account of its notoriety." For the geek showman with $20 to spend, J. Hope in Philadelphia offered fixed rattlers broke to be handled and "Bosco dens" — boxes of snakes for snake eaters.

Nobody knew more about snakes than William Abraham King, a.k.a. "Snake King," who started in the business with a geek show but figured he could make more money selling them than showing them. In 1910, he settled in an area of Texas with lots of snakes. King's reputation for fast shipping of quality snakes earned him the lion's share of the showmen's business. He branched out into monkeys, agoutis, armadillos, coatimundis, javalinas, skunks, foxes, prairie dogs, and kinkajous for wildlife and small zoo operators. For 40-some years his mainstay was snake dens, fixed or hot, the best in the business.

Walter A. Rhodes' "Jaunita the Human Snake from Mexico" illusion show during WWI. Note the sign over the entranceway stating Doctors and School Teachers admitted Free.

It didn't take showmen long to integrate snakes into illusions. Serpentina the Snake Girl became a regular feature on early midways, and Walter A. Rhodes' presentation of Jaunita the Human Snake From Mexico had one of the best banners — it depicted the snake girl riding in a carriage, with the wording "Jaunita in Mexico City." A small sign under the doorway banner read, "Doctors and School Teachers Admitted Free." The few grind-show exhibitors still plying their trade today occasionally revive the snake-girl illusion.

From the first days of sideshows on

Geeks were an attraction that usually stayed on the carnival grounds, but occasionally they could be seen around circuses, too. Azora lured patrons inside this geek pit show on the 1949 Dailey Bros. Circus when it visited New Liskeard, Ontario, for a one-day stand.

circuses, one of the acts inside has been a woman referred to as the "snake charmer." This act not only preys on the fear most people have of snakes, but sexual emotions are also ignited as the snake winds around the body of a scantily clad woman. From a business perspective, snakes were inexpensive and easily transported in small boxes or carrying cases. On a per-dollar per-inch basis, a showman couldn't buy any other animal with such drawing power. Snakes also made good newspaper copy as they were often escaping. Nothing like a 20-foot python loose in a small town to twig the locals to the fact the carnival had arrived.

Anyone not scared of snakes could do the act and also assist in other acts in the sideshow. Sideshow managers who could handle the lecturing, magic, vent, or Punch and Judy, and whose wives could handle snakes and work the sword box, had half the sideshow already covered. It was not unusual for the albino woman in a sideshow to also be the mind-reader and snake handler. In the 1890s, when "Circassian acts" were hot, most sideshow managers bought a Circassian wig for their wife or another lady in the show. The exotic Queen of the Nile snake enchantress was also the Circassian Queen and Viola the Mind That Knows All. From the 1880s on, nearly every circus sideshow or fairground show had a snake act, and in the winter there was plenty of work for snake acts in dime museums and vaudeville. In the 1940s, snakes made their way into burlesque. You can still occasionally see a girl in a strip club do her routine with a snake.

Snakes were also found on the circus midway as zoological attractions in pit shows. Although the geek was mainly a carnival attraction, he also appeared in early circus sideshows and later on midway pit shows. Ringling Bros. World's Greatest Shows listed Rattle Snake Tom, Varmint Subjugator as one of the acts in their 1893 sideshow. Over half a century later, the 1949 Dailey Bros. Circus had the Azora, Madagascar Wonder geek show on their midway.

Circuses today still have pit shows using snakes. With the end of sideshows on North American circuses in the mid-1990s, the snake act has been moved into the center ring. Fair-goers and circus patrons still pay to have their photos taken with a snake. As recently as 2001, the C.N.E. had a good free snake exhibit in a trailer near a fair entrance.

On carnivals, snakes have been presented as zoological attractions and, in the latter part of the 19th century, in a special venue known as the geek show. In the ordinary snake show, you went in and viewed the various species in pits or glass-topped or wire-mesh-topped exhibition boxes. The viewing was usually combined with a lecture, and in some cases a rattlesnake-milking demonstration. One lecturer on a 1900 midway snake show reportedly bellowed, "Here, gentlemen, you see the giant boa constrictor who is in the habit of eating a whole pig for breakfast." Then, focusing his attention on a portly person in the tip, he continued, "For goodness sake, mister, don't go so near the creature!"

A clever back-end showman named Cliff Wilson put up a big snake show behind a huge bamboo front at the 1939 Chicago World's Fair. Wilson's whole show provided an excuse for his very effective snake-oil pitch, and many a patron left the fairgrounds with one of his little bottles after hearing the lecturer say, "The snake sheds his skin four times a year, and when he sheds, the skin emits an oil which is extremely good for the skin." Wilson's success led to a string of showmen pitching snake oil behind bamboo fronts over the next two decades. Pitching snake oil was nothing new, especially to medicine showmen and early carnival sideshow operators, but Cliff's smart twist was to revive the pitch in an upscale environment. Some snake shows never mentioned the word *snake*; they simply used one big, long banner that shouted "MONSTER ALIVE." One such show on the Conklin Shows midway had a bamboo front and long banner but

Jack W. Burke's beautifully framed Wild Cargo snake show on the 1958 Cetlin and Wilson Shows midway.

no talker, just a silent ticket-seller. The come-on was the constant roar from a groaner inside the tent.

Snakes themselves even made it as pitch items. Grind showman Jack Sands, asked if he ever pitched anything in his shows, reflects a moment, then replies, "Actually, one time I did. I sold snakes, baby snakes. I used North Carolina water snakes and they had live young. They'd have them over the run — something about the truck moving up and down — and the snakes would give birth. Maybe 40 or 50 each week. People wanted to buy them, and so I started selling them at $1 apiece. But what the people were doing with them I didn't like. They

This chap with Indian-style wardrobe handling the snakes may have been the "strangest human being" your great grandparents had seen in their lifetime.

Easau was one of the early geeks on midways. This attractive platform show has a striped canvas tent, side walls, and a pit cloth.

were throwing them at others on the midway, using them to scare people. I stopped selling them."

Hollywood, men's magazines, and lurid fiction have long offered up a decadent image of carnival life through stories about girl-show strippers and geeks. Despite these twisted tales and films, the geek show has outlasted all other shows on the midway. Midway grind shows still feature the geek under the "wild man" or "wild woman" banner, or masked as a drug show. There's no more biting the heads off snakes or drinking the blood from decapitated chickens, but you may still see a simulated act of "geeking" as the person in the pit puts a snake's head into his or her mouth. And when the wild and frightening-looking geek lunges for the pit bars, the marks still fly out of the show, some literally jumping over the railings to the ground.

Attractions that showmen billed as "wild men" or "wild women" — featuring performers dressed in loincloths, carrying a spear, with a bone through their nose — quickly developed into snake-eater shows. One such act was working at the Egyptian Hall in London, England, in 1846. The billing read: "Is it animal or human? Link between animal and man? The wild man of the prairies. What is it?" The creature was described as having the top of a human and bottom of an animal, with hair completely covering the body except on the face. What people saw was a hairy caged beast looking like a baboon, uttering blood-curdling yells, and eating raw meat — reportedly live rabbits.

One visitor turned up early to see the "What is it?" and found out the attraction was a character named Hervio Nano, a.k.a. Hervey Leech. The visitor reported, "There it was with his keeper playing toss with an Indian rubber ball. The creature was dressed in only a loincloth and sucked raw flesh and cracked nuts." Hervey Leech was well-known to London theater-goers as "the Gnome Fly." He had been born in Westchester County, N.Y., in 1804 and when fully grown stood only three feet high. He had a normal torso but one leg was only 18 inches long from hip to foot, while the other leg was 24 inches. So he waddled along with the aid of his hands on the ground, similar to how an ape walks. This physical disability didn't seem to interfere with his acrobatic ability — he could jump ten feet into the air and leap onto speeding horses.

Leech worked on various circuses before he headed for the stage, first at the

Veteran showman Dean Potter's "Bloody Mama" snake show at a small fair in Pennsylvania in the 1980s.

Bowery Theater in New York City in January 1840. In the play *Tale of Enchantment, or Gnome Fly*, he played a gnome, a baboon, and a big blue fly in a bottle. Hervey Leech was certainly one of the earliest geeks on record.

An article in the *Clipper* on the Gaskill Carnival Co.'s visit to Atlanta, Ga., in November 1899 reported that in Harry Shield's snake show, Rosco the Australian Snake Eater had put away over nine snakes in six days. Meanwhile, over on Charter's Midway Co., Coglan's Bosco was doing the same act. And the 1899 Bostock carnival also featured a geek act, Posco the Poison Man.

Joe Kara's spin on the geek show on a Canadian midway in the 1950s is "Kuma the Poison Boy." The plain lettered banners without any pictorial allowed you to put almost anything you wanted inside.

The midway geek show consisted of a "wild person" sitting in a pit of snakes (geeks billed as "wild women" were invariably men wearing wigs and makeup). The geek plays with the snakes and in some cases bites and even eats one. At one point the inside showman loses control of the geek and the creature jumps at the crowd, often leaping out of the pit and chasing them out onto the midway. Geek showmen called this "rousting the tip." The tent is cleared, the geek is returned to the pit, and another show begins. All the commotion has helped draw a crowd for the talker to start making another quick opening, turn them to the ticket box, and get them inside the tent.

Showman E.D. Conklin is considered the originator of the Bosco Eat 'Em Alive show; he had the first such attraction on Frank Bostock's first midway in the U.S. around the turn of the century. Bosco the Geek's real name was Will Davis. Nicknamed "Steamboat," he had worked both the Barnum and Bailey and Ringling Bros. Circus as well as assuming the role of Bosco Eats 'Em Alive. He died in 1927 in Fort Madison, Iowa. Another famous geek was Harry Esau, who worked under the name Eau Sau. He was on the Sturgis Carnival Co. in 1901 and billed himself as the "original" snake eater. Esau was still going strong in 1938, working that winter on Harry Lewiston's museum show.

Carey Jones started his four-decade career in 1890, at age 11, as Snake-Oid. He was still out in 1934 on the Johnny J. Jones show. A year later, he was running the Monster Snake show for Dufour and Rogers at the Pacific Expo's midway. *Billboard* reported: "When the midway old-timers heard he was there, they all came by the pit to see him." Jones, who died in 1939, was credited with inventing the Hall of Mirrors show and opening the first movie theater in Muncie, Ind.

During the first years of the 20th century, the geek show was a great money-maker on carnivals. A December 1900 *Billboard* reported: "The art of eating snakes has advanced considerably the past year. If there was a street fair held during the past six months at which there was not a snake eater, that fair should go down in history as a wonder." The writer went on to say that the secretary of the Keokut Street Fair received 21 letters from snake eaters wanting space at his fair. The letters came from eight Boscos, five Esaus, four Unos, two Sunos and one each of Isaw and Rasco. Three years later, Geo Henie's Osay the Snake Eater show grossed $1,200 in one week on the Robinson Carnival Co., making it the second-highest-grossing show when the midway played Atlanta.

Many people felt that geeks were simply alcoholics, but the opposite was true. Showmen preferred their geeks sober. Being a geek was like being a clown — it was an act — and the best geeks were soon in high demand. While in later days the geek may have been some down-on-his-luck chap the carnival showman picked up and put in the snake pit, this was not the case when geek shows first started. Geeks saw themselves as true performers and placed ads just like fire-eaters, fat people, and show talkers in the "At Liberty" and classified ads sections of the trade papers. Most worked on percentage.

Perhaps the root of the geek myth stems from an October 6, 1900, *Billboard* report on a Bosco geek operation. The talker on this show told the crowd Bosco was captured in Australia and ate snakes by choice. On the New England Carnival Co., Bosco got sick and had to be left behind in a town. A hanger-on in the company named Beno was pressed into service; he was described as a "plain unfortunate rummy guy who used to eat twice a week before he took to snakes." According to the report, Beno had spent time in a Cincinnati hospital, and on discharge chose a quaint way of making a living: he drank poisons, had an awl drilled into his head, and let people nail him to a cross in museums. Beno felt pain just like the spectators in front of him, but he had a lot of nerve and a great desire for three square meals and some booze.

When Beno joined the carnival, his crucifixion act was deemed too offensive and he became a useless appendage to the show. But, the carnies let him stay on, eating and sleeping where he could. When Bosco became sick, the show management was concerned — the snake eater had been promoted in the billing and newspaper ads. A quick hunt around the show found Beno asleep behind one of the joints in some cardboard boxes. The carnival signed him up for two weeks' trial as the new snake eater. In the pit with poisonous snakes for the first time, he complained they were too quiet. He slapped them about until the pit was a mass of hissing serpents. One big brown rattlesnake sunk its teeth into Beno's hand. He pulled the snake from the wound, sucked out the poison, and spat onto the pit floor. Then he bit the snake's head off.

Misha Ali Bobia takes a bite out of a snake after tearing off the snake's head. He was a geek for Betty and Bobby Renton's Eeka show in the 1950s and early '60s.

By this time, the carnies that had encircled the pit to see Beno's debut were long gone.

Beno was now the new Bosco, and along with the job he acquired a new self-importance. He took it upon himself to bite the head off a snake for every patron who went into the show. On one slow fair where the show grossed only $50, Beno had eaten $38 worth of snakes. He was told to curb his enthusiasm and bite the heads off only a few times a day. On the lot, he now wanted to eat with the rest of the show folks in the cookhouse, but they weren't thrilled with this idea. The cook gave him his own table, and there he dined by himself when he wasn't in the pit or sleeping off his boozing.

The popularity of the geek show soon got it into trouble. In 1903, the State Senate in Kansas passed a bill banning snake eating at street fairs and carnivals. The law read: "It shall be unlawful for any person to exhibit in a public way in the State of Kansas any sort of exhibition that consists of eating or pretending to eat snakes, lizards, scorpions, centipedes, tarantulas, or other reptiles and animals. The person doing so can be fined $100 and jail time of three to nine months. The person arranging such a show can be fined no less that $25 and no more than $100." Some showmen tempered the geek act. They had their snake-pit men cut out the "glomming" — the act of biting and eating a snake. But this calming of the geek show was shortlived. By 1909, ads again appeared for men or women for snake shows stating: "You must work wild" or simply "Wanted: Glommer for snake show."

The worst thing about working with snakes was being bitten by a "hot" or poisonous snake. Geek shows went through a lot of snakes on a big week, and snake show operators bought snakes by the denfull from dealers they depended upon to ship them snakes every couple of weeks. As a rule, dealers didn't send out hot snakes, but occasionally mistakes happened. In 1932, Zabo, who handled the snakes on H. Backer's snake show on the Mad Cody Fleming Carnival, was bitten by a rattler. He was back on the job the next night, with the incident creating a lot of publicity for the show. Zabo survived, but many geeks and showmen were killed by poisonous snakes.

In 1935 Mrs. C.M. Kindel, president of the Michigan Federation of Humane Societies, wrote an appeal to carnies in *Billboard*: "I wish to take this opportunity of telling you that there is no place in Michigan for carnivals featuring geeks or cannibals that bite off the heads of live chickens. There is little or no suffering involved so far as the chicken is concerned, but the sight is so repulsive and revolting that a number of complaints have arisen."

There were geek showmen, and then there was Al Renton and his sons. Alfred Renton Frisbee grew up in St. Louis, Mo., with a stepfather who managed a chain of theaters. He married a woman whose parents were in vaudeville. In the early teens, he was assistant stage manager at the New York Hippodrome. Next, he worked his magic act for Slim Kelly at Coney Island. Slim suggested that Renton frame an illusion show.

When the public lost interest in the illusion show, Renton became a very good 10-in-1 operator. He had his own 10-in-1 on World of Mirth from 1930 to 1933, then spent 14 seasons with Capt. Sheesley's Mighty Sheesley Shows. After the war, when his sons came back from service, Renton put out the geek shows he called Eeka. His daughter Faye explains the title: "Eeka was my father's name for the geek show, because it was easy to say. He used to spiel: 'Eeka's got the biggest pair of big . . . blue eyes.'" Despite the banner's depiction of a wild, deranged voluptuous woman running through a snake-filled jungle, Eeka was always a man wearing a wig.

Eeka became a big attraction on the carnival circuit. At one point, Renton and his sons Bobby and Chuck each had an Eeka show on the road. Faye recalls that one year they combined their efforts in Detroit and topped midway grosses with only a three-banner front, with the show in a small 20-by-40-foot top. When Renton retired in 1954, Bobby and his wife Betty continued the Eeka show until 1961.

Bobby died in 2000, and Betty was just getting her life back together when she spoke to me about operating the show. She explained how they set up the show for the geek's comfort. They would decide on a location for the pit inside the tent, then had to dig the hole. When they installed the canvas walls and floor that formed the pit, they positioned a hole in the canvas over the one they'd dug in the ground. The geek

WANTED IMMEDIATELY,

FIRST CLASS SNAKE EATER,

One who understands his business thoroughly, not afraid to work. Competent for 'a long season. Touring Europe, also Paris Exposition. I want three hundred snakes, large variety, and two hundred rattlesnakes.

When things slowed down at the Eeka show, Al Renton brought out one of the larger snakes on to the bally and used it to hold the tip's attention while he told them about that "strange girl Eeka" he had inside his show.

Al Renton holds the tip in front of his Eeka geek show in the 1950s. Master banner painter Snap Wyatt did the five-banner front, but later Renton himself painted banners for his geek shows.

stayed in the pit the entire time they were operating, so he needed toilet facilities. The geek always had a blanket with which to cover himself when he had to urinate — the blanket also served as a shield against spectators' spit.

"We used to cut up inner tubes to throw at the public," Betty recalls. "It depended on the tip, how many were in there, whether we actually killed a snake or not. The geek would actually skin the snake and take a bite out of it. He would rip the head off first — it is sweet meat. You could get a couple of days out of a snake if you kept it on ice overnight. When we were done for the night, the snakes used that night went into my refrigerator. That was the one thing that took me quite a while to get used to."

The front of Hall and Christ's Eeka show in the 1970s.

The Rentons would go through a box of 20 snakes each week. The snakes were shipped via UPS in a box marked "LIVE ANIMALS" from a supplier in Louisiana. Sometimes the snakes arrived in poor shape and already had trench mouth; Betty had to nurse them along until they were ready to be used. When Betty worked with Bob and his father, she was the bally girl. Later, when she and Bob had the show, she worked the inside. She says that working the outside of the pit was not a woman's job — it was real tough dealing with the crowd and it wore you out banging the stick on top of the pit.

Betty's main task was crowd control. She stood at the back of the pit with a microphone while Bob worked the outside.

When Bob felt he needed some excitement out front to help draw a new tip, he called for a roust. Betty would bang the stick on the back of the pit and shout, "Down, Eeka!" She'd pretend to try to control Eeka. "I can't keep her down," she'd yell. "I can't control her!" Bob would shout over the microphone outside, "Hold her down, that's your job!" Betty would yell out to him that he'd better get back there: "I can't hold her down much longer!"

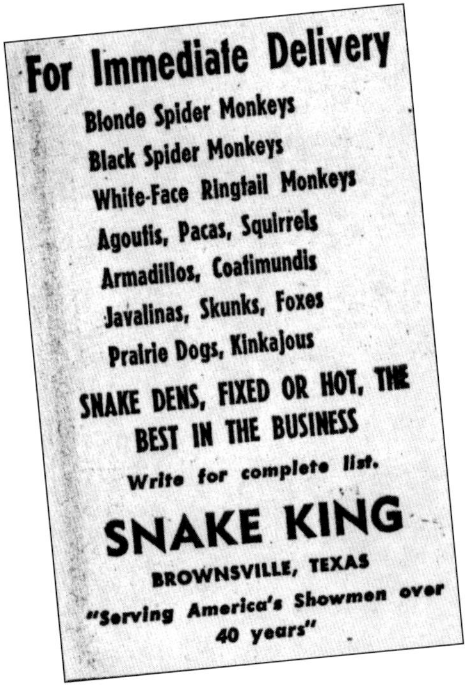

"Eeka would be getting more and more aggressive in the pit and would start stuffing snakes down her pants," Betty says. "Suddenly, Eeka would lunge for the side of the pit and throw a piece of inner tube into the crowd. We would scare them out and Bob would start selling tickets again as fast as he could. Sometimes the roust called for the geek to jump out of the pit and run down the midway with Bob running after him, capturing him, and making a big act of returning him to the pit. On slow nights, you would have to bring the big snake out and bally to get them in."

After the Rentons retired from the geek business, only Hezekiah Trimble was left out there, with his Congo show. Congo wasn't new to the business — I first met him when he was on Cristiani-Wallace in 1962. He would put his hand in an aquarium and pull it out filled with mud. Then he'd put his hand back in, mutter some voodoo words, pull his hand out again, and he'd be cupping dry sand. Billed as the Jungle Creep, that winter he was working in Hubert's Museum in New York City, along with the short-armed Sealo, sword swallower Alex Linton, Professor Heckler's Flea Circus, and boy giant Buck Nolan. Trimble's show was half-magic, half-geek; he would tell his audiences they were witnessing "voodoo, hoodoo, and conjoo!" I asked back-end showman Malcolm Garey about Congo:

"He did some crazy stuff in there. Today, you would go to jail. He would pull all the feathers off a chicken while it was alive. The chicken would be screaming bloody murder, squawking like mad. You could hear it out on the midway. He would hold a chicken between his feet and stretch that chicken's neck out until you would think it was impossible and then — pow! — the neck and head would pop off. That's pretty cruel, even to a chicken.

"He would eat bugs," Garey adds. "He would eat worms. I couldn't watch him eat worms. The crickets were okay, but not the worms. It was pretty bad."

The rise of animal activists in the 1980s put a damper on the traditional geek operation, but showmen quickly came up with a new concept. The new geek was a drugged-out, wheelchair-bound man sitting in the pit with a large snake wrapped around him. The most notorious geek, Billy Reed, was operated by Jack Constantine. The day I saw Billy Reed, he was wearing a large headphone set that made him look more like a crazed Howard Stern. A large snake was coiled around him and slithering toward the pit floor over the arm of his wheelchair.

I spoke to Constantine in 2000 and quickly turned the conversation to his geek. "I named him Billy Reed!" boasts Jack. "Billy Reed was very successful and soon there were many copies of the show. They even copied my mistakes!" I interrupt him to say that other showmen had offered other versions of Billy Reed's origins. "The first drug abuse show I had was booked on Murphy Shows in 1973," Jack reveals. "I had a girl in the pit whose real name was Kathy Reed. I named the show Kathy Reed — 'Come in and see Kathy Reed!' — but she blew. I ended up with this gay guy out of Sedalia, Mo., so I had to rename the show.

"Billy Barton the Ice Man and I are good friends. We were sitting in the dope show trying to think up a new name. He jumped up and blurted out, 'Billy! Billy Reed!' It sounded good, and so I painted out 'Kathy' and lettered in 'Billy.'"

Jack confesses that he wasn't the first to combine the drug angle with the geek. "I have to give credit for that to Randy Rosenson and in turn to Mickey Saiber," says Jack. "Mickey framed a drug show on a big semi, and he had Mike Walker, a 1,000-pound fat man, in there and used the story that drugs did this to him. It went over big. Randy Rosenson saw Saiber's drug show and framed one himself. Randy came up

Congo's Jungle Creep show on the Deggeler Shows midway in the 1980s. Every few seasons Deggeler bought Congo a new school bus to live in and transport his show.

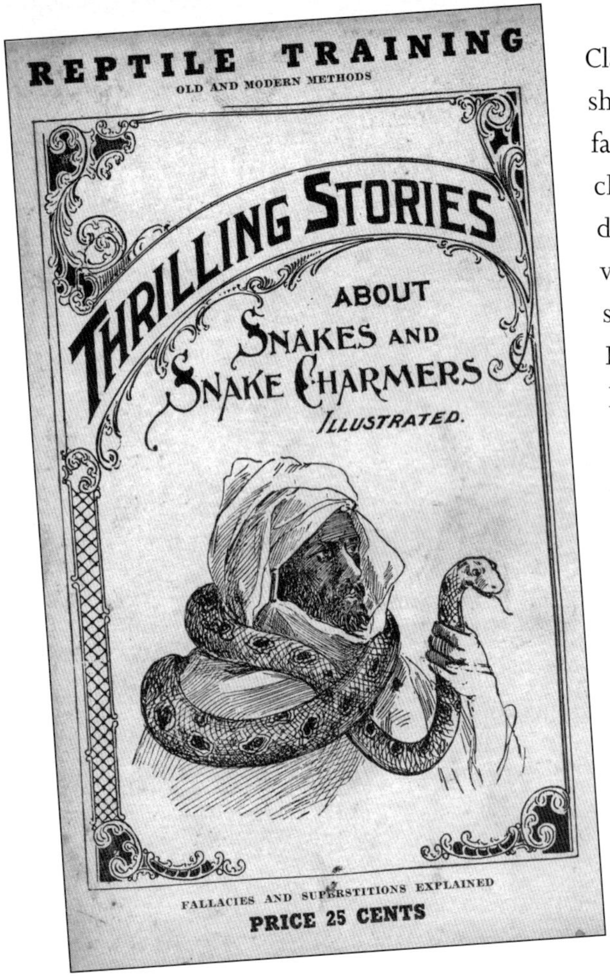

with the concept of the drugged-out guy and also the snake. I copied him because he was my first partner. Of course, after I called mine Billy Reed and was successful, there were all kinds of them. I still have the show. It still makes money. I presently call mine Chris. It was out last year."

Billy Reed, Willie Wright, Willie Clark, and a half-dozen other drug-abuse shows eventually were viewed by enough fairgoers that the concept had to be changed again. "When I first had the drug show with Billy Reed, the thing was to let the crowd build up inside the show and they would be watching Billy," Jack explains. "He would put the head of the snake in his mouth, roll his eyes, and then pretend to fall asleep. Suddenly, he jumped at the bars with the snake and scared the shit out of the people. They were jumping over the railings and running out of there every which way, and of course, that helped to build the next crowd. Once I had to go up and get this black lady who had a fit in the corner of the truck and was scared to come out past the geek!

"It was constant beefs and you couldn't walk away from it for a minute. I thought, 'If I can run this, I can run anything.' Then we calmed it down, but it didn't do the money. When you took the scare off it, the money stopped coming in. Charlie, who worked for me, got the idea to make the geek into a blockhead. The story went that he could drive a big spike up his nose because cocaine had made such a big hole in his nose cavity. That was a gross-out act, but it worked. Then other showmen started having their geek use an electric drill!"

The closest I can come to explaining the geek may lie in several stories Malcolm Garey told me about the geeks he had. We were looking at photos in his living room, and after I'd paused at one for some time, Malcolm says, "That was Fat Pat, my female geek. She was with me two years. The second year at the end of the season she asked me, 'Can I have the snakes?' 'Sure, I guess.' She put all the snakes in a couple of pillowcases. She and her boyfriend went off to get a motel room. The season was over and I was closing up the show. She had left something inside, and so I went down to the motel to give it to her. She opened up the door and she had let all the snakes loose in the hotel room. They were crawling everywhere!"

How did Garey ever find someone like that? "Oh, she was walking down the midway and we got talking and she told me she liked snakes," he recalls. "I was getting ready to fire the guy I had. He was a winner! One night some people walked in the show and quickly came back out and told me it was a rip-off. I said, 'What are you talking about?' They said, 'There's nobody in there!' I couldn't believe them

— nobody in there? I went in and they were right. I closed the show. A little while later, a ride jock comes up and says, 'Hey, your wild man is over at the Dairy Queen. He's got his leopard-skin swimsuit, wig, and all his makeup on!' I said, 'I'll buy you a case of beer if you will go back down there and get him for me, but I want you to bring him back here to the show. I don't care what it takes.'

"They went down and tied him to a tree branch and carried him back here. This was on Coleman Shows up in New England. They came down the midway with him screaming and cussing. They took him into the show and dropped him back in the pit. I had an eyebolt in the middle of the pit that the geek was supposed to be chained to. I put a padlock on the chain and locked him to the eyebolt this time. Old man Coleman came in and said, 'I don't want to see you do that again!' We cleaned the midway. The carnies were all complaining we took all the people off the joints and down to the back end. People left the joints in the middle of their game!"

Malcolm is constantly coming up with new show ideas. He tells the story behind another photo depicting a guy in the pit with a spiderweb painted on his face.

"I did something with a geek show that I hadn't seen other showmen do," he says. "I did a Spiderman Show. Instead of snakes, lizards, or chickens, I had spiders. So I put this guy in the pit with them. He's not too swift. One day I went in there and he was sitting there with a big grin on his face. I asked him what was so funny and he opened his mouth, stuck out his tongue, and this big tarantula was sitting there! I told him, 'That's pretty good! Keep that up!'"

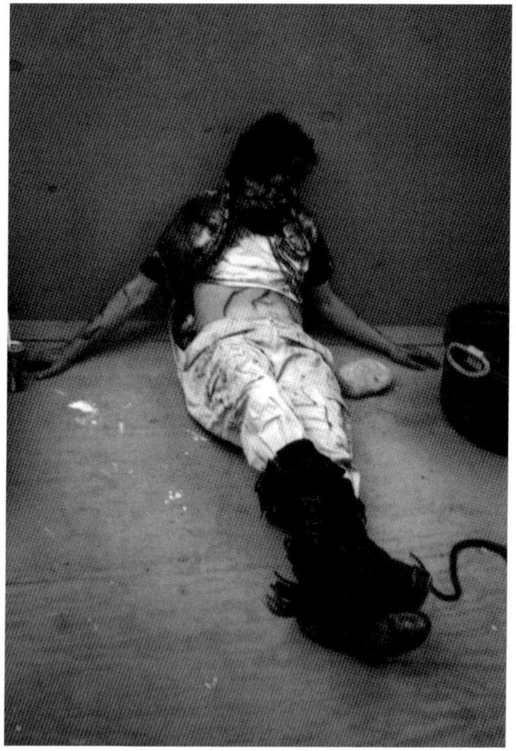

Malcom Garey's "Spiderman the Geek" in his 1970s grind show. One night after the show was over an old lady in a pick-up truck pulled up to the midway and Spiderman hopped in. He was never seen again.

The Most Particular Man on Earth About His Snakes is

HINDOO WILL

I have been furnishing his Snakes for over twelve years. If I can please him I can please you. Last year with George L. Dobyns Shows. With it again this year. There must be a reason.

SNAKE KING

Brownsville, - - - - - Texas.

HOTEL
PARADISE

EPILOGUE

It's Not Over Till the Fat Lady Sings

"Yo, geek!" was the cry of the '90s among teenagers. We have come a long way in 100 years on carnival midways. Fueled by memories of the Chicago World's Fair in 1893, North Americans — like pythons shedding old skin — began to discard negative Puritan attitudes toward entertainment as a new century began. No longer did entertainment have to be whitewashed as "educational" — it could be enjoyed for the pure fun of it. By the end of World War I, going out on a weekly basis to fairs, carnivals, amusement parks, dance pavilions, and vaudeville and movie theaters, as well as visiting tent circuses, repertory and minstrel shows, and hundreds of other roving distractions, was part of normal life on this continent.

Opposite: Pete Kortes' sideshow troupe working a date in Hawaii. Back: Willy Muse (Iko-Ecko), photographer Chimera, unknown, Jack Connors, unknown, Thelma and Doris Patent (albino twins), Don McDaniels, Mimi Garneau (sword-swallower). Middle: George Muse (Iko-Ecko), Rasmus Nielson, Barney Nelson, Athelia (pin head), Grace McDaniels, Alva Evans. Front: Magician Harry Hanuoko, Lady Ethel, Prince Dennis.

The bally on Slim Kelly's 10-in-1 show on the 1941 Goodman Wonders Shows featured George Vokal on the left of the bally stage. George smoked a cigarette and blew the smoke out of a hole in his back, but the blow-off contained an even stronger attraction: a person who exposed a third sex!

The parents and grandparents of today's "boomers" viewed shows and spectacles with a healthy curiosity. On today's midways, if we come across a two-headed baby, we no longer wonder if the baby is alive, but unenthusiastically calculate if this fake is worth spending 50 cents on. When it comes to midway shows and circuses, our minds are so besieged by "political correctness" and false images thrown at us by politicians, do-right committees, and the animal activist crowd that the sheer fun of the showground is at risk. Audiences these days consider themselves so sophisticated that a sideshow is beneath them. No one's

Above: In the 1980s grind showmen found it hard to give up 50% or more to carnival owners. Showman Lee Kolozsey tried different venues. He set up his giant rat, big snake, and headless woman shows at the 1996 Lollapalooza tour in New Orleans, La.

Teenagers trying to decide whether to see Jack Constantine's "Strange Babies Show" at the Hamburg, N.Y., fair in 1999. Signage on the front stating that these were facsimiles may have them confused.

going to make them line up in front of a bally stage and be herded into a tent. They're more concerned with being seen themselves than being a passive observer. That's a tough environment for any showman.

The only public encouragement midway showmen have received in recent years has come from the tattooed-and-pierced crowd, who have embraced live and unconventional entertainments including the sideshow and circus arts.

Shows on midway back ends started to thin out by the late '60s, when fairs began demanding higher percentages from carnivals. Carnival owners had to pass the cost on to their tenants, and owners of back-end shows consequently had to pay more than 50 percent of their gross, as well as fees for parking, electricity, garbage pickup, and so on. Today, at most fairs, there are no shows among the rides, games, and food stands. Perhaps fewer than two dozen back-end shows are still touring, whereas there are hundreds of fairs and midway dates. Of these shows, two or three are tented museums, the rest, small grind shows with either a single animal or a single human

Sammy Speed and Billy Reed came along just in time to revive the faltering careers of midway geeks. Several of these drug abuse shows continued to gross out audiences and even more important, make money!

attraction inside. As for actual performances, we have several girl-to-gorilla shows, a half-dozen live performers in Ward Hall and Chris Christ's museum sideshow, and live acts in Tim Demer's illusion show and Steve Cramer's motordrome. Among the grind shows, you can still see a midget lady, the world's largest and smallest horses, alien bodies, a savage alligator, a home in a big tree, several big pigs, and a half-dozen young men claiming to have had one bad drug-trip too many. Except for the odd midget and fat person, there are no freaks on exhibition.

At some point in the '60s, free love and staring at freaks collided. Looking at someone with a deformity became unfashionable. Parents dragged their kids past the last of the freak shows on their way to the fair grandstand to watch the more correct mud wrestling and auto-demolition derbies. Girl shows were leaving the midway just as go-go clubs, topless bars, and hotel lounges with strippers flourished.

Displays of torture items and depictions of their use on victims — even papier-mâché and wax victims — were viewed with the same disdain as gawking at the elephant-footed girl or the alligator-skinned man. Caught in the same wave of midway sanitizing were glomming geek shows. The wild man took up his new sedate career inside the dope show with "Billy Reed . . . He Is Still Alive" leading the way (and proving that showmen were still versatile). Parents today shun exhibitions of caged animals the way their parents accelerated their pace past freak shows. We no longer see wildlife shows, though the "evil" snake is still on display. People prefer to read about freaks in the tabloids rather than view them in person.

Crowd empathy was not the only culprit in ending the big 10-in-1s on midways. As much as some people preferred not to look at freaks, those who did found there wasn't much left to stare at. Emmett the Alligator Skin Man and his wife Percilla the Monkey Girl, Jeannie Tomaini the Half Lady, Sealo the Seal Boy, and Melvin Burkhart the Anatomical Wonder were in retirement by the 1970s, and all have died in recent years. Today, most infant deformities can be

During a Bros. Grim Milwaukee performance, Tim Cridland (Zamora the "Torture King" laying on top of three sword blades) cringes as strongman John Hartley breaks a cement block on his chest. Tim has appeared on several television specials with his human pain endurance and pin cushion acts. He was a Jim Rose troupe member responsible for the high faint counts at each show.

The World's Strangest Married Couple, Emmett Bejano the Alligator Skin Man and his wife Percilla the Monkey Girl, in the mid-1990s outside the carnival museum at the annual I.I.S.A. trade show in Gibsonton, Fla. Their passing, along with Jeannie the half lady and Melvin Burkhart, marks the end of the sideshow performers who started their careers in the 1930s.

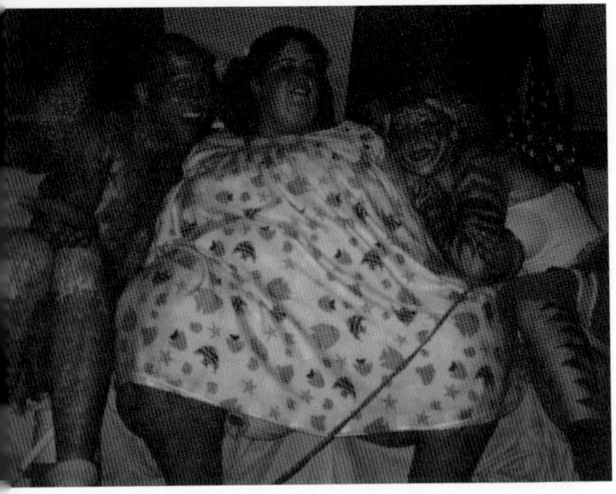

Multi-talented Enigma (Paul Lawrence) and his wife Katzen, the Cat Girl, cuddle fat lady Little Fannie Bryson while entertaining on the Bros. Grim sideshow. They are the new "World's Strangest Couple," now that Emmett and Percilla are gone, and they continue to work tattoo shows and in clubs.

A stalwart of the Jim Rose troupe has been "The Amazing Mr. Lifto," Joe Hermann. Here he swings a concrete block from his nipple rings on the 1991 Lollapalooza stage. Some guys in the crowd fainted from seeing this. Even more hit the turf when he swung a heavy anvil from a ring in his penis. His reputation soon spread.

corrected shortly after birth. What freaks medical science has let fall through the cracks survive on welfare and government assistance. Most sideshow freaks took pride in being a burden to nobody — the sideshow allowed them to escape being institutionalized or stuck inside a home. Carnivals and circuses gave them independence, self-worth, friends, and a support system to help them achieve as normal a life as possible. Compare some poor individual wheelchair-bound in a house to someone with shoulder stubs for hands and virtually no legs who could drive a car pulling a house trailer and own their own sideshow. Who would you pity?

Just as there is no freak pool for showmen to draw from, there has also been an acute shortage of working acts. A one-time pool of hundreds of knife-throwers, sword-swallowers, fire-eaters, magicians, and talkers has dwindled to a few dozen. Tape-recorded spiels may have successfully eliminated talkers on grind shows, but talkers were still a necessity on 10-in-1s. Few young people are willing to put in the long work hours demanded by fairground work, nor are they interested in accepting low-paid apprenticeships around shows.

In this book, I have tried to present a history of midway shows we will never see again. Left for my next book in this series is a detailed account of sideshows and grind shows. You will read more about Bobby Reynolds, Ward Hall, and Chris Christ, the last of the sideshow presenters. For the past few seasons, Ward and Bobby have each proclaimed, "This is my last year!" But both are still out there. Perhaps each one wants to be known as the last American sideshow operator.

The circus and carnival sideshow businesses are like Siamese twins who share internal organs. Their history is rich and colorful. It's time for this world of "tips" and "blow-offs" to be explored more deeply. Certainly the Mule Face Woman has an interesting tale, but so do the sideshow impresarios, sword swallowers, pitchmen, magicians, and Punch and Judy workers. These theaters of the bizarre were truly America's most unique small businesses. One *Billboard* writer described '40s sideshows as a five- and ten-cent store —

Left: Danielle Stampe, a.k.a. Slymenstra Hymen from the heavy metal band GWAR (God What Awful Racket), blasts fire over the audience at the Bros. Grim sideshow during the 2000 circus parade festivities in Milwaukee, Wisc. Danielle also tours her own sideshow troupe known as the Girly Freak Show.

there was something for everyone, and everything was for sale.

In the '80s, sideshows disappeared from circus and carnival midways. As the shows faded, artists and collectors realized they were seeing the last of not only a unique form of show business, but also of the physical evidence of it. Banners, signage, and exhibits quickly found homes in collections. Generations of young non-conformists adopted lost or eccentric fashions, lifestyles, and mediums. Freaks and geeks have been Generation X's find. Teenagers shoved swords down their throats and burned their faces trying to eat fire. Nail boards didn't outnumber skate-boards, but I have seen more nail boards in the last six years than I have in 40 years around shows. Avant-garde sideshow troupes like the Jim Rose Circus Sideshow and Tim Cridland's Torture Parade have abandoned the midway tent for the bar and nightclub circuit. Sideshow acts have opened for rock stars, and grind shows toured as part of the Lollapalooza tour. Circus, sex, burlesque, and the sideshow arts can still be viewed in café basements and on theater stages.

The old saying "It's not over until the fat lady sings" still holds true. Save the eulogy — the art of the sideshow is still breathing.

Above: The last of the carnival sideshowmen, Chris Christ in the ticket box with partner Ward Hall doing the talking on the front of their large traveling museum. Longtime employee Petey Trihune eats fire to stop the tip. In 2002 they are heading away from east coast venues to tour in the mid-west. They have added several inside performers to make their show the last sideshow on tour with "live" acts.

In the 1990s new sideshow artists have emerged from various performance circles. Matt "Molitov" Bouvier was fronting a band with his fire eating while his partner Felecity Perez spent time in experimental theater and the Lusty Lady nude dance clubs. Together they present sideshow numbers like sword swallowing, fire eating, and knife throwing.

GLOSSARY

AUTOMATON: An automaton is anything that can move or act by itself. Showmen have presented small figures that dance, do acrobatics, play chess, etc. The figures' movements are created by intricate gears, levers, and clockworks machinery inside them. Today large animated figures lure crowds into dark rides and fun houses on the midway.

BACK END: The area at the back of the carnival midway containing the shows. Now it means the back of the lot.

BALLY: The free show in front of a carnival attraction to hold the crowd while the talker explains the attraction and then urges the crowd to buy tickets.

BALLYHOO: Showmen have shortened the word ballyhoo to bally. The word "Ballyhoo" comes from the 1893 Chicago World's Fair where talkers Americanized an Arabic word the performers from the far east used amongst themselves when the talker called them outside to demonstrate what the show was about.

BLOCKHEAD: The word describes an act in which the performer drives nails or inserts other sharp objects inside his nasal cavity.

BLOW-OFF: The last act in a 10-in-1 or sideshow, for which an extra fee is charged. Also means to "get rid of" or can refer to the circus audience itself as it leaves the big top after the performance.

BOUNCERS: "Unborn" or pickled punk showmen that didn't want to use human specimens or couldn't acquire them for their shows could buy rubber babies from medical supply houses and make their own "freak babies." The bouncer title comes from the fact rubber bounces. Today the term applies to any freak baby that is not real, regardless of what it is made from (rubber, vinyl, wax, papier-mâché).

BUBBLE SHOW: Movie shows displayed on the 180-degree surface of one side of a vinyl dome kept inflated by air came on midways in the late 1960s. Carnies called the dome a "bubble" and the show a "bubble show."

CARNIVAL: The name given to a collection of rides, food stands, games, and shows set up in a location for the public's amusement. Carnivals usually set up for a week at each location.

CIRCUS: Tent and indoor circuses offer patrons a show of a set duration in which animal and human performers entertain them. Early tent circuses also offered a separate menagerie and sideshow. Today most tent circuses present only the big top performance either in one ring (European style) or in the traditional American three-ring format. The traditional tent circus plays one-day shows or seven towns a week.

CONTROLLED GAMES: Games at carnivals where the operators determine the winners and losers. The era of controlled games on carnivals and circuses has long past. Carnival games today are based on odds like any casino or lottery.

COOCH SHOW: A type of girl show that featured complete nudity. Posing shows featured some nudity but no movement, and large revue shows featured one or two strippers but not complete nudity.

DING: Any extra charge or additional request for money inside a show.

DIORAMA: Miniature scenes, often three-dimensional, of cities, villages, and buildings.

FREAK: The term used to describe someone who is physically unlike the majority of the populace. Those labeled as freaks included extremely fat people, tall people, dwarfs, midgets, Siamese twins, bearded ladies, people with three legs or additional toes or fingers, people with extra-large feet, scaly skin, or more than normal body hair. Freaks dominated the sideshow exhibition business on carnivals and circuses from the 1870s to the 1960s.

GEEK: A performer who acts like a wild jungle man or woman and who eats snakes and other small animals while confined to a pit in a show tent.

GILLY: To carry anything onto or off a show lot. Railroad carnivals that used box cars and baggage cars to move in were called gilly shows because everything had to be unloaded from the rail car to a truck or wagon and hauled to the lot, where it was unloaded onto the ground. The process was repeated on tear down. Rail shows that used wagons that loaded on flat cars eliminated all this extra handling.

GLOMMER: The name given to a geek that bites or eats snakes, chickens, etc. The act of doing so is "glomming," which also means to take or grab something.

GRIND SHOW: Small midway shows that operate continuously. Customers don't stay long and the tip is turned over repetitively all day long. Originally presented in small tents or on platforms, today most grind shows are built on trailers or trucks.

GRIND TAPE: By the 1960s, talkers on shows, especially grind shows, were replaced by taped spiels. Operators started using 30- and 60-second continuous loop tapes to draw in their customers.

ILLUSTRATED SONGS: A big part of nichelodeon, vaudeville, and moving picture performances from 1904–1910. A vocalist accompanied on piano sang a song with the words projected on a screen behind them.

JIG SHOW: Common carnival term for minstrel or all-black revue show, now considered derogatory. Derived from jig dancing.

JOINT: Any booth on a carnival midway. Small eating stands with limited or no seating are called "grab joints" — you get your food and eat it elsewhere.

KINESCOPE: A type of stereopticon or early motion picture projector.

LUNETTE: One of the first floating girl illusion shows on carnivals was called "Lunette." Probably derived from luna (moon) and "ette" (part of a female name like Paulette). Carnival showmen referred to all these suspension illusion shows as Lunette shows.

MARK: Carnival patron.

MIDNIGHT RAMBLE: Black revue shows gave a special sexed up show on the last night the carnival was in town. It was heavily promoted during regular shows. Black revue operators may have taken the idea from early tent minstrel shows that gave a special "after show" or "concert" often featuring a blues singer and more risqué dancing.

MIDWAY: A midway show and a carnival show are the same thing. The word "midway" stems from the name "Midway Plaisance" given to the amusement area of the 1893 Chicago World's Fair. Circus people call the area out front of the main circus tent, where the ticket wagon, concession stands, pit shows, pony rides, and the side show is located, the "midway."

MOOCH BOX: To "mooch" on a show is to beg. This is a carnival term for the ding or donation box in a ding show.

MOTORDROME: A circular walled area, usually made of wood, in which motorcycle drivers ride their bikes and do various stunts.

PANOPTICON: The name given to an early musical and pictorial clock. In Europe the term referred to wax and curiosity shows on the fairgrounds.

PITCH BOOK: A small booklet sold by various freaks and acts inside the sideshows and dime museums. Early ones were multi-page biographies. The term also refers to any booklet sold (pitched) inside a show like sex booklets sold inside "Unborn" shows.

PLANT SHOW: Carnies shortened "plantation show," an early name given to black revues on carnivals, to "plant show."

PUNK: Any youngster around a show. Also the name given to pickled babies (pickled punks).

SINGLE-O SHOW: A show on the midway with just one exhibit or attraction inside.

SKILL-O: A type of controlled midway game involving a small gaming wheel that sits flat on a table.

STEREOPTICON: A projector used to show slides.

TAB SHOW: Short for tabloid show, a cut-down or condensed musical similar to a small revue with burlesque show features. Most tab shows ran about an hour and were often combined with movies in theatres.

TALKER: The person who talks you into seeing a midway show. In the early days he was referred to as the boomer, door talker, barker, or spieler.

10-in-1 SHOW: A sideshow presentation made on carnivals with ten acts in one tent. A few seasons before the First World War, several midway show operators who had three or four single attractions and pit shows combined these acts under one tent. Showman Walter Sibley is credited with being the first to do this, and was beating out most of the competition at fairs. By the 1920s most carnivals were carrying a 10-in-1, while some featured 20-in-1s. The 10-in-1 became the basic midway sideshow in operation.

TIP: The crowd gathered in front of a concession, a pitchman, or the bally platform of a show. The show talker's first task is to "gather a tip" (stop the people in front of his attraction). Then he delivers his spiel and "turns the tip" (makes them buy tickets).

VAUDE: The showman's shortened name for vaudeville. Vaudeville theaters evolved out of the dime museums of the 1880s, and survived as a theatrical entertainment form into the early 1950s. A vaudeville show consisted of eight variety acts. Vaude audiences have seen everything from performing elephants to musical glass players.

VENT: Shortened term for a ventriloquist act.

INDEX

BIBLIOGRAPHY

Books

Abel, Richard, and Rick Altman. *The Sounds of Early Cinema.* Bloomington, Ind.: Indiana University Press, 2001.

Addams, Chas. *Dear Dead Days: A Family Album.* New York: Putnam, 1959.

Altick, Richard D. *The Shows of London: A Panoramic History of Exhibitions 1600-1862.* Cambridge: Harvard University Press, 1978.

Ausstellungskatalog: Drehorgen: Schaurig-Schon. Karlsruhe, Germany: Badisches Landesmuseum, 1994.

Balzec, Richard. *Peepshows: A Visual History.* New York: Harry N. Abrams, 1998.

Barry, Richard H. *Snapshots on the Midway of the Pan-Am Exposition, Buffalo.* New York: Robert A. Reid, 1901.

Barth, Tack, Doug Kirby, Ken Smith, and Mike Wilkins. *Roadside America.* New York: Fireside, 1986.

Beaver, Patrick. *The Spice of Life: Pleasures of the Victorian Age.* London: Elm Tree Books, 1979.

Berrouet, Laurence, and Gilles Laurendon. *Magiciens des Boulevards: Bateleurs Artistes et Bonimenteurs d'Autre Fois.* Paris: Pari Gramme, 1994.

Birdoff, Harry. *The World's Greatest Hit: Uncle Tom's Cabin.* New York: S.F. Vann, 1947.

Bonderson, Jan. *A Cabinet of Medical Curiosities.* New York: W.W. Norton, 1997.

Bowers, David Q. *Nickelodeon Theatres and Their Music.* New York: Vestal, 1986.

Braithwaite, Paul. *Peep Shows.* Bristol, England: Privately published, 1994.

Broome, Richard, and Alick Jackomos. *Side Show Alley.* St. Leonards, Australia: Allen and Unwin, 1998.

Burke, Thomas. *The Streets of London.* London: B.T. Batsford, 1940.

Cameron, David Kerr. *The English Fair.* Gloucestershire, England: Sutton Publishing, 1998.

Challamel, Augustin. *Les Amuseurs de la Rue.* Paris: Librairie Ducrocq, 1929.

Chapuis, Alfred, and Edmond Droz. *Les Automates: Figures Artificielles d'Homme et d'Animaux. Historie et Technique.* Neuchatel, Switzerland: Editions Du Griffon, 1949.

Chesney, Kellow. *The Victorian Underworld.* Trowbridge: Redwood Press, 1970.

Christopher, Milbourne. *The Illustrated History of Magic.* New York: Thomas Y. Crowell, 1973.

Chubbuck, Ted. *The Sound of the Jenny.* New York: Vantage, 1972.

Cross, Gary. *A Social History of Leisure Since 1600.* State College, Pa.: Venture, 1990.

Dadswell, Jack. *Hey There Sucker.* Boston: Bruce Humphries, 1946.

De Bussy, Charles. *Les Forains a Travers les Ages.* Avignon, France: 1930.

De Nansouty, Max. *Les Trucs du Theatre, du Cirque et de la Foire.* Paris: Armand Colin, 1909.

Dennet, Andrea Stulman. *Weird Wonderful: The Dime Museum in America.* New York: N.Y. University Press, 1997.

Dering, Florian, Margarete Groner, and Manfred Wegner. *Heute Hinrichtung: Jahrmarkts und Varieteatraktionen des Schaustellar - Dynastie Schichtl.* Munchner, Germany: Stadtmuseum, 1990.

Discher, Wilson M. *Pleasures of London.* London: Robert Hale, 1950.

Emmons Gould, Della. *Jay Gould's Million Dollar Gems.* Minneapolis: T.S. Denison, 1974.

Evans, Henry Ridgeley. *History of Conjuring and Magic.* Kenton, Ohio: International Brotherhood of Magicians, 1928.

Fieldler, Leslie. *Freaks: Myths and Images of the Secret Self.* New York: Simon & Schuster, 1978.

Fischer, Jean-Louis. *Monstres, Histoire du Corps et de Ses Defauts.* Paris: Syros-Alternatives, 1991.

Frost, Thomas. *The Old Showmen and the Old London Fairs.* London: Chatto & Windus, 1881.

Garnier, Jacques. *Forains d'Hier et d'Aujourd'hui.* Orleans, France: Jacques Garnier, 1968.

Gorham, Maurice. *Showmen and Suckers.* London: Percival Marshall, 1955.

Gorman, John. *Banner Bright: An Illustrated History of Trade Union Banners.* Essex, England: Scorpion, 1986.

Gould, George M., and Walter L. Pyle. *Anomalies and Curiosities of Medicine.* New York: Bell Publishing Co., 1896.

Gresham, William Lindsay. *Monster Midway.* New York: Rinehart, 1948.

Guralnick, Peter. *Sweet Soul Music.* Boston: Little Brown, 1986.

Habenstein, Robert W., and William M. Lamers. *The History of American Funeral Directing.* Milwaukee: Bulfin Printers, 1955.

Hale, Grace Elizabeth. *Making Whiteness: The Culture of Segregation in the South, 1890-1940.* New York: Pantheon, 1998.

Hammer, Carl, and Gideon Rosker. *Freak Show.* San Francisco: Chronicle, 1996.

Hark, Ina Rae. *Exhibition: The Film Reader.* New York: Routledge, 2002.

Haskins, James. *Black Theatre in America.* New York: Thomas Y. Crowell, 1982.

Heard, Nigel. *International Fairs.* Lavenham, England: Terence Dalton, 1973.

Holtman, Jerry. *Freak Show Man.* Los Angeles: Holloway House, 1968.

Hopkins, Albert A. *Magic, Stage Illusions and*

Scientific Diversions Including Trick Photography. New York: Arno Press, 1977.
Hornaday, William T. *Taxidermy and Zoological Collecting.* New York: Scribner, 1912.
Hoyt, Harlowe R. *Town Hall Tonight.* Englewood Cliffs, N.J.: Prentice-Hall, 1955.
Hubmann, Franz, and Helmut Qualtinger. *Der Wiener Prater Oder die Schonste Illusion des Gegenwart.* Wien, Germany: Christian Brandstatter, 1986.
Humphries, Barry. *Bizarre.* New York: Putnam, 1959.
Hyde, Ralph. *Panoramania!* London: Trefoil Publications, 1988.
Jennings, John J. *Theatrical and Circus Life or Secrets of the Stage, Green Room, and Sawdust Arena.* St. Louis: M.S. Barnett, 1882.
Johnson, Fred G. *Side Show Banners.* (Exhibition Book) Chicago: State of Illinois Art Gallery, 1989.
Johnson, Randy, Jim Secreto and Teddy Varndell. *Freaks, Geeks, & Strange Girls: Sideshow Banners of the Great American Midway.* Honolulu: Hardy Marks, 1995.
Jones, David C. *Midways, Judges, and Smooth-Tongued Fakirs.* Saskatoon, Sask.: Western Producer Prairie Books, 1983.
Joys, Joanne Carol. *The Wild Animal Trainer in America.* Boulder, Co.: Pruett, 1983.
Kasson, John F. *Amusing the Million: Coney Island at the Turn of the Century.* New York: Hill & Wang, 1978.
King, Jr., W.A. *Rattling Yours... Snake King.* Brownsville, Texas: Privately printed, 1964.
Kirby, Irwin, with Lou Dufour. *Fabulous Years: A Showman's Tales of Carnivals, World's Fairs, and Broadway.* New York: Vantage, 1977.
Knight, Arthur. *The Liveliest Art: A Panoramic History of the Movies.* New York: Mentor, 1957.
Kunhardt, Jr., Philip B., Philip B. Kunhardt III, and Peter W. Kunhardt. *P.T. Barnum, America's Greatest Showman: An Illustrated Biography.* New York: Knopf, 1995.
Landeshauptstadt Munchen: 175 Jahre Oktoberfest 1810-1985. Munchen, Germany: Bruckmann, 1985.
Langham, James. *More Than Meets the Eye.* London: Evans Bros., 1951.
Laurie, Jr., Joe. *Vaudeville From the Honky Tonks to the Palace.* New York: Henry Holt, 1953.
Le Roux, Hugues and Garnier, Jules. *Acrobats & Mountebanks.* London: Chapman & Hall, 1890.
Leslie, Anita, and Pauline Chapman. *Madame Tussaud: Waxworker Extraordinary.* London: Hutchinson, 1978.
Levenson, Randal. *In Search of the Monkey Girl.* New York: Aperture, 1982.
Lewis, Arthur L. *Carnival.* New York: Trident, 1970.
Lewis, George W. *The Ape I Knew.* Caldwell, Idaho: Claxton, 1961.
Lewiston, Harry. *Freak Show Man.*
MacDougall, Curtis D. *Hoaxes.* New York: Dover, 1940.
The Magic Lantern Society of Great Britain. *Magic Images.* London: Print Studio of the Architectural Assoc., 1990.
Malone, Jacqui. *Steppin' on the Blues: The Visible Rhythms of African American Dance.* Urbana and Chicago: University of Illinois Press, 1996.
Mannix, Daniel P. *We Who Are Not as Others.* New York: Simon & Schuster, 1976.
Martin, Howard. *Victorian Grotesque.* London: Jupiter, 1977.
McKechnie, Samuel. *Popular Entertainments Through the Ages.* London: Frederick A. Stokes, 1931.
Metcalfe, Francis. *Sideshow Studies.* New York: The Outing Publishing Co., 1906.
Mickel, Jere C. *Footlights on the Prairie.* St. Cloud, Minn: North Star, 1974.
Morgan, Bob. *The Showies: Revelations of Australia's Outdoor Side-Showmen.* Mitcham, Australia: Privately published, 1995.
Morley, Henry. *Memoirs of Bartholomew Fair.* London: Ballantyne, 1880.
Muller, Gunter. *Des Schone Alle Odenburger Kramermarkt.* Oldenburg, Germany: Verlag Isensee, 1982.
Muncey, R.W. *Our Old English Fairs.* London: Sheldon Press, 1935.
Museo la Specola Florence. *Encyclopedia Anatomica.* Koln, Germany: Taschen, 2001.
Museo Nazionelle dell' Arte Tradizioni Popolari. *La Plazza Universalo, Giochi, Spettacoli, Machine di Fiere e Luna Park.* Roma: 1987.
Musser, Charles. *The Emergence of Cinema: The American Screen to 1907.* Berkeley: University of California Press, 1994.
Nassaw, David. *Going Out: The Rise and Fall of Public Amusements.* New York: Basic Books, 1993.
Noell, Anna Mae. *The History of Noell's Ark Gorilla Show.* Tarpon Springs, Fla: Noell's Ark Publisher, 1979.
Norman, Tom, and George Norman. *The Penny Showman: Memoirs of Tom Norman 'Silver King.'* London, 1985.
Oettermann, Stephen. *The Panorama: History of a Mass Medium.* New York: Zone, 1997.
Opschonders, Roland, and Florian Dering, and Justina Schreiber. *Im Banne der Motoren.* Munchen, Germany: Buchendurfer, 1995.
Pilat, Oliver, and Jo Ranson. *Sodom by the Sea: An Affectionate History of Coney Island.* New York: Doubleday, 1941.
Placsek, John F. *The Development of the Circus and Menagerie 1825-1860.* Thesis. 1974.
Quigley, Christine. *Modern Mummies.* Jefferson, N.C.: McFarland & Co., 1998.
Reid, Robert A. *Sights and Scenes at the Lewis and Clark Centennial Exposition, Portland, Oregon.* Portland: Woodard Clarke & Co., 1905.
Rendle, T. McDonald. *Swings and Roundabouts.* London: Chapman & Hall, 1919.
Rydell, Robert W. *All the World's a Fair: Visions of Empire at American International Expositions 1826-1911.* Chicago: University of Chicago Press, 1984.
Sappol, Michael. *A Traffic in Dead Bodies.* Princeton: Princeton University Press, 2002.
Scrivens, Kevin, and Stephen Smith. *The Travelling Cinematograph Show.* Tweedale, England: New Era, 1999.
Sloan, Mark, Roger Manley, and Michelle Van Parys. *Dear Mr. Ripley: A Compendium of Curiosities from Believe It or Not! Archives.* Boston: Little Brown, 1993.
Slout, William L. *Olympians of the Sawdust Circle.* San Bernardino: The Borgo Press, 1998.
Smith, F. Berkeley. *How Paris Amuses Itself.* London: Funk & Wagnalls, 1903.
Thompson, C.J.S. *Giants, Dwarfs and Other Oddities.* New York: Citadel, 1968.
Thompson, C.J.S. *The Mystery and Lore of Monsters.* New York: Bell, 1931.
Toll, Robert C. *Blacking Up: The Minstrel Show in Nineteenth-Century America.* New York: Oxford University Press, 1974.
Vergnugen, Viel. *Offentliche Lustbarkeiten im Ruhrgebiet der Jahrhundertwende.* Essen, Germany: Ruhrlandmuseum, 1992.
Waller, Gregory A. *Main Street Amusements.* Washington: Smithsonian Institute Press, 1995.
Ward, Brian. *Just My Soul Responding: Rhythm and Blues, Black Consciousness, and Race Relations.* Berkeley: University of California Press, 1998.

Watkins, Mel. *On the Real Side: Laughing, Lying and Signifying*. New York: Touchstone, 1994.
Withers, Ernest C., and David Wolfe. *The Memphis Blues Again*. New York: Penguin, 2001.
Wright, Richardson. *Hawkers and Walkers in Early America*. Philadelphia: J.B. Lippincott, 1927.
Zikmund, Miroslav, and Jiri Hanzelka. *Amazon Head Hunters*. Prague, Czechoslovakia: Arta, 1963.

Trade Journals

Billboard, 1911.
NY Clipper, 18 December 1860.
Dr. Judd. *Billboard*, December 1903.
NY Clipper, 24 December 1853.
NY Clipper, 17 November 1860.
NY Clipper, 4 August 1860.
NY Clipper, 15 December 1860.
NY Clipper, 6 January 1861.
NY Clipper, 21 November 1885.
"Circus and Sideshow" and "Miscellaneous." *NY Clipper*, 7 November 1885.
NY Clipper, 16 January 1886.
Ad for Goss tent, *NY Clipper*, 1887.
NY Clipper, 20 August 1886.
Metallurgy Electro Co. ad, *NY Clipper*, March 1892.
NY Clipper, 23 July through September 1892.
J. Augustus Jones ad, *NY Clipper*, July 1892.
Billboard, 1910.
NY Clipper, December 1891.
Monford ad, *NY Clipper*, 3 September 1892.
NY Clipper, August 1891.
Ament ad, *NY Clipper*, October 1893.
Billboard, Spring 1901.
Billboard, 14 March 1903.
Billboard, 1909.
Billboard, 1896.
Tate ad, *Billboard*, 1942.
Julius S. Hansen ad, *NY Clipper*, 10 September 1887.
"Gorilla Man."*NY Clipper*, Fall 1891.
"The World." New York City newspaper, 6 November 1887.
Nelson ad, *NY Clipper*, 9 August 1890.
Billboard, 16 May 1903.
Fawcet Robinson ad, *NY Clipper*, 1 October 1888.
Western Papier-mâché Co. ad, *NY Clipper*, 1893.
Shaw ad, *Billboard*, August 1896.
Weil ad, *Billboard*, 1955.
Chas Buell ad, *Billboard*, March 1926.
Daniel Boone ad, *NY Clipper*, 20 February 1892.
Bostock ad, *NY Clipper*, 10 June 1893.
Billboard, 12 March 1904.
Frank White. *Billboard*, Winter 1900.
Billboard, 21 October 1921.
Billboard, 1952.
McAllister stereopticons ads, *NY Clipper*.
Billboard, 6 December 1902.
William Judkins Hewitt. "Movies as shows on carnivals midways are over." *Billboard*, 27 October 1917.
Billboard, 21 March 1903.
Harriet Laurie obituary, *NY Clipper*, 29 September 1888.
NY Clipper, May 1873.
Billboard, 20 October 1917.
Ackerman ad, *Billboard*, January 1918.
Nelson ad, *Billboard*, 28 August 1915.
Buell ad, *Billboard*, 1940.
"Hitler's Genuine Personal Limousine." *Billboard*, 26 November 1949.
Billboard, 22 January 1955.
NY Clipper, 29 December 1888.
John Michael Schliesser ads, *Billboard*, 1915.
NY Clipper, 19 April 1873.
NY Clipper, 12 April 1873.
Christophel ad, *Billboard*, 1934.
Billboard, 13 April 1959.
Billboard, 29 June 1959.
Billboard, 1 April 1900.
Billboard, 7 November 1903: p.17.
Flack ad, *Billboard*.
Billboard, 13 November 1915.
Billboard, 1926.
Mahatma, August 1901.
Billboard, December 1903.
Billboard, 14 March 1903.
Billboard, 15 December 1917.
Billboard, 1909.
Billboard, 8 September 1917.
F.B. Kellor ad, *Billboard*, December 1902.
Charles Weston ads, *Billboard*, 5 December 1903.
Horace Goldin ad, *Billboard*, 10 September 1924.
Billboard, 15 October 1921.
C. Colvin ad, *Billboard*, 1919.
"At Liberty" section, *Billboard*, 1921.
Billboard, 1902.
Star De Belle. "Ballyhoo Bros. Exposition Shows, a Century of Profit." *Billboard*.
Mullikin Co. ad, *Billboard*, 12 July 1947.
NY Clipper, 3 November 1860.
Billboard, 1910.
Billboard, 1921.
Black fair ad, *Billboard*, 21 July 1900.
Amusement Business, August 1964.
Billboard, 1928.
Color, 1957.
Billboard, 1915.
NY Clipper, 22 December 1888.
Billboard, 20 February 1903.
Billboard, 3 April 1915.
Billboard, March 1914.
Billboard, 15 December 1917.
Billboard, 28 March 1925.
"Outlaw's Father Trouper." *Billboard*, 11 May 1935.
Billboard, 1936.
Tom Hughes ad, *Amusement Business*.
Charles Stanley ad, *Billboard*, 29 July 1957.
Amusement Business, October 1969.
Amusement Business, 23 August 1973.
NY Clipper, 5 April 1873.
NY Clipper, November 1899.
Billboard, December 1900.
Billboard, 6 October 1900.
Billboard, 21 February 1903.
Billboard, 1935.

PHOTO CREDITS

Amusement Business, 30 June 1984, p. 41: 218.
Author's collection: xii, xv, xvi, xix, xxi, 4 (left), 5 (left), 6 (left), 7 (right sketch), 8, 12, 15 (right), 16 (inset), 20, 23, 24, 25, 27 (left), 29, 30, 32, 33, 34, 35 (bottom), 36, 39, 40, 42, 43, 45, 50, 52, 53, 56, 59, 60, 61, 62, 63, 64, 73, 76, 77 (bottom far right), 79, 80, 81 (right), 82, 84, 85 (right), top 86, 87, 91, 93, 99, 100, 101, 102, 103, 105, 106, 108, 109, 111, 112, 114 (bottom), 115 (top), 116, 119, 120, 121, 123, 126 (bottom), 130, 131, 134 (top), 137, 141, 142 (bottom), 146, 148, 150, 151, 157 (bottom), 158, 161, 163, 164, 165, 166 (right), 167, 168, 169, 170, 172, 173, 174, 175, 177, 179R, 187, 191, 194 (top), 199, 200, 201, 202, 203 (right), 207, 210, 212 (right), 214, 215, 216, 217, 221, 225, 227, 228 (left), 229, 230, 231, 237, 241, 243 (left), 245 (right).
Bob and Gail Blackmar: 27 (right), 46, 47, 136, 138, 143, 155 (left), 240.
Matt Bouvier and Felecity Perez: 248.
Joe Bradbury: 166 (left).
David Braithwaite: 3, 10.
Capac Historical Society, Capac, Mich.: 190, 192, 193, 195, 196, 197, 198.
Barbara Fahs Charles Collection: 44 (top), 72 (right), 74, 75, 88, 89, 134 (bottom), 135 (bottom), 203 (left).
Chicago World's Fair souvenir photo book: 6 (right).
Circus World Museum, Baraboo, Wisc.: 21, 38 (right), 44 (bottom), 48, 54, 68 (right), 71, 77 (top), 90, 95, 194 (bottom), 228 (right).
City of Ottawa Archives: 49.
Bill Cooker: 35 (top), 83, 145, 220.
Richard Cox Archives: 85 (left).
Fred Dahlinger, Jr.: 55, 57 (top).
Jim Dillman: 176 (top).
Jimmy Dixon: 144.
William Eakin: 114 (top).
Harry Fee: 118, 126 (top), 127, 128.
Richard Flint: 9 (top), 14, 15 (left), 18, 22 (bottom).
Faye Renton Frisbee: 133, 232, 234.
Malcolm Garey: 239.
Glenbow Archives, Calgary, Alberta: 58, 125, 206, 222, 224.
Jan Gregor: front flap, 92, 246 (bottom).
Paul C. Gutheil: 248 (top).
Ward Hall and Chris Christ Collection: 41, 98, 139, 156, 160, 223, 235, 242, 244.
Ken Harck: 26, 28 (bottom), 78, 104.
Jack Hartley: 245 (left), 246 (top), 247.
Indiana Historical Society, Indianapolis, Ind.: 66, 135 (top).
Kinder Von RAS: 185, 186 (left), 219.
Lee Kolozsey: xiv, xx, 81 (left), 140, 157 (top), 243 (right).
Ralph Lopez: 113.
Mahatma: 132.
Scott McLelland: 17.
Henry and Patricia Meyers: 212 (left).
Henry Morley, *Memoirs of Bartholomew Fair*: 5 (right), 7 (top left and bottom left), 9 (bottom), 11 (left).
Jeff Murray: 153.
The National Fairground Archive, Sheffield University, Gt. Britain: 2, 4 (right), 57 (bottom).
Robert Noell Jr.: 122.
Lucky Orr: 179 (left), 180, 181, 182, 183.
Bob Paul: 86 (bottom), 115 (bottom), 142 (top), 176 (bottom), 204, 208, 209.
Bill Peacock: xvii, xviii, 184, 186 (right), 188.
Fred Pfening II: 22 (top), 51.
John Polacsek: xvi (ad), 67, 68 (left), 77 (bottom left and bottom middle).
John Schoenijahn: 226
John Shipley: 149, 152, 154, 162, 213
George Smith: 155 (right).
Ted Stickley: 16 (poster).
Strand magazine: 11 (right).
Myron Vickers: 13.